A CULTURAL JOURNEY THROUGH ANDALUSIA

A CULTURAL JOURNEY THROUGH ANDALUSIA

FROM GRANADA TO SEVILLE

Gwynne Edwards

CARDIFF
UNIVERSITY OF WALES PRESS
2009

www.uwp.co.uk

British Library Cataloguing-in-Publication Data
A catalogue record for this book is available from the British Library.

ISBN 978-0-7083-2207-9

Printed in Wales by Dinefwr Press, Llandybïe

Contents

Preface

Andalusia is probably the region of Spain which is most familiar to the foreign visitor, though that familiarity may well be superficial, based on the holiday resorts of the Costa del Sol with their mile upon mile of characterless hotels and apartments, supermarkets and pubs with English names run by English exiles – in short, Blackpool with sun and sangría. The real Spain, the Spain which is rich in history and tradition, is not, however, far away. Even in the coastal resorts the holidaymaker who is interested only in having a good time may see a flamenco show which, however inferior in quality, comes from a tradition which is uniquely Spanish and rooted deep in Spanish history and tradition. Again, the foreign tourist will catch a glimpse of a poster advertising a bullfight – no doubt a run-of-the-mill event which he or she has no intention of seeing, but which would not exist were it not for the fact that, like flamenco, the bullfight has a long and colourful history. As well as this, the hotel in which the foreign visitor is staying may well have ornamental pools, fountains and decorative tiles which are the modern equivalent of a style and a way of life introduced many centuries ago by the Moors.

These influences from the past may, then, be glimpsed superficially in the present, but to appreciate that past to the full one has to visit those places where, in the case of buildings and monuments, it can still be seen, and where, as far as performance is concerned, it still occurs. The true architectural glory of the Moors can be found in Córdoba, in Seville, in Granada's wonderful Alhambra and in many other less frequented and less familiar towns throughout Andalusia. True flamenco, in all its fiery passion, may be experienced too in particular venues, as indeed may the solemnity and anguish of the Crucifixion in the Holy Week processions in Seville and Granada, or the colour and tension of the bullfight in the famous bullrings of Seville and Ronda.

The aim of this book is, without introducing complex theoretical arguments, to provide the educated reader and traveller with an account of the historical and cultural richness of Andalusia which penetrates beneath the superficial and stereotyped image, and to reveal too the way in which particular aspects of the region's culture have evolved over the centuries into their present form. It is the result of many visits over a long period of time, and of an enthusiasm for southern Spain which the reader will, it is hoped, come to share.

Note on place names

The reader may encounter in Spain the Spanish spellings Sevilla and Andalucía, but here the commonly used English-language versions, Seville and Andalusia, have been used.

Acknowledgements

The author and publisher gratefully acknowledge the permission granted by the following to reprint extracts from:

Spanish-language works by Federico García Lorca

© Herederos de Federico García Lorca from *Obras completas*, ed. Miguel García Posada (Barcelona/Valencia: Galaxia Gutenberg/Círculo de Lectores, 1996).

Translations by Gwynne Edwards © Herederos de Federico García Lorca and Gwynne Edwards. All rights reserved. For information please contact William Peter Kosmas at *kosmas@artslaw.co.uk*

Quotations from Richard Ford, *Handbook for Travellers in Spain*, 1966 edition (distributed by Pythian Books), by kind permission of Centaur Press.

Quotations in English translation from Victor Hugo, *Œuvres Complètes, Poésie I*, 1985 edition, by kind permission of Robert Laffont Publishers.

Photographs of the Alhambra © Eleri Thomas, Mark Liddington

Illustrations

1. The Courtyard of the Water Channel in the Generalife. Copyright: Eleri Thomas.
2. The Courtyard of the Myrtles, described by Washington Irving. Copyright: Eleri Thomas.
3. The Albaicín in Granada. Copyright: Mark Liddington.
4. A forest of arches and columns: the Mezquita in Córdoba. Copyright: Visual&Written SL/Alamy.
5. Flamenco passion. Copyright: Daniel H. Bailey/Alamy.
6. Carmen: the prettified image. Copyright: Photos 12/Alamy.
7. Blood and sand: the drama of the bullfight. Copyright: LOOK Die Bildagentur der Fotografen GmbH/Alamy.
8. The Giralda in Seville. All rights reserved.

Every effort has been made to trace the copyright holders of material reproduced in this volume. In the case of any query, please contact the publisher.

xi

Introduction

Since the 1960s Spain has become a familiar stamping ground for millions of foreign tourists, the majority in search of sun, sex and alcohol, and what they consider to be a fun time. Benidorm, Fuengirola, Lloret and Torremolinos have become even more familiar to the British than Blackpool, Brighton and Skegness, and just as unrepresentative of the true Spain as are these English resorts of Britain as a whole. Even so, the more discerning tourist has in recent times been attracted to the real Spain, exploring by car, train or organized coach tours such historically fascinating places as Burgos, Mérida, Toledo, Salamanca and Santiago de Compostela; lesser-known towns such as Cuenca, Teruel and Tortosa; and the stimulating southern cities of Córdoba, Granada and Seville. In the past such exploration was, more often than not, the monopoly of privileged and moneyed individuals for whom Spain was a part of the Grand Tour of Europe. Today the process has become more democratic, the opportunity to visit and be entranced by Spanish magic available to all.

Spain is unique in many ways. It is, first of all, the only European country to have been overrun and inhabited for more than seven hundred years by Muslims. Proof of their presence is to be found in towns and cities as far north as Burgos, home of El Cid, Toledo and Zaragoza. But the southern region of Andalusia is where the Muslims had their base, first in Córdoba, then in Seville and finally in Granada, until this last stronghold of Muslim influence fell to the Christian armies in 1492. These three cities were the hub of Muslim culture and artistic achievement in Spain, and to this day the wonderful Mezquita, or Great Mosque, in Córdoba, the Alcázar in Seville and, above all, the Alhambra in Granada attract millions of visitors every year.

Spain is also fascinating in the sense that the Christian–Muslim opposition of the past has an echo in the present-day conflict between Islam and the West. Although Muslims and Christians often lived in harmony in Spain, the Christian victory of 1492 led to the ruthless expulsion of the Muslims from the country and, in conjunction with it, to a building programme in which, as a demonstration of Christian power, mosques

1

were demolished and churches and palaces constructed in their place. Such is the cathedral in Seville, the largest Christian building in the world; the cathedral built inside the Mezquita in Córdoba; and the huge Renaissance palace of Charles V in the grounds of the Alhambra. The coexistence of such architecturally different styles, especially in Andalusia, is a lasting testament to the different values of Islam and the Christian West.

Just as the Muslims had entered southern Spain in the eighth century, so in the fifteenth there arrived from Egypt large numbers of immigrants, subsequently known as 'gypsies', who, five hundred or more years earlier, had left their homeland in India and made their way into Asia, Europe and Africa. Persecuted by the law and forced to live in communities on the margins of the cities, they lamented their fate in songs which expressed their anguish to the full and which, influenced as well by refugee Jews and Muslims, acquired the wailing sound which today we either love or loathe. Later on, flamenco extended its boundaries, moving first into cafés, and then into theatres and even cinema. But, whatever its form and performance space, it is uniquely Spanish, and the southern towns and cities of Córdoba, Seville, Jerez de la Frontera and Cádiz remain its source of inspiration. Muslim architecture and flamenco together create a heady mix.

If flamenco is strongly ritualistic, so are the bullfight and the Holy Week religious processions, both once more essentially Spanish. Although the bullfight also exists in southern France and Portugal, the great bullrings are in the Spanish cities, including Seville. The British are appalled by the bullfight mainly because they insist on regarding it as a sport and are largely ignorant of its ancient origins when bulls were slain as part of a ritual sacrifice. That sense of ritual remains in what is today a highly theatrical performance played out on a sandy stage in a series of acts in which costume, movement, music and lighting – sunlight and shadow – are key elements, and in which the conflict between beast and man, instinct and reason, is ever more intense. It is no surprise, given its dramatic character, that the bullfight should have absorbed creative artists such as Picasso and Hemingway.

To the foreigner, the Holy Week processions, as theatrical in their way as the bullfight, may seem very strange. Who are these gowned figures whose pointed hats bring to mind the Ku Klux Klan? Who are the men who crouch beneath the huge floats, bearing them slowly on their backs and shoulders to the point where they bleed? What could be more dramatic than the sound of the trumpets and drums which accompany the slow procession, suddenly stop and then break out again? As in flamenco and the bullfight, the emotions are raw – in this case the anguish and suffering associated with the Crucifixion – and the spectacle alive with feeling and colour, the very opposite of northern restraint. Such processions take place throughout the whole of Spain, of course, but they are especially impressive in Seville and Granada where thousands of people fill the streets as they pass by.

Just as flamenco, the bullfight and religious spectacle have emerged from the soil of Andalusia, so has one of the world's most memorable literary characters: Carmen, the archetypal seductress associated with Seville's Royal Tobacco Factory. Seville was also in the seventeenth century the home of a school of magnificent artists. Velázquez was born there in 1599, produced his earliest work there and later became painter to the king in Madrid. Bartolomé Murillo, nineteen years older than Velázquez, was also born in Seville, and many of his paintings are displayed there today. Francisco de Zurbarán, another great painter, was born in 1598 in the small town of Fuente de Cantos, but moved to Seville at a relatively early age, while Juan de Valdés Leal, born in Seville in 1622, completed his apprenticeship in Córdoba but later moved back to Seville, where he died in 1691. Alonso Cano, born in Granada in 1601, subsequently studied painting in Seville. It goes without saying that, in terms of colour, luminosity, religious fervour and theatricality, the work of all these artists captures the spirit of the region and the age.

Granada was also the inspiration for two of the twentieth century's greatest creative artists: the composer Manuel de Falla and the poet-dramatist Federico García Lorca. Born in Cádiz, de Falla settled in Granada in 1920 and quickly established a close friendship with the much younger Lorca, both of them fascinated by the folklore and the traditional music of southern Spain, including flamenco. Indeed, much of de Falla's music, even though it was composed before his arrival in Granada, is deeply influenced by Granada, by its gypsy associations and the rhythms of flamenco. As for Lorca, born in Fuente Vaqueros near Granada in 1898, he spent much of his life in the city, inspired by its mixture of Christian, Muslim, Jewish and gypsy elements. He often recited his poems in the Alhambra which for him symbolized the beauty and sophistication of a civilization long gone. Many of his plays resonate with the spirit of an Andalusia steeped in tradition, and in 1922 he and de Falla played leading roles in the organization of the Festival of Deep Song, celebrated over two days in the Alhambra itself. The music, theatre and poetry of these two

3

quintessentially Andalusian artists possess to the full the magic and the mystery of the region which inspired them.

In the twentieth century as a whole, Seville has prospered much more than Córdoba and Granada and is today one of the most attractive cities in Spain. In 1929 it hosted the Fair of the Americas, an Ibero-American exhibition intended to celebrate the achievements of Spain, Portugal and Latin America. In 1992, it hosted Expo '92, another prestigious exhibition. Both have enhanced the city's appearance in terms of beautiful buildings, the former rather more than the latter. But by far the most significant event in twentieth-century Spanish history was, of course, the civil war and its aftermath. One of the most striking aspects of the war is the way in which, in some respects, its commencement paralleled the Muslim invasion of 711, for, like that incursion, the military forces attempting to overthrow the Madrid government in 1936 crossed into Spain from north Africa and quickly seized the southern cities of Córdoba, Seville and Granada. Furthermore, as in the case of the Muslims, the military uprising was both political and religious, for the generals sought to recover their country from the socialists, whom they regarded as infidels, the sworn enemy of the Catholic Church. Again, the three-year war and its immediate aftermath was as bloody as any previous conflict between Christian and Muslim; and even if it differed in the sense that Spaniard was now pitted against Spaniard, the parallel is both curious and fascinating. Seville, once the centre of Muslim domination, became the headquarters of General Queipo de Llano, from which he made regular and fiery broadcasts both to his troops and to the enemy. It was on his orders that Lorca, arrested in Granada at the beginning of the war, was taken to a house outside the village of Viznar, near Granada, and shot at dawn. How strange that such an admirer of Muslim culture should have met his death near the city which boasted the Alhambra, the greatest Muslim monument in the whole of Spain!

As the preceding outline suggests, Andalusia is a tapestry in which the different threads of history, music, ritual and art come together in a vibrant and colourful whole. Indeed, it is in the end extremely difficult to separate them, for the Muslim imprint was and is a vital element of modern Christian Spain. Flamenco artists were often bullfighters and bullfighters flamenco artists, and flamenco songs are still to be heard in the Holy Week religious processions. In short, the south of Spain is a region which has an irresistible magic and a unique dramatic appeal and theatricality.

1

Muslim Spain

Córdoba, situated on the river Guadalquivir, forms the apex of a triangle which is completed by Seville, some 130 kilometres to the south-west, and Granada, a similar distance to the south-east. It is less well known than the two other cities, yet nowadays is an essential part of the coach-tour itinerary of leading travel firms. To the north is the Sierra Morena, the mountain range through which, via the pass called the Desfiladero de Despeñaperros, travellers and traders – including Don Quixote – have made their way for centuries from the dry plains of Castile to Córdoba. To the south of the city is the Campiña, an area of fertile rolling countryside rich in olive groves, vineyards, wheat and sunflowers. And the region is rich in history too. To the east and south-east of Córdoba are the towns of Jaén, Baeza and Úbeda, all distinguished by fine cathedrals, Arabic baths, and magnificent Renaissance palaces; to the south Priego de Córdoba with its splendid baroque architecture. These are places which are off the main tourist routes, but they provide a vivid testament to the fascinating past of this part of Andalusia.

At one time, Córdoba, with half a million inhabitants, was the centre of Muslim power in Spain, rivalling Baghdad in its splendour. Imagine twelve royal palaces, a thousand mosques, 800 public baths, colleges, libraries, country houses, exotic gardens and paved streets. Prior to this, some two thousand years ago, the city had been an important provincial Roman capital, producing the writers Lucan and Seneca, and some of the grandeur of that time can still be seen in the sixteen arches of its bridge, the Puente Romano. Of the magnificence of these earlier times much has been lost. The Moorish water-supply systems, at which the Moors were so expert, fell into decline and disrepair after they were expelled from Spain. Many mosques were demolished and transformed into churches. Economically, because it was upstream from Seville, Córdoba did not benefit greatly from the wealth which poured into southern Spain following the discovery and exploitation of South America. Later still, the city suffered a great deal in the nineteenth-century war against the French, as well as in the last century, during the civil war, when it fell into the hands of General Franco's nationalists. Since the death of Franco in 1975 and the subsequent transition to democracy, Córdoba has made more progress and is today reasonably prosperous, as well as attractive. Its fame lies, however, in one magnificent reminder of its Moorish past: the Mezquita, the Great Mosque, one of the finest examples of Muslim architecture in the world, once seen, never to be forgotten. So how was it that the Moors, *los moros*, came to Spain in the first place?

From the fifth to the eighth century, Spain had been occupied by the Visigoths, who had earlier overwhelmed the Romans, but after three centuries of undisputed power, their authority had been weakened by increasing internal disagreements and quarrels over succession. The first Muslim invasion of the country occurred in the spring of 711, when an army of 7,000 men, consisting of Berber and Arab tribesmen, crossed the straits from north Africa, landed near Gibraltar, and in the subsequent battle overcame the forces of King Roderick, then ruler of Visigothic Spain. According to a rather appealing legend, Roderick had seduced the daughter of Count Julián, Visigothic governor of Ceuta in Morocco, and he therefore took his revenge on Roderick by describing to the Muslims the riches available in Spain, thereby whetting their appetite to seize the country. At all events, Roderick's army was easily defeated, Córdoba fell to the invading forces in October 711, Seville in the following year and, by 714, when other Muslim armies followed suit, most of the country had fallen into Muslim hands – an incredible outcome, given the often harsh and difficult terrain. In the greater scheme of things, the conquest of Spain was part of a long process of Arab expansion from the Middle East in a north-easterly, south-easterly and westerly direction, the Arabs who travelled west moving into north Africa, from where the crossing into the south of Spain was an easy additional step.[1]

The vast area of Spain occupied by the Muslims – only the far north remained in Christian hands – was known as al-Andalus (not to be confused with present-day Andalusia). At the time of the invasion and for almost forty years afterwards, al-Andalus owed its allegiance to Damascus, from which the caliph, a member of the Umayyad family and a descendant of Muhammad, ruled his vast empire. In 750, however, the Umayyads were massacred and power shifted from Damascus to Baghdad. As a consequence of this, Abd-ar-Rahman, a member of the Umayyads then living in Morocco, crossed into Spain and in 756 was proclaimed emir of al-Andalus, which also declared its independence from Baghdad.

Córdoba had been the capital of al-Andalus from the time of the initial Muslim invasion and continued to be so for another three hundred years or so. During the reign of Abd-ar-Rahman (756–88), the caliphate of Córdoba became much more prosperous; towns increased in size, irrigation techniques – which can still be seen today – allowed for the cultivation of new crops, including oranges, rice, sugar cane and cotton, and commerce made great strides. On the other hand, Abd-ar-Rahman faced the difficult problem of keeping the peace and easing the tensions amongst the different elements of the population over which he ruled: Arabs, of whom there were different kinds; Berbers, whom the Arabs regarded as inferiors; and Christians who had decided to remain in Muslim territory and who were known as Mozárabes or 'would-be Arabs'. Despite these problems, Abd-ar-Rahman's reign was a successful one, and, partly as a result of it, there were relatively few internal problems between 788 and 912, when Abd-ar-Rahman III (912–61) came to power. During his reign, however, al-Andalus began to face problems from different directions. First, the Muslim governors who ruled particular areas of al-Andalus often refused to obey the emir, and the threat which they posed was also accompanied by that of Muslim rulers in north Africa. And, secondly, the Christians who had fled to the northern areas of the country in the face of the Muslim invasion of 711 were growing ever stronger and more determined to recover their homeland, so that between 740 and 961 periodic advances southwards were made by them. Even so, by the time of his death, Abd-ar-Rahman III had succeeded in uniting al-Andalus once more, and in 929 had dropped the title of emir and assumed that of caliph, thereby asserting his independence from all higher Muslim authority and giving the caliphate of Córdoba an even greater dignity.

The successful reign of Abd-ar-Rahman III continued when his son, al-Hakam II (961–76), succeeded him, and by the time of his death the power of the Umayyad dynasty and the prosperity of al-Andalus were at their height. His son, Hisham II, was, however, only eleven years of age when he came to the throne, and more and more power was cunningly assumed by the ambitious Ibn-Abi-Amir, who administered the property and revenues of the young caliph and who in 981 took the title of al-Mansur bi-'llah. For the most part a military man, al-Mansur is said to have been involved in fifty-seven military victories and even to have destroyed the church and shrine of St James (Santiago) at Compostela in north-west Spain. After his death in 1002, al-Andalus remained unchanged for a while, but between 1008 and 1031 it was racked by internal strife, thirty towns acquired independent rulers, and the once mighty caliphate of Córdoba effectively came to an end. Indeed, power moved now to Seville under al-Mu'tadid (1042–68) and al-Mu'tamid (1068–91), and Córdoba became merely a part of the territory under Seville's jurisdiction. The disunity which existed in al-Andalus also allowed the Christian rulers of the north to advance further south, and in 1085 they succeeded in capturing Toledo, virtually in the centre of the country.

During the rule of the Umayyads, intellectual and cultural life in general prospered. The Muslims were particularly interested in law, but they also produced many books and treatises on history and biography. There were fine poets, writing on purely traditional themes, including love, but elaborating expression in a way which is reminiscent of the arabesques in their architecture. In the ninth century, the singer Ziryab arrived from Baghdad and founded the Andalusian school of music and song. Indeed, although Córdoba had broken away from Baghdad in the eighth century, links with the East were largely maintained, especially during the reigns of Abd-ar-Rahman III and al-Hakam II. The latter's library, containing more than 400,000 volumes, was one of the largest in the Islamic world, proof enough of the intellectual life of the caliphate of Córdoba. But the truly outstanding achievements of the period were in the fields of art and architecture: first, the Mezquita in Córdoba itself, much of which remains as it was in the tenth century; and secondly, the palace-city of Medina Azahara, to the north-west.

For the foreign visitor, the Mezquita is a sight to behold and is certainly one of the most impressive buildings in the whole of Spain. During the reign of the Visigoths, a Christian church existed on the site. When the Muslims arrived and occupied Córdoba in 711, they took over one half of the church for their own worship, and around 785 Abd-ar-Rahman purchased the other half, had the entire church demolished and initiated the construction of what would become the Mezquita, the third largest mosque in the Islamic world.

The visitor should understand in the first place that the mosque was built in four separate stages by four Muslim rulers – Abd-ar-Rahman I, Abd-ar-Rahman II, al-Hakam II, and al-Mansur – between 785 and around 1000. We enter the Mezquita by an entrance in the north wall which is known as the Penitents' Gate (the Puerta del Perdón) and find ourselves in a courtyard or patio which leads through the Archway of Palms (the Arco de las Palmas) into the prayer hall. This is the part of the building which was constructed by Abd-ar-Rahman I on the site of the original church. The courtyard, which can be found in any mosque, is where worshippers can cleanse themselves before proceeding into the prayer hall, but in Córdoba it also served as an overflow, for all Muslims in the city were expected to attend on Fridays. The presence of fountains in the courtyard points to its function as a place for ritual washing, while the green of the orange trees and the heady perfume of their blossom create an atmosphere of great beauty and tranquillity. To the right of the entrance to the courtyard is the bell-tower, 93 metres in height, which was built later, in the fourteenth century, on the site of the original minaret. It is an impressive spectacle, but more impressive still is the sight which greets us as we move from the courtyard into the prayer hall.[2]

We see in front of us a forest of columns and arches: ten rows of columns extending from north to south (the building runs in this direction) and separating eleven naves. The columns are clearly of Roman or Visigothic origin and were brought to the site of the Mezquita from other places. They were, however, too short to allow a roof of any great height to be placed directly on them, and in order to achieve the height they required, the Muslim architects created a double arch: a lower horseshoe arch which opens out from the top of the supporting column, and above it a second semicircular arch which bears the weight of the roof. The design, therefore, had a largely practical purpose, but the effect is extremely beautiful, enhanced by the alternating yellow stone and red brick which fill the space between the higher and lower arches. When this part of the building was constructed, there was no wall, as there is now, between the courtyard and the prayer hall. One can imagine the lovely effect which the light would have created as it flooded directly onto the columns and the red and yellow arches.

By the time Abd-ar-Rahman II came to power in 822, the Muslim population of Córdoba had increased greatly, which in turn required that the Mezquita be extended. A second stage of the building was therefore added to the first, taking it in a southerly direction by a distance of seven more columns. The extension meant, of course, that the end wall of the original prayer hall had to be taken down, but ten columns were retained in order to provide support. In general Abd-ar-Rahman II adopted the construction methods and style of his great predecessor, so that there is no great difference between the old and the new parts of the mosque. As a result of the extension, however, the side walls of the prayer hall now measured 64 metres in comparison with the original length of 37 metres.

The third part of the building, constructed by al-Hakam II between 961 and 966, was a continuation of the second, again removing the end wall and taking the prayer hall further south by a distance of twelve bays. The overall length of the Mezquita was now 104 metres – in other words, more than the length of a football pitch. This new section of the mosque was also more beautiful than the other two parts of the building, not least in relation to the arches. The lower horseshoe arch mentioned previously became multi-lobed and was therefore much more intricate in appearance, rather like a piece of lacework. In addition, the area between the lower and the upper arch was no longer the alternation of yellow stone and red brick already mentioned. It was now richly decorated and patterned with designs. And, although the columns supporting the double arches remained simple, they were of different colours, some light, some dark, and cleverly arranged for aesthetic effect. As we stand at the northern end of al-Hakam's extension, we cannot but be impressed by the impression it creates of elegance and lightness. And, if we look up, that sense of elegance is further enhanced by the ceiling, in which there are four domes, each with a pyramid roof and six small windows. Each dome is supported by a series of curved ribs which divide the ceiling into sections, each of which is elaborately designed. Not without cause was al-Hakam II regarded as a highly cultured man and a true lover of the arts.

At the southern end of the Mezquita, in direct line with the Penitents' Gate at the northern end, we come to the *mihrab*, the small prayer room which is the spiritual centre and the most important part of any mosque. Normally, the *mihrab* faces Mecca, but in the Mezquita, because the building follows the line of the church on whose site it was built, it rather incongruously points towards Timbuktu. The entrance to this small, seven-sided chamber consists of a horseshoe arch, above which are seven smaller parallel arches, each tri-lobed at the top. The whole of the area between the lower and the higher arches is brilliantly decorated with gold mosaics set in coloured backgrounds of green, yellow and red. Circular forms, usually consisting of leaf and flower designs and arranged in geometric patterns, can be seen throughout. As for the mosaics, al-Hakam wanted his mosque to be more glorious than any other and therefore succeeded in obtaining the services of a specialist from Constantinople who arrived in Córdoba with 600 kilograms of gold mosaic cubes. He was assisted in his work by slaves who, after his departure, were able to continue his work. As we stand in what is still an extremely impressive building, we should try to imagine what it was like in al-Hakam's time. On the penultimate day of Ramadan, for example, it would have been lit by 2,400 lamps and candelabra and would have been quite dazzling.

The fourth and final part of the Mezquita was built on the orders of al-Mansur, the work commencing around 978 and responding once more to an increase in Córdoba's Muslim population. Because the southern end of the mosque faced the river and the western side the caliph's palace, further expansion was only possible on the eastern side. Al-Mansur therefore widened the existing building by adding eight naves or aisles. The court-yard was also widened, and the Mezquita thus achieved the size it possesses today. But al-Mansur's extension was by no means as splendid as al-Hakam's. His prayer hall was much simpler, and the stripes on the arches were painted. In short, al-Mansur revealed in general a lack of imagination which was, perhaps, typical of someone who was essentially a military man.

The visitor to Córdoba should also make every effort to visit Medina Azahara, the once magnificent palace 8 kilometres north-west of the city and now largely in ruins. It was built by Abd-ar-Rahman III, the project financed, so the story goes, by money left to him by one of his favourite concubines, az-Zahra (the Radiant One). Work began in 936, took more than forty years to complete, and involved as many as 10,000 workmen at any one time. The palace was roughly 2,000 metres in length and 900 metres wide. It covered three terraces on a hill above the Guadalquivir valley and clearly enjoyed magnificent views. The complex contained 4,000 marble columns, the majority imported from north Africa, and, apart from the palace itself, had a zoo, an aviary, fish ponds, gardens, a mosque, a university, a barracks for 12,000 soldiers, 300 baths, markets, workshops, and a harem of 6,300 concubines.

In its time, Medina Azahara embodied the wealth and sophistication of Muslim Spain, but its life was short, for in 1010, a mere fifty years after its completion and while al-Andalus was subject to internal conflicts, it was sacked and burned by Berber mercenaries. In subsequent centuries, the stonework which remained was used in the construction of buildings else-where, notably the nearby monastery of San Jerónimo, built in the fifteenth century, and the fourteenth-century Alcázar in Seville. Eventually, Medina Azahara became covered by weeds, its former glory almost extinct, but in 1944 the remains of part of the palace were revealed by excavations.

One enters the site by the north gate, the Puerta Norte, which leads in turn to the army barracks, Dar al-Yund. To the south of this, reconstruction has focused on the Royal House, where important visitors were received, and, within it, on the main hall, the Salón Rico, decorated with beautiful marble carvings. Further down the slope, to the south-east, is the mosque, of which only the ground-plan now exists. Indeed, apart from the recon-structed palace, only foundations, a few horseshoe arches and gardens suggest the one-time size and splendour of this palace-town, but it is not difficult to imagine how visitors from the east were impressed by Medina Azahara.[3]

Seville, capital of Andalusia and 130 kilometres south-west of Córdoba, also lies on the Guadalquivir. On the eastern side of the river is the old city, distinguished by its three great monuments: the cathedral, the Giralda and the Alcázar. To the east but quite near them is the old Jewish quarter, the Barrio de Santa Cruz, with its white, labyrinthine streets; the city hall, the Ayuntamiento, built between 1527 and 1534; and the Casa de Pilatos, the House of Pilate, one of the finest palaces in Seville and which contains magnificent examples of Mudéjar style – the style practised by Muslims living under Christian rule. To the south of the Alcázar is the old Tobacco Factory, the Fábrica Real de Tabacos, where the fictional Carmen worked and which is now part of the university, and to the north the Calle de las Sierpes, Serpent Street, one of Don Juan's favourite haunts. The northern part of the city, known as La Macarena, is a working-class area less frequented by tourists but full of interesting squares, churches and convents. To the south of the old city is the beautiful and extensive María Luisa park and the magnificent Plaza de España, only ten minutes' walk from the cathedral. The Plaza de España was designed to celebrate the Spanish Americas Fair of 1929, but the fair itself coincided with the Wall Street crash and was less successful than it otherwise might have been. Returning north to the river bank, we encounter the striking Golden Tower, the Torre del Oro, built in 1220 by the Muslims in order to protect the area. And close by is the bull-ring, the Plaza de Toros de la Maestranza, built in the eighteenth century and one of the most famous in Spain.

Across the river, opposite the bullring, is the district called Triana, once home to the great flamenco gypsy families of the south of Spain but now much changed. And a short distance to the north is La Cartuja, originally a monastery of the fourteenth century but later put to other uses and restored at vast expense in connection with the celebration in Seville of Expo '92.

As we have seen, the once mighty caliphate of Córdoba had come to an end around 1031, when power moved to Seville, first under al-Mu'tadid and then under his successor, al-Mu'tamid. Al-Mu'tadid, in fact, succeeded in enlarging the kingdom of Seville to the west and south-west, and also waged war against Córdoba and Granada. Under both rulers the court of Seville became the most brilliant in Spain, but the fall of Toledo to the Christians in 1085, and the generally deteriorating situation in al-Andalus itself, led al-Mu'tamid to seek military assistance from Yusuf ibn-Tashufin, ruler of the powerful Almoravid state in north Africa. The end result was that, aware of the weakened condition of al-Andalus and having taken Granada in 1090, Yusuf ibn-Tashufin removed al-Mu'tamid from power and in 1091 took possession of both Córdoba and Seville. The

Almoravids would remain in power for fifty-four years. Indeed, during his reign, which lasted until 1106, Yusuf extended his power northwards, as far as Zaragoza by 1110, though he failed to recapture Toledo. Subsequently, however, the Almoravid grip on al-Andalus began to weaken, and by 1145 had come to an end. There followed a period of instability until, around 1170, the Almohads, yet another powerful African dynasty, seized power.

From 1162, Abd-al-Mu'min, leader of the Almohads in north Africa, had entertained the idea of taking possession of Muslim Spain, but his plan was not put into effect until 1171, after his son, Abu-Ya'qub Yusuf, had succeeded him. The process continued under his successor, Abu-Yusuf Ya'qub al-Mansur, until his death in 1199, but by this time the Christians were growing ever stronger, and in 1212, when Muhammad an-Nasir was the ruler of al-Andalus, they won a famous and decisive victory at Las Navas de Tolosa, south of Toledo. When Muhammad died a year later, his fifteen-year-old son, Abu-Ya'qub Yusuf II, was unable to halt the Almohad decline, and when he also died in 1223, leaving no heir, power was virtually handed to the Christians. They occupied Córdoba in 1236 and Seville in 1248. By around 1270 Muslim control in Spain had vanished, with the exception of Granada, which prospered from 1235 under the Nasrid dynasty.

In spite of frequent political instability, cultural activity prospered almost without interruption in the period described above. Two of the most famous Andalusian writers of the time were Ibn-Zaydun (1003–70), whose love poems were dedicated to princess Wallada, and Ibn-Hazm (994–1064), who, with other poets, described different aspects of love in the treatise *The Ring of the Dove*. As the work of these writers suggests, the themes of Muslim poetry were often to do with pleasure seeking, be it drinking, women, beauty, love and the enjoyment of Nature, all described in highly refined and sophisticated verse. In love poems, in particular, the emphasis was firmly on the sensual. As well as love poets, there were many Arab grammarians in al-Andalus; there were dictionaries, anthologies of various kinds, biographies, works on law and history, volumes of short stories and religious works to do with the teaching of Muhammad. And in the twelfth century there were philosophers of great merit, such as Ibn-Tufayl (1105–85), born in Guadix, near Granada, and Ibn-Rushd (1126–98), author of a commentary on Aristotle. But what still remains of Almoravid and Almohad architecture?

During the rule of the Almoravids, no major building projects were undertaken, for they favoured the production of smaller things, such as silk fabrics and ivory caskets and boxes. The Almohads were, in contrast, a much more austere people who favoured a simpler lifestyle and condemned what they regarded as the luxury enjoyed by the Almoravids. When they came to power in 1171, they at once demolished the Visigothic cathedral in which the Christians who remained in Seville were allowed to worship, and constructed on the site a huge mosque. When the Christians once more took possession of the city in 1248, the mosque was adapted for Christian worship; it subsequently became unsafe and the current cathedral, 104 years in the building, replaced it. The Giralda tower, now crowned by a bell-tower, was, though, the minaret of the Almohad mosque and remains one of the most interesting monuments in Seville, as well as a remarkable testimony to its Muslim past.

The minaret was built between 1172 and 1198 and was originally 76 metres high, topped by four gilded brass balls, one on top of the other. When these were dislodged by an earthquake in 1356, a small brick bell-tower was built in their place, and in 1558 this was in turn replaced by a more impressive bell-tower, which increased the height of the original minaret by 18 metres. On the very top is a statue which weighs more than a tonne but which, nevertheless, turns with the wind. Indeed, the name Giralda means 'weathervane'. As for the minaret itself, we can see from the outside windows that it consists of seven rooms, one above the other. The outer walls are divided into three areas: the lower part smooth, the upper two decorated with a criss-cross or 'lozenge' pattern. The top section, shorter than the other two, has ten interlocking arches. In general, the Giralda has a simple grace and elegance, and the added bell-tower merges perfectly with the minaret below it. The bell-tower contains twenty-five bells, each with its own name, the largest called San Pedro.[4]

The Alcázar, which must be seen by any visitor to Seville, was probably built in the eighth century but has since undergone many changes. Under al-Mu'tadid, in the eleventh century, it became the centrepiece of an extremely sophisticated court; it is said to have contained a harem of 800 concubines and boasted terraces where flowers grew in the skulls of beheaded enemies. Most of the present-day building dates from the four-teenth century, when the Christian king, Pedro the Cruel, brought Muslim craftsmen from Granada to decorate the palace to his own taste. The result is a brilliant example of Mudéjar, the style practised by Muslims living under Christian rule, but further additions were also made in the fifteenth and sixteenth centuries.

The main façade of Pedro the Cruel's palace consists of two storeys, the upper distinguished by double and triple windows, and is a fine example of Mudéjar workmanship. From the entrance we proceed into a central courtyard known as the Patio of the Maidens, the Patio de las Doncellas, the name of which brings to mind the Christian practice of presenting the Muslim rulers with a hundred virgins every year. This is a magnificent, galleried courtyard, its two levels containing beautiful arches supported on slim marble columns. On the lower level the walls above and between the arches are filled with intricate decorative patterns, while the upper level, restored by the Catholic Kings, is in Plateresque style. Around the courtyard are various rooms, of which the Hall of the Ambassadors, the Salón de Embajadores, is strikingly beautiful.

Completed in 1366, this two-storey building, intricately decorated with mosaic tiles, gilt and stucco painted in pink, yellow and blue, is a blaze of colour. Each wall of the lower storey has three perfectly shaped archways with horseshoe arches, topped by the most delicate tracery. The top storey has a magnificent domed ceiling in which strips of wood enclose areas of stucco painted red, green and gold. The effect, as we look up, is that of stars twinkling in the night sky. The royal portraits which we see in the lower storey were installed during the reign of Philip II in the sixteenth century. It was in the Hall of the Ambassadors that Philip's father, Charles V, married Isabel of Portugal, and where, prior to that, Pedro the Cruel murdered his half-brother, Don Fadrique.

From the Hall of the Ambassadors, we can enter the Patio of the Dolls, the Patio de las Muñecas, so called because of the two small, doll-like faces which decorate one of its arches. Beautifully decorated, though on a smaller and more intimate scale, this building was the domestic centre of the palace, for the royal bedrooms are adjacent to the courtyard. Originally, the harem was probably to be found here. The elegant columns are thought to have been brought from Medina Azahara, for, as we have already seen, stonework and columns from that once magnificent city were frequently transported for building elsewhere.

From the side of the Patio of the Maidens furthest from the Hall of the Ambassadors, we proceed into an area of the Alcázar which is quite different from the rest: the chapel and the apartments of Charles V, dating from the sixteenth century. The style of these more recent buildings has none of the beauty and elegance of Moorish or Mudéjar architecture. No longer are the walls embellished by intricate geometrical patterns and brilliant colours; they are, instead, covered by rather uninteresting tapestries, the work of Flemish craftsmen. As in the case of the Alhambra in Granada, the contrast between light and elegant Muslim architecture and the much heavier, weightier Renaissance monuments and buildings constructed during the reign of Charles is both striking and to the detriment of the latter.

The gardens of the Alcázar, a haven of peace created by fountains, myrtle bushes, flowers and different kinds of trees, are to be found behind the apartments of Charles V and the Patio of the Maidens. They extend along the entire width of the complex and are reminiscent, on a smaller scale, of the gardens of the Generalife in the Alhambra. Beneath the palace are a number of cisterns known as the Baths of María Padilla, the beautiful mistress of Pedro the Cruel. A rather attractive story has it that the young men at Pedro's court drank María's bathwater in order to find favour with the king. Later, in the eighteenth century, Philip V ordered the construction of a cistern in which he fished while preparing to die through religious flagellation.

One of Seville's most visible and famous monuments is the Golden Tower, the Torre del Oro, situated on the bank of the Guadalquivir some 300 metres west of the Alcázar. Built by the Almohads in 1220, it is a twelve-sided building which was then part of a fortified wall which ran from the river to the Alcázar itself. In fact, some parts of the wall, with its towers, can still be seen, and we can imagine how well defended against enemy attacks Seville must have been. Indeed, the Golden Tower was matched by a second tower on the other side of the river, the two joined by a massive chain which was designed to prevent ships sailing upstream. Built of brick and stone, the Golden Tower has a massive base and was originally three storeys high, the turret being added in 1760. As for its name, one well-worn theory is that it stems from the belief that Pedro the Cruel stored his treasure there; another is that it stored the gold brought by Christopher Columbus from the New World. The far more likely explanation is that its name is derived from the gilt tiles which once covered its walls and which gleamed brightly in the light of the sun.

The House of Pilate, the Casa de Pilatos, so called because it was thought to resemble the house of Pontius Pilate in Jerusalem, is particularly interesting because it was not built until the sixteenth century, well after Muslim rule in Spain had come to an end. It is, though, a perfect example of the Mudéjar style which continued to be practised by Muslim craftsmen living in Spain after the fall of Granada in 1492 and which is also to be seen in the Alcázar. And, in the House of Pilate, Mudéjar style is also brilliantly combined with Renaissance influence, inspired by Fadrique de Ribera's visit to Italy and the Holy Land in the early part of the sixteenth century. Along with the Alcázar, the House of Pilate should certainly be at the top of any visitor's list.

After entering the building through a portal of marble commissioned by Fadrique de Ribera in 1529, we pass through a courtyard to the main inner patio. The two-storey layout and the low balustrade above the lower storey are typically Renaissance, but the arches and the slender marble columns of both the lower and the upper storeys are wholly Muslim in style, as is the wonderfully intricate design between and above the arches. The brilliant patterns created by the tiles in caramel, yellow, green and purple evoke an oriental rug.

The combination of Italian and Muslim elements can be seen throughout the rooms of the building. In the Salón Pretorio, to the right of the patio, the highly decorated wooden panelling inlaid with ivory and the clusters of wooden cones which hang like stalactites from the ceiling are pure Muslim in style. And in the chapel reached via the Judges' Rest Room, the Salón del Descanso de los Jueces, is a beautiful Gothic ceiling whose ribs are set against a Mudéjar stucco background. The upper floor of the building is reached by a tiled staircase above which is a gilded dome in the form of a half-orange, splendidly decorated with an intricate pattern of wood and colourful inlays. This lovely ceiling has its counterpart in some of the upper rooms in which there are also Mudéjar ceilings. And the Muslim influence is completed by the gardens which lie to either side of the building and where palms, orange trees, rose bushes and fountains create the mood of tranquillity so evident in other Muslim gardens.

Even though Seville is one of the most beautiful cities in Spain, far more attractive in general than either Córdoba or Granada, Granada it is which has the greater celebrity and appeal to the imagination, and this on account of what is clearly the most magical Muslim monument in western Europe. The Alhambra, once the royal palace of the Nasrid rulers until their defeat by the Catholic Kings, Ferdinand and Isabella, in 1492, has been celebrated throughout the centuries in literature, painting and music to a far greater extent than either Córdoba's Mezquita or Seville's Alcázar. In Granada itself, postcards and ornamental tiles contain the following refrain:

> Give him alms, woman,
> For there is nothing in life
> More painful than
> To be blind in Granada.[5]

The words refer to a blind beggar saddened not so much by his inability to see the buildings of the city as by his exclusion from the beauty of the Alhambra which stands above it: a beauty evoked by the fourteenth-century Muslim poet, Ibn Zamrak:

I am the garden adorned by beauty: look and you will understand me.
This mansion is sublime, for Fortune has made it greater than any other.
What joy it offers to our gaze, awakening the desires of our noble ruler.
These dazzling columns, hidden and so full of magic, have no equal.
The brilliant stars, weary of circling the heavens, descend and rest below,
    slaves awaiting the king's command.
The marble, smooth, transparent, illuminates, like pearls, the darkened
    corners.
No garden is as green; no place possesses such abundant sweetness.

For those of us who can feast our eyes on such beauty, it is not difficult to understand the blind beggar's anguish.

The city of Granada, east of Seville and south-east of Córdoba, stands on several hills, some 670 metres above sea level, and consists of a high and a low city. On one of the hills is the 'barrio' or district known as the Albaicín, a maze of steep, narrow, twisting streets and white houses, steeped in Arabic influence. To the south-east of it, on still higher ground, is the Sacromonte, a once famous gypsy quarter now largely derelict. And to the south of the Albaicín, separated from it by the River Darro, is the Alhambra, the 'red fortress', built on the Sabika Hill, high above the city. Between Granada and the sea to the south is the mighty Sierra Nevada, rising to a height of almost 3,500 metres, its peaks covered with snow, while at its base there extends the rich agricultural plain known as the Vega, some 227,000 hectares in area and rich in orange and olive trees. Its fertility is due to two rivers, the Darro, already mentioned, and the Genil, which descends from the Sierra Nevada, enters the city on the southern side and merges with the Darro. From the walls of the Alhambra the surrounding landscape is a marvellous sight.

As we have seen, Seville had fallen to the Christians in 1248, and by 1270 only Granada remained in Muslim hands. The first Nasrid ruler of the sultanate of Granada, Ibn-al-Ahmar, also known as Muhammad ibn-Yusuf ibn-Nasr, had assumed power in 1235 and enjoyed a relatively long reign of thirty-six years. It was, however, a difficult time, for the increasing threat posed by the Christian advance was often accompanied by internal dangers rooted in personal envy and ambition. In this respect, one of Ibn-al-Ahmar's successors, Muhammed III, reigned for only seven years, from 1302 until 1309, when he was ousted by his own brother, Nasr, but he in turn was overthrown after only five years by his nephew, Ismael, who eleven years later was himself stabbed to death. His successor, Muhammed IV, was murdered after eight years in power, and Yusuf I, who ruled for twenty-one years until 1354, was murdered while at prayer. Intrigue and treachery were never far away.

This said, Yusuf's successor, Muhammed V, ruled until 1391, apart from three years in exile, enjoyed an unusually peaceful time and, as we shall see, contributed greatly to the development of the Alhambra. After his death, the greatness of the Alhambra and the good fortune of Granada itself came to an end, for during the next one hundred years the story proved to be one of constant internal division, as well as of increasing external pressure from the Christians. Yusuf II, Muhammed's successor, was dead within two years, apparently poisoned by a ceremonial robe sent to him by the sultan of Fez. Yusuf III was immediately removed from power by his own brother but recovered his position sixteen years later, in 1408. In the seventy-five years which followed Yusuf's death, there were ten different rulers, while in the region around Granada town after town fell to the Christian advance. When in 1469 Ferdinand of Aragón married Isabella of Castile, thus uniting the two most powerful kingdoms in Christian Spain, the completion of the process known as the Reconquest was not far away.

An opportunity to launch a final assault against Granada itself arose when in 1476 the sultan of Granada, Muley Hasan, refused to pay the Catholic Kings the customary tribute – the equivalent of protection money. The campaign, though, proved to be long and difficult and involved setbacks on both sides. In 1481, for example, the Moors captured the Christian town of Zahara, to the west of Ronda, but in retaliation the Christians seized the Moorish-occupied town of Alhama, only 50 kilometres from Granada, the immediate effect of which was to bring about the downfall of Muley Hasan as sultan of Granada. Although replaced by his son, Muhammed XII, better known as Boabdil, Muley Hasan was able to return to Granada when Boabdil was himself captured by the Christians in 1483. When Muley Hasan died two years later, he was succeeded by his brother, Muhammed XIII, but he was much disliked, and Boabdil, having been released from captivity, was persuaded by Ferdinand to return to Granada in the hope that his presence there would lead to further discord. The outcome was, indeed, civil war, but Boabdil and his uncle reached an agreement whereby they ruled different areas of the sultanate. Consequently, Ferdinand launched an assault against the town of Loja which fell to the Christians after five weeks of fierce fighting. Boabdil, himself wounded in the fighting, was informed that, as soon as he once more became ruler of Granada, he would be obliged to surrender it to the Christians. In 1487 he did indeed succeed in entering the city while Muhammed was away attempting to defend Málaga. When Muhammed returned to Granada, he found the city gates closed against him and

Boabdil once more in control. Two years later, Muhammed was forced to surrender to the Christians. He was soon freed and allowed to settle in Fez, but there he was regarded as a coward, he was imprisoned and blinded, and he ended his life as a beggar.

The final Christian attack on Granada commenced in 1491 and was motivated in no small part by Boabdil's failure to fulfil his promise to surrender the city to Ferdinand and Isabella. Instead, he proceeded to attack various Christian towns, and so it was that the Catholic Kings resolved to take Granada by force. Initially, they began to destroy the Vega, the lush and fertile plain which supplied the city with its food. Boabdil, observing this process and the growing panic of his subjects, then entered into secret negotiations for Granada's surrender. According to the agreement, concluded on 25 November, Muslims would be allowed to keep their property and maintain their religion, customs, law, and dress. Boabdil and his family would be guaranteed their safety, and he would be allowed to rule a small neighbouring kingdom as a vassal of Ferdinand and Isabella – a generous gesture, given his earlier actions against them.

Boabdil surrendered the keys of the city in the Alhambra's magnificent Hall of the Ambassadors on 1 January 1492. The Christians, headed by the cardinal of Spain, entered the city on the following day, and, after meeting Ferdinand and Isabella, Boabdil left the Alhambra and the city. The story goes that, as he did so, he looked back and wept, and, in so doing, was chastised by his mother, Fatima, with the words: 'It is proper that you weep like a woman for what you failed to defend like a man.' The place where Boabdil is said to have wept, some 10 kilometres from Granada, has been known ever since as 'The Last Sigh of the Moor' ('El último suspiro del moro'). Boabdil's tears for the loss of his beloved Granada also marked, of course, the end of almost 800 years of Muslim power in Spain.

Most visitors to the Alhambra nowadays arrive by car or by bus, following a circuitous route which ends in the car park on its eastern side. It is far more interesting to approach it on foot, beginning in the Plaza Nueva in the city below and climbing the Hill of Gomérez, the Cuesta de Gomérez, until, after passing through the Alhambra Wood, where the tall elms are mistakenly thought to have been planted by the duke of Wellington, we reach the massive Gateway of Justice, the Puerta de la Justicia, one of the many towers constructed around the Alhambra walls and today one of the two entrances to the complex. Passing through the Gateway of Justice, we encounter the Gateway of Wine, the Puerta del Vino, and then a large open area known as the Square of the Wells, the Plaza de los Aljibes, to the west of which, and on the western side of the

Alhambra itself, is the Alcazaba, which was known in Arabic as Qa'lat al-Hamra, the Red Fortress, the name later given to the entire area. The ten towers placed in the walls of the Alcazaba clearly point to its fortress-like nature.[6]

When Ibn-al-Ahmar, the first of the Nasrid rulers, came to power in 1235, he initially established his court not on the site now occupied by the Alhambra but on the hill of the Albaicín to the north of it. Not long afterwards, however, he took the decision to relocate to the Sabika Hill, on the other side of the River Darro, for a fort already existed there, of which the two existing towers known as the Vermillion Towers, the Torres Bermejas, were a part. Ibn-al-Ahmar then proceeded to rebuild and transform the original fort into what became the Alcazaba by adding towers and defensive walls within which there would have been a barracks and, of course, accommodation for the royal family. Of the towers, the most imposing is the watchtower, the Torre de la Vela, which is more than 27 metres high and some 16 metres wide. Situated at the western end of the Alcazaba, it serves as a wonderful lookout point from which one can see the Albaicín to the north, the city of Granada down below to the west, the great agricultural plain known as the Vega, and, in the distance, the snow-capped peaks of the Sierra Nevada. Until fairly recent times, the workers in the fields would have heard the bell of the watchtower ring out, instructing them to open the irrigation sluices and, even nowadays, on 1 and 2 January it is rung to remind the inhabitants of Granada that on 2 January 1492, the city's surrender to the forces of the Catholic Kings marked the end of Muslim domination of Spain. The way in which, over centuries, the great bell has imposed itself on the consciousness of the citizens of Granada is suggested in the words of a traditional song:

> I want to live in Granada
> If only to hear
> The bell of la Vela
> As I go to sleep.

The visitor to the Alhambra should bear in mind that, initially, midway through the thirteenth century, the Alcazaba stood on its own. It was essentially a fortress-town, isolated from the city below and strongly defended by its walls, towers and location. The palace buildings which attract us today had still to be built.

In order to enter the latter, we turn back from the Alcazaba, cross the Square of the Wells and proceed to the group of rooms known as the Mexuar, completed in all probability in the second half of the fourteenth century, well after the death of Ibn-al-Ahmar. The first room we encounter

21

is the Hall of the Mexuar, the Sala del Mexuar. This served as a council chamber where a Muslim council would have met to discuss important matters of the day and where the sultan would have heard petitions of various kinds. Although many alterations have been made to the room in the course of time, an impression of its original character can still be formed, for the upper part of the walls are much as they were in both colour and intricate plasterwork, while Arabic inscriptions across the length and breadth of the room – 'Enter and fear not to ask for justice, for you will find it' – point to the judicial matters which were conducted there. The gallery at the back is, however, a much later addition, probably sixteenth century.

The other rooms which make up the Mexuar are the Oratory of the Mexuar, the Oratorio del Mexuar; the Courtyard of the Mexuar, the Patio del Mexuar; and the Golden Room, the Cuarto Dorado. All three rooms, for a variety of reasons, present considerable difficulties as far as dating is concerned. The oratory, a prayer room at the far end of the Hall of the Mexuar, was so severely damaged by an explosion in 1590 that it had to be rebuilt. The northern end of the courtyard contains features which range from thirteenth-century capitals to sixteenth-century ceilings, while its southern wall was either built or rebuilt in the second half of the fourteenth century. And the Golden Room displays above the window the emblems of the Catholic Kings, which suggests that they played an important part in the restoration of the room after the capture of Granada by the Christians. This said, there is much that evokes the beauty and harmony of Muslim architecture. On the northern side of the courtyard, for example, are three perfectly proportioned arches supported by slender columns of marble, and above the arches the most beautiful and elaborate decoration. The wall on the opposite side of the courtyard is, if anything, even more beautiful, for it contains two doorways framed by extremely attractive tiles, and higher up are two arched and perfectly proportioned double windows separated by a single smaller arched window. The wall itself is faced with wonderfully intricate plaster decoration and is surmounted by overhanging eaves, also finely carved. In short, the various rooms of the Mexuar provide us with a fascinating introductory glimpse to the beauty of the Alhambra.

Like the Mezquita in Córdoba, the different parts of the Alhambra were built by different rulers at different times. From the Mexuar we move, then, to the right into the Palace of Comares, the Palacio de Comares, which, even if some of it existed prior to the accession to the throne of Muhammed V in 1354, was greatly improved by him during his reign of thirty-seven years. The Palace of Comares consists of three areas: the visually stunning Courtyard of the Myrtles, the Patio de Arrayanes; the

Hall of the Ship, the Sala de la Barca; and the brilliantly decorated Hall of the Ambassadors, the Salón de Embajadores.

The Courtyard of the Myrtles, rectangular in shape, is enclosed on all four sides. The pool which occupies the centre of the courtyard, and which is almost as long as the courtyard itself, is flanked on its two long sides by the myrtle bushes which give the place its name. If we stand at the southern end of the courtyard, the effect is truly startling, for the buildings at the opposite end of the pool are reflected in the water: the façade of the Hall of the Ship, with its seven perfectly and finely decorated arches, and behind and above it, the massive Tower of Comares, the whole, of course, inverted in the shimmering surface of the pool. And if we stand at the northern end of the courtyard, the southern façade is similarly reflected: a marble-columned colonnade of seven arches, above it the outer wall of a room with seven arched windows and above this a gallery with seven arches which balance those on the ground floor. The effect is one of perfect symmetry and proportion. The seven-windowed room would in Muslim times have been the place from which the sultan's family could, without being seen, observe what was happening below, including the foreign ambassadors who were waiting for an audience with the sultan in the Hall of the Ambassadors. At that time the water in the pool would have lapped against the base of the columns at either end of the courtyard, creating the illusion of a floating palace. The effect must have been magical. Needless to say, the Courtyard of the Myrtles has attracted the attention of artists for many centuries.

The Hall of the Ship stands at the southern end of the courtyard and in front of the Hall of the Ambassadors, both of which were brilliantly decorated by Muhammed V. The Hall of the Ship was destroyed by fire in 1890 but was restored to its original state in the 1960s. Its rather unusual name has two possible explanations. Because the Spanish word for ship is 'barca', this may have been confused with the Muslim word 'baraka', which means 'blessing', and which appears numerous times in the entrance to the hall, suggesting that hospitality was extended to visitors. On the other hand, the word 'barca' may be connected with the ceiling of the room, which has the appearance of an upturned boat. It is, without question, the most striking feature of the hall.

To enter the Hall of the Ambassadors from the Hall of the Ship is to understand the effect which this marvellous room must have had on those granted an audience with the sultan. The biggest and most splendid room in the whole of the Alhambra, it is perfectly square, each side measuring some 10 metres, with a high ceiling. At ground level in three of the walls there are three arched windows which face north, east and west, and above them, high up in the wall, are five smaller arched windows. The sultan's throne would have been placed in front of the middle window in the northern wall, as indicated by the inscription: 'Yusuf ... chose me as the seat of the kingdom. The ruler of this kingdom makes it a great and divine throne.' Standing at the opposite end of the room, imagine the effect on a visitor entering the room from the Hall of the Ship. He would have seen the sultan seated on his throne and bathed in the light coming through the windows behind and above him – a powerful and dazzling effect enhanced by the gold of the walls and the square of patterned marble which forms the floor. The original stained-glass windows were destroyed in an explosion in the sixteenth century, but even today the effect of the light streaming through the glass is impressive.

Given the great beauty of the Hall of the Ambassadors, its ceiling is considered by many to be its outstanding feature. The Muslim carpenters of the fourteenth century constructed a domed roof made of 8,017 pieces of wood on which cedar reliefs consisting of symmetrical panels were superimposed. Originally comprising red, light green and white colours, the ceiling represented the seven heavens of the Muslim paradise, its star-like patterns lighting the way to God at the centre. The religious significance of the building should not be underestimated, for inscriptions on the walls – 'Only God is the Victor' – are a reminder of it, as well as the fact that the splendour of this palace was created by men whose skill and artistic talent was afforded them by God.

The Courtyard of the Lions, the Patio de los Leones, lies to the right of the Palace of Comares and is probably the best-known part of the Alhambra, celebrated worldwide in painting and photography. Around the actual courtyard are four buildings: the Hall of the Mozárabes, the Sala de los Mozárabes; the Hall of the Abencerrajes, the Sala de los Abencerrajes; the Hall of the Kings, the Sala de los Reyes; and the Hall of the Two Sisters, the Sala de las dos Hermanas. Apart from the latter, the whole of the complex belongs to the reign of Muhammed V and has the overall design of a villa with a central courtyard. The Hall of the Abencerrajes seems to have been Muhammed's winter dining-room, and the Hall of the Two Sisters his permanent living quarters. Because the buildings also contained the rooms of the women of the royal household, this part of the Alhambra is often mistakenly alluded to as the harem, but in reality it was often used to conduct the political and diplomatic activities of the kingdom.

We enter the Hall of the Mozárabes from the Courtyard of the Myrtles. The ceiling, which originally consisted of highly decorative plaster work, was destroyed by the same explosion which in 1590 blew out the stained-glass windows of the Hall of the Ambassadors, and was subsequently replaced by a baroque ceiling. What really attracts our attention here, though, is our first glimpse of the Courtyard of the Lions through the slender columns of the pavilion which project into the courtyard from the Hall of the Mozárabes. The effect is rather like that of looking through a cluster of palm trees towards a cool and inviting oasis. In times past the courtyard contained many plants, which obscured from the visitor the marble bases of the columns of the surrounding buildings, thereby creating the illusion of a golden forest.

Moving in an anti-clockwise direction, we come to the Hall of the Abencerrajes. In the centre of the room is a twelve-sided fountain at ground level, but the most arresting feature here is the ceiling with its central eight-sided star supported by stalactite corner mouldings and sixteen windows around its sides. The intricate decoration of the whole, suffused with a golden light, suggests an enormous honeycomb. It is the most impressive ceiling in the whole of the Alhambra. The name of the hall is derived from that of an illustrious Granada family, some of whose members were, according to legend, slain there. The most colourful version describes how Boabdil, the last sultan of Granada, was falsely informed that his queen was engaged in an affair with a member of the Abencerraje family. Convinced of the truth of this story, Boabdil then summoned thirty-six Abencerrajes to the Courtyard of the Lions and had them beheaded. The red stains on the bottom of the fountain in the Hall of the Abencerrajes are reputed to be their blood, though the far less intriguing fact is that they are actually iron-oxide stains.

From the Hall of the Abencerrajes we proceed to the Hall of the Kings, on the opposite side of the courtyard from the Hall of the Mozárabes. The room is divided into sections by five arches across its width, while their supporting side columns create a corresponding number of alcoves along its length. Viewed from one end, therefore, it gives the impression of five areas of light and shade. The sultan and his companions would have spent their time in the central alcove, looking out no doubt onto the Courtyard of the Lions. On the ceiling of this alcove there are paintings of human figures which are thought to be the first ten rulers of the Nasrid dynasty and which contradict the common belief that the representation of living beings was forbidden by the Koran.

The fourth room in the complex, the Hall of the Two Sisters, is both the oldest and the most beautiful. Its name is thought by some to derive from two captive sisters who, witnessing lovemaking in which they could not take part, died from sheer frustration, but it seems more likely that the name has its origin in the two great marble slabs which form part of the floor. The lower part of the hall is square in shape, some 8 by 8 metres, but higher up it becomes octagonal in order to accommodate the octagonal ceiling. Each of the eight sides of this ceiling contains two windows which, until the explosion of 1590, were of stained glass, which meant in turn that the most beautiful light would have flooded into the room below. The ceiling, made of over five thousand pieces of wood and plaster and covered with stalactite and scroll-like effects which change colour in rela-tion to changing light, was clearly intended to evoke heaven. The lower parts of the walls are decorated with tiles and, above them, running around the four walls, is the poem by Ibn Zamrak, quoted earlier, which cele-brates the beauty of the room. It is not surprising that, in the latter part of the fourteenth century, the Hall of the Two Sisters should have replaced the Hall of the Ambassadors as the sultan's throne room.

Extremely beautiful too is the Balcony of Lindaraja, the Mirador de Lindaraja, which is a kind of gazebo situated on the northern side of the Hall of the Two Sisters. From its beautiful, double-arched window one looks out onto the peaceful Garden of Lindaraja. The ceiling consists of a glass dome held in place by the most attractive wooden tracery, while the walls are wonderfully decorated and tiled at the base with perfectly proportioned coloured tiles. We can well image why this lovely room was occupied by the sultana and other members of the royal family.

As for the courtyard itself, twelve marble lions, arranged in a circle and spraying water from their mouths, support a large, twelve-sided bowl, around which is an inscription which states that the lions' ferocity would be much greater were it not for their respect for the sultan. From this central fountain four slightly raised marble paths, each containing a narrow channel, carry water to the surrounding buildings. It is easy to understand how, in this haven of beauty and tranquillity, the Muslim inhabitants of the Alhambra took their ease.

At the north-west corner of this group of buildings we encounter the baths, which played an important part in the lives of the Muslim rulers of the Alhambra. They were, like Roman baths, divided into three sections which corresponded to the various stages of bathing: the hot room, the warm room and the rest room. In the first two of the three rooms, small canals contained water which, heated by a chimney below, turned into steam and therefore had the effect of a modern sauna. In the rest room, the reclining bathers were entertained by singers and musicians positioned on the balconies above. It seems quite likely that these entertainers were blind and so unable to see the female members of the royal family in a state of undress.

The buildings which constitute the Alhambra clearly formed a relatively small royal city which, quite apart from the palaces of the Muslim rulers, contained living quarters, administrative buildings, mosques, schools, baths, barracks, stables, cemeteries and gardens. Below it lay the city of Granada, with a population of some 150,000 inhabitants, sprawling down the hill as it does today. As for the various palaces of the Alhambra, it is clear that their basic design consisted of, as in an ordinary Muslim house, a central courtyard surrounded by living quarters. At the back of the rooms there was often another small room, or 'oriel', as in the case of the Balcony of Lindaraja, where visitors could be welcomed and entertained without intruding on the activities of the family around the courtyard.

One of the essential and distinctive features of Muslim architecture, evident in both the Alhambra and other buildings, is, of course, the slender and elegant columns. They appear to bear no weight at all, and the delicate and finely patterned structure which they support seems as light as the icing on a wedding cake. The overall effect is one of great beauty and serenity. A second distinctive feature of Muslim art, evident everywhere in the walls and ceilings of the Alhambra, as well as in the Muslim build-ings in Córdoba and Seville, is the arabesque, which is essentially non-representational. Arabic art in general is abstract, based on pure line and rhythm. When we walk through the rooms of the Alhambra, we can see that the fine and elaborate decoration on plaster and tiles suggests stars, flowers and intertwining plants, all arranged in complicated but symmetrical and harmonious patterns. The aim of such intricate and beau-tiful design was to create a framework which was worthy of the dignity of man and, in particular, of the sultan, who was, in effect, the most precious jewel of all. But even more important, of course, was its celebration of the magnificence of God.

A third important and characteristic feature of Arabic art and decoration in general is the so-called stalactite, which is particularly prominent in the Hall of the Mozárabes and the Hall of the Two Sisters. In one sense, the base of the stalactite had a purely practical function, for it tied a domed ceiling to the supporting walls. On the other hand, it had a symbolic signif-icance, for the sky was considered by the Muslims to be formed of ether. In both rooms mentioned above, the domed ceiling represented the sky, and the stalactites descending from it at the corners of the room therefore symbolized the ether which flowed from the sky to the earth and which solidified in the process of so doing.

Although the main impression created by the Alhambra is that of its outstanding beauty, it is just as important that we appreciate its overall simplicity of design. The arrangement of buildings around a pool, the placing of archways and doorways, the layout of courtyards, are essentially relatively simple, as in the case of the southern façade of the Courtyard of the Myrtles, where the bottom seven arches are perfectly balanced by those at the top. But the effect of this simplicity, which is repeated again and again throughout the Alhambra, is to create a wonderful and satisfying sense of peace and harmony. This, however, is not a purely aesthetic effect, for to stand in any part of these palaces is also to experience an inner calm and tranquillity, a sense of infinite peace.

In much Islamic art the secular and the spiritual go hand in hand. The point has been made earlier that in times past the Courtyard of the Lions was filled with plants. This effectively transformed it into an enclosed garden, and in this context we need to appreciate that in Islamic thought a garden is an image of paradise. For those who lived in the buildings around this courtyard, the water channels which cross it were therefore symbolic of the four rivers of paradise, while the twelve lions around the fountain were synonymous with the twelve suns of the zodiac, the twelve months of the year. For Islam, furthermore, paradise consists not only of running water and beautiful flowers, but also of the effect created by the interaction of the natural world and lovely buildings and of the way in which they are affected by light. Light itself is thought to be an essential element of paradise, and the architects of the Alhambra made every effort to use it to its full advantage. In general, then, the palaces may be seen as having served both a practical and a spiritual purpose, for, if they served as living quarters and as an administrative centre, they also delighted the soul and spirit, combining this world with the next.

If the visitor is impressed by the buildings of the Alhambra, he or she will also admire the extensive gardens of the Generalife which lie close at hand. The name has been interpreted in various ways, the most appealing of which is probably 'the garden of lofty paradise'. In order to reach the gardens, we cross the bridge over the Hill of the Pebbles, the Cuesta de los Chinos, and then pass through a long walkway flanked by cypress trees, until we finally reach an old palace and, in particular, the Courtyard of the Water Channel, the Patio de la Acequia, and the Water Stairway, the Escalera de Agua.

The Courtyard of the Water Channel is so called because a water channel, spouting water which forms delicate, shimmering, arch-like patterns, runs almost its entire length. It is an enchanting spectacle, but during the time of the Nasrid dynasty the effect was rather different, for the water came from only two spouts at either end of the channel. The sound of splashing water would therefore have been much quieter, but the water in the channel would have produced the same mirror-like effect as we have seen elsewhere in the Alhambra, for its surface would have been much less disturbed than is the case nowadays. On either side of the channel, also running along its entire length, is a proliferation of shrubs and flowers, adding to the dazzling impression.

The courtyard is flanked by buildings on all four sides. On the northern side is part of an old Moorish palace which dates from about 1319 and which is fronted by an arcade of five perfectly proportioned arches, the middle one larger and higher than the other four. At the southern end of the courtyard another building balances that at the opposite end, but it is less impressive. On each of the long sides of the water channel are two narrow parallel buildings, one of which has a 'mirador' or viewing point. The Water Stairway, above the courtyard on its eastern side, is, as its name suggests, a flight of steps which has water flowing down its stone balustrades. Beyond this, at the top of the hill, is the Moor's Chair, the Silla del Moro, once a watchtower and now in the process of reconstruction. It affords the most magnificent views over the Alhambra, the Albaicín, the city itself and the Sierra Nevada in the distance. In the account above of the Hall of the Abencerrajes, one of the members of the Abencerraje family was described as having had an affair with the wife of the sultan, Boabdil. Their meeting place, intriguingly, was the small garden called the Courtyard of the Cypresses, the Patio de los Cipreses, a small garden immediately behind the eastern side of the Courtyard of the Water Channel. One can well imagine the secret encounters of the Sultana Zoraya and her lover in this secluded walled garden, both of them transported by their feelings, lulled by the sound of running water and oblivious to the catastrophe that lay ahead.

The Generalife, the only garden to have survived from the many which covered the slopes around the Alhambra, was designed for the pleasure and relaxation of its Muslim rulers. As has been mentioned previously, however, a garden was for Islam a symbol of paradise, its appeal as much spiritual as sensual, and in this respect it is useful to refer to a treatise on gardening written by Ibn Luyun at the beginning of the fourteenth century. According to this writer, a house should be constructed on elevated ground and surrounded by gardens. The house, in order to receive maximum sunlight, should be south facing, but steps should also be taken to provide shade and tranquillity. With this in mind, a pool or well should be situated above the house so that water could descend through water channels, and there should also be an abundance of trees and shrubs shading the paths around the area. The house or pavilion at the centre of the garden should be surrounded by rose bushes, myrtles and all manner of beautiful flowers, the whole designed to please the eye. In addition, there should be vines and other fruit trees from which one could pick and eat the fruit. In short, the garden should appeal to all the senses – hearing, sight, smell, taste and touch – thereby creating a true heaven on earth.

In order to create such a garden, it goes without saying that a constant supply of water is essential. Because the hill on which the Alhambra is situated originally had no water, its Muslim rulers took steps to ensure that it did, and the River Darro, which today flows downhill on the northern side of the Generalife, was diverted from its original course by a distance of 18 kilometres. The construction of dams, channels, ponds and wells quickly transformed a barren hill into a fertile paradise.

Muslim influence is very evident too in the Albaicín, the area to the north of the Alhambra, separated from it by the River Darro and character-ized by its steep, labyrinthine streets. The word 'Albaicín' is itself of Arabic origin, a shortened form of 'Rabad Al-Baezin', which means 'the suburb of those from Baeza', referring to Muslim fugitives who in times past fled to Granada from the town of Baeza, some one hundred kilo-metres to the north. We reach the Albaicín, starting off in the Plaza Nueva in the city, and following the Street of the Darro, the Carrera del Darro, which runs alongside the river. The Muslim heritage of the Albaicín becomes clear almost immediately, for some 200 metres along the road we arrive at the ruins of the evocatively named Bridge of the Cadí, the Puente del Cadí, across the river from the western tip of the Alhambra and in the past a means of reaching it. In this area too we encounter the Arabic baths, the Baños Árabes, which date from the eleventh century and point to the early presence here of the Moors, earlier than in the Alhambra itself. Now carefully restored, the baths consist of hot, warm and cold rooms, as well as a dressing room. The walls contain horseshoe arches of brick supported by columns of marble, while the ceilings are barrel-vaulted and distinguished by star-shaped skylights, the whole a vivid re-creation of the Albaicín's past.[7]

Continuing a little way along the same road and then turning left along the Calle de Zafra, we come to the Church of San Juan de los Reyes, which was originally a mosque, and whose belfry, the former minaret, contains typically Moorish decoration. If we then go further along the Calle San Juan de los Reyes and turn left into the street called the Cuesta del Chapiz, we soon discover the Casa del Chapiz, which now functions as the School of Arabic Studies but which was once an Arabic palace. Not far from here is the Plaza del Salvador, in which the Church of San Salvador still has the courtyard and the horseshoe arches which point to its former existence as a mosque. To the west of this church, in the Calle Santa Isabel la Real, is the Convent of Santa Isabel, which occupies the site of a former Moorish palace, La Daralhorra, itself built on the site of the castle of the Zirid King Badis, who lived there two centuries before work began on the construction of the Alhambra. To the north of the convent are the remains of the great walls which once surrounded and defended the Albaicín, just as the Alhambra was also protected by its walls and towers.[8]

The visitor to the Albaicín should also know something about the 'carmen', the villa with an enclosed garden, many of which are to be found adorning its slopes. Once more, the word is of Arabic origin and refers to a dwelling which cannot usually be seen by the passer-by, but within whose outer walls flowers, shrubs and running water combine to produce an effect of great beauty and tranquillity. The 'carmen' is, in effect, the Generalife in miniature, and reminds us once again that in Islamic thought the garden is a paradise on earth. Villas and gardens of this kind are not, though, restricted to the Albaicín. They can be seen elsewhere on the hills around Granada, as in the little house in which the composer Manuel de Falla once lived, close to the Alhambra. To sit in the garden of a 'carmen', in absolute silence, and with the sun's last rays turning the snow-capped peaks of the Sierra Nevada red, is to be transported to another world.

The area known as the Sacromonte, to the north of the Alhambra, will be discussed in more detail later in relation to flamenco, but it too has a Muslim connection. St Cecil, the first bishop of Granada in the first century, was once said to have been an Arab who subsequently converted to Christianity. The theory has been shown to be false, in fact a hoax, but there can be no doubt that, as many buildings in the area suggest, the presence of the Moors there was a long-standing one. Many of them display the Star of David, which in the sixteenth century was commonly associated with Muslims as well as Jews. And the Church of St Michael is built on a site which originally contained an Arab tower.

Although Córdoba, Seville and Granada are the jewels in the crown as far as major Muslim buildings and monuments are concerned, there are many other examples of Muslim civilization both in and beyond Andalusía. North of Madrid, for example, is the fortified town of Buitrago, whose outer wall with its five towers formed the defence of a pre-eleventh-century Muslim citadel. North-east of Madrid, in Zaragoza, is to be found the Aljafería, a castle dating from the eleventh century which functioned also as a summer residence. In Mérida, to the north-west of Córdoba, there are remains of an 'alcazaba', a Muslim citadel, belonging to the Umayyad period. To the north of Jaén, east of Córdoba, is an extremely well-preserved fortress, in all probability of the tenth century. And in Málaga, south-west of Granada, the mighty Alcazaba, high on the hill and built in the eleventh century, is a favourite tourist attraction.

As well as fortresses of this kind, many buildings, in particular churches, still contain clear reminders of the earlier existence of a mosque. One example is the Church of San Cristo de la Luz in Toledo. This was built as a mosque around the year 1000. A small square building, 8 metres along each side, its interior is distinguished by multi-lobed arches, and one of its external walls by interlocking horseshoe arches. In that respect it is highly reminiscent of al-Hakam's extension to the Mezquita in Córdoba. Similarly, in Niebla, west of Seville, the Church of Santa María de la Granada was once a mosque built by the Almohads. It still has a multi-lobed entrance, the bell-tower was once a minaret, and one of the side walls still contains a *mihrab* or small prayer room. In the town of Almería, east of Granada, the Church of San Juan was once the chief mosque, built in the architectural traditions of the caliphate of Córdoba. Not surprisingly, its *mihrab* invites comparison with that of the Mezquita. The Aljafería in Zaragoza contains a well-preserved mosque which also reveals the influence of Córdoba, for this is clearly evident in the horseshoe arch of its entrance, in the multi-lobed arches of the prayer hall and again in its *mihrab*. Near Bollulos de la Mitación, not far from Seville, are the remains of an Almohad mosque whose minaret is reminiscent of the Giralda, and in the Alcázar in Jerez de la Frontera the present-day Chapel of Santa María la Real was also once a mosque.

Finally, there are also numerous examples of Arabic baths. The baths in the Albaicín have already been mentioned. Similar, often well-preserved or restored examples can be seen elsewhere, as in Jaén, where they date from the eleventh century. In short, Andalusía in particular, but other more northern areas of Spain too, still provide ample evidence of both the extent and the sophistication of a Muslim civilization that was unique in western Europe, and that would leave its mark long after the completion of the reconquest of their country by the Christian army of Ferdinand and Isabella in 1492.

2

After the Muslims

The fall of Granada to the Christians in 1492 marked the end of an almost 800-year campaign in which they attempted to recover from the Muslims the territory which had previously been exclusively theirs. The Reconquest, as this process is generally known, had been slow and laborious, partly because the terrain was harsh and difficult, especially in the central mountainous areas of the country, and partly on account of internal divisions within the Christian kingdoms themselves. This said, the marriage in 1469 between Isabella, half-sister to Henry IV of Castile, and Ferdinand, prince of Aragón, was a decisive step in bringing the Reconquest to a close for, when they succeeded to their respective thrones in 1474 and 1479, this brought together the two most powerful kingdoms and stiffened the resolve of the so-called Catholic Kings to launch a final assault on the last Muslim stronghold. The two most prominent factors in the Reconquest, both before and during the time of Ferdinand and Isabella, were a desire to regain land and to oust or convert the non-Christian, but the triumph of the Catholic Kings in 1492 marked a further, crucial step in this process, for it was also the year in which Columbus discussed with them the voyage which led to the discovery and the subsequent conquest by the Spanish of the West Indies and parts of South America, campaigns in which material and spiritual objectives – territory, treasure and the spread of Catholicism – also went hand in hand, while, in the reigns of Charles V (1517–56) and especially Philip II (1556–98), spiritual fervour made Spain a symbol of religious orthodoxy. Indeed, the fact that Boabdil handed over the keys of the Alhambra to Ferdinand and Isabella in the Hall of the Ambassadors and that Columbus discussed his voyage with them in the very same room seems both ironic and symbolic, a true turning point in Spanish history. But it was not a turning point that has been universally welcomed. In the summer of 1936, for example, the great Spanish poet and playwright, Federico García Lorca, gave his opinion on the fall of Granada to the Christians more than 500 years earlier:

> It was a disastrous event, even if in the schools we are taught the opposite. A wonderful civilization, and a poetry, architecture and sensitivity which was

unique – all that was lost and was replaced by a poor, cowed city, a 'miser's paradise', where the worst middle-class in present-day Spain is occupied in causing trouble ...[1]

Under the Catholic Kings, the Muslims who remained in Granada and its environs – by far the largest number in the whole of Spain – were initially allowed to practise their own religion, laws and customs, and those who wished to emigrate, in most cases to north Africa, were given permission to do so. Conversions to Christianity were, of course, encouraged in these early stages, but from 1499 a new and much more rigorous policy began to be enforced, which led in 1500 to a three-month revolt in the Alpujarran region, to the south of Granada. From this point on, tensions between Christians and Muslims continued to grow, and from 1526, during the reign of Charles V, the Muslim religion ceased to be recognized officially. Indeed, Muslims were persecuted in all kinds of ways, not least by having their land seized and their industries, such as silk production, taken away from them. Still later, a royal decree of 1567 – Philip II was now king of Spain – forbade the Muslims, or Moriscos as they were now called, the use of their language, their traditional rites, their form of dress and their characteristic dances. Its effect was to produce in 1568 a rebellion of the Moriscos in the Alpujarra mountains which lasted for two years and involved as many as 30,000 rebels. When it was finally overcome, further repressive measures were taken by the authorities, for the Moriscos were uprooted from the area and dispersed to different parts of the country. As well as this, the activities of the Inquisition, which had increased from around 1550, became even more rigorous in relation to rooting out and punishing unbelievers. Worst of all, a decree was issued in 1582 which proposed the expulsion of the Moriscos from the country. When it finally came into effect in 1608, during the reign of Philip III, some 300,000 out of a Morisco population of 320,000 left Spain for other countries. The consequence was that a vast number of workers skilled in agriculture and the production of textiles was lost forever, with predictable adverse repercussions in the Spanish economy.

The advance of the Reconquest, the seizure of Muslim cities, and the accompanying religious fervour had their effect, of course, on Córdoba, Seville and Granada, but at different times. Córdoba, besieged and captured by Ferdinand III of Castile in 1236, was the first of the three to fall, an event which had important repercussions on the Mezquita. Any visitor nowadays, dazzled by the beauty of Muslim architecture as he or she enters this wonderful building, is bound to be equally startled by the presence at its centre of a Catholic cathedral and, close by, two chapels.

The Royal Chapel, the Capilla Real, belongs to the reign of Alfonso X, often known as Alfonso the Wise, of Castile (1252–84). In 1263, just twenty-seven years after the capture of Córdoba, he instructed that those Muslim craftsmen who lived in the city should spend some of their time working in the Mezquita, as a reward for which they would be exempted from paying taxes. The Royal Chapel is, therefore, a Christian chapel built and decorated in Muslim or Mudéjar style. The presence of the royal arms, the towers of Castile and the lion of León, bear witness to its Christian origin, but its intricately decorated stucco walls, its lobed niches and its domed roof, with crossed ribs and plentiful stalactite decoration, reveal very clearly the work of Muslim craftsmen.

The Chapel of Villaviciosa, the Capilla de Villaviciosa, stands next to the Royal Chapel and was built in 1371, during the reign of Henry II, king of Castile (1369–79), and in the part of the Mezquita built by al-Hakam II. Because it was again constructed and decorated by Moorish craftsmen, it harmonizes perfectly with the original building. The columns which separate the naves are so arranged that their different colours and patterns of marble and jasper form an ordered sequence. As well as this, the arches are multi-lobed, extremely ornate and richly decorated. But the chapel is especially noteworthy for its ceiling which is distinguished by its crossed stone ribs and beautiful decoration.

The cathedral is, of course, the largest Christian building in the mosque. Work on its construction commenced in 1523, during the reign of Charles V, and continued for many years. Situated more or less in the centre of the mosque and backing on to that part of it built by al-Mansur, its walls and roof rise above those of the mosque itself, proclaiming in that sense the triumph of Christianity over Islam. Within the cathedral there are around thirty chapels, such as the Capilla de San Pablo and the Capilla de Santa Teresa. Some areas of the ceiling are painted in Italian Renaissance style, Old Testament scenes are carved on pulpits, and the pulpits themselves are Baroque. In general, the cathedral is a mixture of Gothic and Renaissance styles and, on that account, strikes a rather incongruous note in the midst of the beauty of the Mezquita as a whole. Indeed, when Charles V saw what work had been done, he is reported to have said: 'You have built what others could have built anywhere, but you have destroyed something that was quite unique.'[2]

The most striking part of the cathedral is generally thought to be the 'coro' or choir, which is distinguished by its wonderful wood carving in mahogany, brought from the New World and now darkened by more than 200 years of use and exposure. This is the work of the Sevillian craftsman,

Pedro Duque Cornejo, and his assistants, begun in 1748, when Cornejo was already seventy years old and virtually completed in 1758, when he was eighty. It consists of a large three-seater bishop's throne, part of the central lectern, and 106 choir stalls, each decorated with scenes from the Bible. Barely an inch is left uncovered, for animals, birds, flowers and many other ornate designs adorn columns, corners and arm-rests. Although Cornejo died in his eightieth year, he had the pleasure of seeing all but the finishing touches to his visionary work.

Post-Reconquest influence is also to be seen in other important buildings throughout Córdoba. Such is the Alcázar Real, a fortress-palace situated near the river and the Roman bridge. Despite its Arabic name, work on it began in 1328, almost 100 years after the fall of the city to the Christians, but 164 years before the fall of Granada to the army of Ferdinand and Isabella. They, in fact, lived in the Alcázar for substantial periods of time during the Granada campaign, and Columbus is also said to have had an audience there with Isabella in 1486, six years before his first voyage to the Indies and South America. From the end of the fifteenth century, the Alcázar was used by the Inquisition, which, as we have seen, increased its activities thereafter, and in more recent times it functioned as a prison. Because of such varied use, its original beauty is considerably faded, but the Moorish-style gardens, with their rectangular pools, trees, bushes and flowers, are particularly attractive, even if they were not added until the fifteenth century. Below the floor of the Alcázar's hall are the remains of baths which, with their star-shaped vents, are thought to be Arabic in origin. In short, the Alcázar Real, like many post-Reconquest buildings in the south of Spain, both imitates the style of Muslim architecture and incorporates genuine Muslim features.

Another beautiful and intriguing building, the Palace of the Marqués de Viana, belongs to the fifteenth century but occupies the site of the palace of the last caliph. Operating nowadays as a museum, it has 181 rooms and twelve beautiful patios filled with a dazzling array of trees, shrubs and flowers. Despite the fact that the building itself contains all kinds of treasures from later periods, the ceilings of many of the rooms reveal the intricate decoration and geometric patterns that are typically Mudéjar, while the patios and gardens suggest what the original caliph's palace must have been like in Muslim times. Intriguingly, the last caliph is said to have caught one of his wives in conversation with a Spanish officer whom he then had murdered and buried somewhere in the palace.

Many of Córdoba's churches also point to the fact that, after the fall of Córdoba to the Christians, they were either built on the site of a mosque or incorporated Mudéjar elements. The Convent of the Crucified Christ, the Convento de Jesús Crucifijado, for example, has a finely decorated Arabic ceiling and various columns of Muslim origin in one of its patios. The Church of Santa Marina, which dates from 1236, has a sacristy whose entrance is distinguished by beautiful arabesques and stalactites. The Church of San Lorenzo was built on the site of a mosque and its tower is the former minaret. And even though the façade of the Church of San Miguel is in a rather severe early Gothic style, its southern entrance consists of a delightful horseshoe arch.

The mixture of Muslim and Christian elements throughout Córdoba point to the city's fascinating history. Although it is not one of Spain's major cities and for many years fell into decline, overshadowed by Seville to the south, much has now been done to make it attractive to the visitor, particularly in terms of its rich heritage. It remains, therefore, an intriguing city whose mystery and magic has in more recent times been suggested in the opening lines of a Lorca poem:

> Córdoba.
> Distant and alone …
> On the plain, in the wind,
> Black mare, red moon.
> Death watches me
> From the towers of Córdoba.[3]

The greatest testament to Christian supremacy in Seville is, of course, the cathedral, which, covering an area of 11,520 square metres and rising to a height of 42 metres, rivals St Peter's, Rome, and St Paul's, London, and, according to recent calculations, surpasses them as the largest place of Christian worship in the world.[4] As we have seen in the previous chapter, the Almohad mosque which stood on this site was adapted for Christian worship after the capture of Seville in 1248. It functioned in this way for 150 years but then became unsafe on account of earthquakes and was replaced by the cathedral, building work commencing in 1401 and lasting for over a century.

The presence of an earlier mosque on the site is suggested by the fact that at the northern end of the cathedral is the Courtyard of the Orange Trees, the Patio de los Naranjos, reminiscent of the courtyard which forms the entrance to the Mezquita in Córdoba. Here, as there, Muslim worshippers would have performed ritual washing, having entered the courtyard through the Penitents' Gate, the Puerta del Perdón. This gate dates back to the Almohad period but many changes belong, of course, to the time when

37

the cathedral was built and afterwards. The great doors themselves, made of larchwood and bronze, are from the fifteenth century, the stucco work around them from the sixteenth. The courtyard itself, almost as wide as the Cathedral, contains rows of well-spaced-out orange trees which provide welcome shade in the blazing heat of summer, while the marble fountain in the centre again points to the original purpose of the courtyard. The present entrance to the cathedral is not, though, the Penitents' Gate but a doorway to one side of the Giralda.

Along the eastern side of the courtyard is a library, the Biblioteca Colombina. It contains some 63,000 books, 3,000 of them a bequest by Hernando Colón, the younger son of Cristóbal Colón, Christopher Columbus. The bequest is an appropriate pointer both to the son's extensive reading and to his father's close association with Seville. On the western side of the courtyard is a large seventeenth-century chapel, the Iglesia del Sagrario, which now functions as a parish church.

We enter the cathedral through the Doorway of the Crocodile, the Puerta del Lagarto, so named after the crocodile which for many years was suspended above the doorway. This is a wooden replica of the original crocodile which, together with a giraffe and an elephant, was sent to Alfonso X by the sultan of Egypt when he requested Alfonso's daughter's hand in marriage. She, however, refused to marry him, and Alfonso kept both his daughter and the sultan's gifts. The crocodile, subsequently stuffed, was suspended as it is now, and, together with one of the elephant's tusks, was believed to bring good luck. When both objects disintegrated over time, they were replaced by imitations in wood.

The main or central body of the cathedral is formed of three large and important structures, next to each other along the length of the nave in an easterly-to-westerly direction. On the eastern side is the Royal Chapel, the Capilla Real, dedicated to Ferdinand III, who captured Seville in 1248 and whose body lies in the chapel in a silver casket. The chapel also contains Ferdinand's sword, his spurs, the buckles of his belt and a silver reliquary in which, it is said, one of his fingers is preserved. Below the chapel is a crypt, in which there is an ivory statue, 43 centimetres tall, known as the Virgin of the Battles, the Virgen de las Batallas. It appears that Ferdinand carried this image into battle, along with another of the Virgin, both fixed to his saddle and protected by his shield. The crypt also contains caskets in which are placed the remains of various Castilian monarchs, of which the most famous is Pedro the Cruel, so closely associated with the construction of the Alcázar. Quite clearly, this part of the cathedral allows us to form a vivid impression of the Christian conquest of Seville.

To the west of the Royal Chapel and immediately next to it is the Chapel of the High Altar, the Capilla Mayor. Immediately in front of the altar are wonderfully crafted wrought-iron gates, forged in the early sixteenth century, their gilt surface glowing in the changing light. Even more striking, though, is the massive altarpiece or 'retablo' which stands behind the altar. At 21 metres high and 18 metres wide, it is the largest in the world. It contains forty-five niches, each of which displays scenes from the life of Christ and the Virgin, all immaculately carved in walnut, larch and chestnut between 1482 and 1564 by Spanish and Flemish artists. In front of this magnificent altarpiece and behind the altar is a statue of the Virgin known as the Virgen de la Sede, the Virgin of the Chair, made of cypress wood, in part silver plated, in part painted, and dating from the thirteenth century.

The third part of the central nave, next to the Chapel of the High Altar, is the choir, the *coro*. There are 117 wooden choir stalls, the work of several craftsmen, set out in two rows, the upper for the canons, the lower for those receiving benefices. Each seat has carvings different from the others and there are also 216 statues carved in wood. One of the seats, distinguished by its royal arms, was reserved for the king of León and Castile.

Around the sides of the cathedral, especially on the southern side, are a large number of chapels, all of them interesting for different reasons. The Sacristy of the Chalices, the Sacristía de los Cálices, for example, contains forty or so paintings, five by Murillo, including a very fine Holy Family, and also paintings by Zurbarán, Pacheco, Valdés Leal and Titian.[5] Perhaps the most impressive piece, though, is the Crucifixion by the Sevillian sculptor, Juan Martínez Montañés, completed in 1603. It stands at the end of the room, the pale colour of the body emphasized by the deep red of the background against which it is suspended.

Next to the sacristy we encounter the tomb of Christopher Columbus, a much later monument completed in 1891. The coffin is supported by four larger-than-life heralds who represent the four kingdoms of Castile, León, Navarre and Aragón, and the lance of León is seen to be piercing a pomegranate, which is the symbol of Granada, the image therefore representing the final defeat of Islam by the Christians. Whether or not the body of Columbus is contained in the coffin is a matter of conjecture. After his death in Valladolid in 1506, Columbus's remains were moved in 1509 to Seville, where they were buried in the monastery of Santa María de las Cuevas, on the island of La Cartuja. Subsequently, the bodies of Columbus and his eldest son, Diego, were transferred, at the request of Columbus's widow, to the Carribean island of Hispaniola – nowadays

Haiti and the Dominican Republic – where they were interred in the cathedral and, on his death, the body of another son, Luis, was buried along with them. Later on, building work caused the three coffins to be removed, opened and the names confused, as a consequence of which all three bodies were placed in one coffin. Still later, when Santo Domingo fell into French hands, the coffin was removed to Cuba, but when Cuba was also lost in 1898, it was transported back to Spain and placed in the tomb in Seville cathedral. The remains of Columbus may, then, be found here, but the issue is clouded further by the fact that in 1879 another coffin inscribed with Columbus's name was unearthed in the cathedral in Santo Domingo. This then disappeared, so the question concerning the actual whereabouts of his remains is still unanswered.

A number of chapels also run along the northern side of the cathedral. The first of these, in the north-west corner, is the Chapel of St Anthony, the Capilla de San Antonio. The outstanding feature here is another painting by Murillo, the celebrated *Vision of Saint Anthony of Padua*, which belongs to the artist's later period. It depicts St Anthony's vision of the infant Christ emerging from a golden cloud. In 1875 the figure of the saint was removed from the painting by a thief and was discovered in New York when an attempt was made to sell it there. It has, of course, been replaced in the painting, but it is possible to see where the repair has been carried out.

Interesting too is the Chapel of Santiago, the Capilla de Santiago. It contains the painting of a battle scene, *Santiago Matamoros*, by the seventeenth-century artist, Juan de Roelas, in which Santiago (St James) is seen descending from Heaven on a white charger and slaying Muslims – hence the title – at the battle of Clavijo. In that respect, it embodies the religious fervour which, in part at least, inspired the Reconquest and which also lay behind the building of cathedrals and churches, often on the sites of mosques. Next to the Chapel of Santiago is the Altar of Our Lady of Bethlehem, the Altar de Nuestra Señora de Belén, then a doorway which leads back into the Courtyard of the Orange Trees, and finally, to the right of it, the Chapel of the Maidens, the Capilla de las Doncellas, named after a society which provided dowries for impoverished young women.

While the cathedral is Seville's most impressive and arresting testament to the Christian triumph over Islam, many other buildings convey the same message. In the northern part of the city, to the north-east of the cathedral, for example, is the Convent of Santa Paula, founded in 1475. It has an extremely beautiful entrance which combines Christian and Mudéjar elements, while inside is a highly decorative ceiling in Muslim style by a

Christian carpenter, Diego López de Arenas. There are also three tombs, splendidly decorated in blue, green, brown and white panelling. The building suggests once more that, despite the Christian triumph, Muslim influence was too ingrained in the Spanish experience to be eradicated.

The Church of San Marcos, some 200 metres to the west of the Convent of Santa Paula, occupies the site of a mosque and reveals Arabic influence in its Mudéjar tower, its Mudéjar-Gothic entrance and, inside, well-preserved horseshoe arches. Also close by is the Church of Santa Catalina, again built on the site of a former mosque. It has a Mudéjar tower based on the design of the Giralda, and inside the entrance is a beautiful and well-preserved horseshoe arch. A short distance to the west, the Church of San Pedro, the church where Velázquez was baptized in 1599, displays Mudéjar craftsmanship in the lobed brickwork of its tower, the interior has a Mudéjar wooden ceiling and west door, and the vault of one of its chapels contains intricate geometric patterns which are distinctly Arabic. The Church of San Gil, 800 metres to the north, is one of the earliest Christian churches in Seville and was probably built on the site of a mosque. Further to the west, the Convent of Santa Clara, near the river and built in the thirteenth century, has a chapel with a lovely Muslim-inspired ceiling.

Apart from churches, there are three buildings in the southern part of the city which embody particular aspects of post-Muslim Spain. Two of these, both founded in the seventeenth century, reveal the religious concerns of that time. To the east of the cathedral and quite near it is the Hospital for Venerable Priests, the Hospital de Venerables Sacerdotes, a home for elderly priests which now functions as a cultural centre. It dates from 1675 and, like many other charitable organizations of the time, points both to the more compassionate nature of the Catholic Church and to its willingness to look after its own. To the south-west of the cathedral and a mere stone's throw from it is the Hospital de la Caridad, the Hospital of Charity, which dates from 1674 and still functions as a refuge for the sick and the aged. Its founder, Don Miguel de Mañara, is said to have led an extremely dissolute life, but he then underwent a religious conversion in response to two colourful events. While returning home after a drinking session, he encountered a funeral procession and, on asking about the identity of the corpse, discovered it to be himself. In the second incident, he pursued a woman whose face was concealed by a veil and, when he removed it, found himself face to face with a skull. As for the building itself, the façade is baroque and contains five pictures in blue-and-white ceramic, allegedly designed by Murillo. Inside the entrance are two square patios filled with plants and, beyond them, the church of the hospital, in which there are paintings which are entirely expressive of the religious spirit of seventeenth-century Spain. Seven of these are by Murillo and include *Loaves and Fishes*, *St John of God Carrying a Sick Man* and *St Isabel of Hungary Curing the Lepers*. But the most striking paintings here are by Juan de Valdés Leal, who was born in Seville in 1622, subsequently spent much of his time there and died in the city in 1691. One of the paintings, *In the Blink of an Eye*, depicts a skeleton stepping over red robes and symbols of power, its bony hand pointing to the words of the painting's title. The other picture, facing the first, is entitled *No More, No Less* and portrays a dead bishop in full regalia whose flesh is being eaten away by insects and worms. While the religious paintings of Murillo are often in the more sentimental vein of seventeenth-century religious feeling, those by Valdés Leal are uncompromisingly harsh, much more concerned with the empty pursuits and materialism of the world at large, a theme which figures prominently in seventeenth-century Spanish literature.

As far as Granada is concerned, many of the buildings and monuments constructed after the city fell into Christian hands, as well as changes made to existing buildings, reflect both Spain's religious character and her increasing power and influence in the world, especially in the sixteenth century. After 1492 the chief mosque of Granada, situated some 400 metres west of the Alhambra, was adapted for Christian worship, but it soon proved to be too small; the mosque was demolished and work on the cathedral began in 1521, under the supervision of Enrique de Egas, and continued for many years. Although the building as a whole is far less impressive than many other Spanish cathedrals, it has a solid-looking Gothic façade, while inside there are five broad aisles and a central dome which rises to a height of more than 30 metres. The most striking feature of the interior is the Great Chapel, the Capilla Mayor, which contains the high altar. Above the pulpit, on either side, are the kneeling figures of Ferdinand and Isabella at prayer, and higher up the busts of Adam and Eve by the celebrated seventeenth-century artist, Alonso Cano, who was born in Granada. On a higher level again are seven paintings of episodes in the life of the Virgin, also by Cano, and, above these, fourteen stained-glass windows.

More interesting than the cathedral, especially from a historical point of view, is the Royal Chapel, the Capilla Real, which is attached to the cathedral as though it were an integral part of it. In fact, it was built between 1505 and 1507, before work on the cathedral commenced, as a tomb to house the bodies of Ferdinand and Isabella and their family. Isabella died in 1505, two months after she had given the order for the construction of the building, and Ferdinand eleven years later, in 1516. Initially, in accordance with her instructions, she was buried on the Alhambra Hill in the Convent of San Francisco (now part of the *parador* hotel) until the Royal Chapel had been completed. Her body, as well as that of Ferdinand, was placed in the tomb there in 1522. They lie in an underground crypt in lead coffins, alongside which are coffins containing the remains of their daughter, Juana la Loca, Joanna the Mad, her husband, Philip of Austria, and the prince of Asturias who died before he was two years old. Above them is a monument displaying the effigies of all four monarchs in a recumbent position.

The fine altarpiece or 'retablo' behind the altar is by Felipe de Vigarny, a Burgundian from Langres, and was completed in 1522. On either side are images of Ferdinand and Isabella praying, and, near these figures, panels depicting, respectively, Boabdil surrendering the keys of Granada and the conversion of the Muslims to Christianity. The Capilla Real is, in short, alive with history.[6]

When Ferdinand died in 1516, the legal heir to the throne was his daughter, Juana, but, given her mental instability – after her husband's sudden death at the age of twenty-eight, she refused to be parted from his coffin – the throne passed in 1517 to Juana's son, Charles, who was born in Ghent in 1500 and who had spent his entire childhood in the Netherlands. On his father's side, Charles was, of course, a Hapsburg, and when his grandfather, the emperor Maximilian, died in 1519, he soon became Holy Roman emperor as well as king of Spain. He was therefore ruler of an empire which embraced the Netherlands, Austria, Germany, Hungary, Spain, Naples, Sicily and the South American territories discovered by Columbus. Spain, which Charles made the centre of his activities for seven years from 1522, became in that sense the hub of the greatest empire in the world at that time. Charles's policy, after his accession, also proved to be essentially imperialist, focused on extending his territories. It was an age, then, in which the sense of power was very much to the forefront.

The Sacristy of the Royal Chapel contains paintings from Isabella's private collection, many of them bearing witness to her religious fervour, such as the *Triptych of the Passion*, *Head of Christ* and *Virgin with Child and Angels* by the Flemish painter, Dirk Bouts, a nativity scene and a *Pietà* by Rogier van der Weyden, *Christ before the Sepulchre* by Perugino, and *Gethsemane* by Botticelli. As well as this, the Sacristy contains Ferdinand's sword, Isabella's crown and the banners which were displayed during the conquest of Granada.

During the reign of Charles V – he was Charles I of Spain but Charles V of the Holy Roman Empire – various monuments and buildings associated with him were built in the Alhambra and its surrounding area.[7] When, for example, we set out from Granada's Plaza Nueva, climbing the Hill of Gomérez, we soon come across the Gateway of the Pomegranates, the Puerta de las Granadas, a massive Renaissance construction designed for Charles by Pedro Machuca, who had been a student of Michelangelo, and built in 1536. Surmounted by the two-headed Hapsburg eagle, the gateway also displays three pomegranates, the symbol of the city itself. The size and solidity of this monument immediately reminds the visitor both of Spain's power in the world at this time and of the enormous contrast between Christian and Muslim architecture.

Moving on, we soon encounter another monument of the same period, the Fountain of Charles V, the Pilar de Carlos V, again designed by Pedro Machuca and completed in 1545. It displays in its upper part the imperial shield of Charles V, and at either end the heraldic shield of Don Íñigo López de Mendoza, the second count of Tendilla and first marquis of Mondéjar at the time of the fountain's construction. The three heads spouting water are said to represent spring, summer, and autumn.

As far as the palaces of the Alhambra itself are concerned, Ferdinand and Isabella are known to have stayed there on occasion after the fall of Granada, and Ferdinand continued to do so after his wife's death and his marriage to Germaine de Foix, niece of the king of France, in 1506. Indeed, before his own death in 1516, important changes were made to parts of the complex. Many of the Alhambra's towers were reduced in height and reinforced in order to make them more resistant to artillery fire. As a result, the Alhambra has the appearance of a military fortress when viewed from the outside. Within the complex, Germaine de Foix occupied an apartment above the Golden Room in the Mexuar, and certain changes were also made to the Golden Room itself. The emblems of the Catholic Kings appear on a mullion which divides the window, as well as on a frieze on which the ceiling rests, and the ceiling itself was redecorated. Ferdinand and Isabella also gave land to the Franciscan Order so that they could build a monastery within the walls of the Alhambra. This has since become a splendid *parador*, a luxury hotel. When they ousted the Nasrid dynasty from the Alhambra, they also appointed the count of Tendilla and his family as its hereditary governors.

In 1526, ten years after the death of Ferdinand and his own accession to the Spanish throne, Charles V married his cousin, Isabella of Portugal, and from May to late autumn of that year, the newly-weds spent their time in the Alhambra. Charles had new apartments built on the northern side of the Balcony of Lindaraja – they block the view to the mountains from the balcony itself. Above one of the original Muslim towers on the outer walls of the Alhambra he also constructed the Queen's Dressing Room, the Tocador de la Reina. It provides magnificent views, and in the floor to the right of the entrance is a marble slab with sixteen perforations, a Muslim device which allowed perfumes to enter the room from below. In addition, the baths to the left of the Hall of the Two Sisters were restored and redecorated for his own use, and the Hall of the Mexuar, which had been used as a council chamber by the Muslims, was converted into a chapel.

Such changes and alterations to the fabric of the Alhambra were nothing, however, in comparison with the enormous palace which Charles ordered to be built close to the Mexuar and the Courtyard of the Myrtles.[8] As we approach the Muslim complex, the vast bulk of the Palace of Charles V is, indeed, the first thing that imposes itself upon us in an area which is otherwise remarkable for its beauty and delicacy. Work on the palace commenced in 1526, the year of Charles's marriage, under the guidance of the same Pedro Machuca who had designed the Gateway of the Pomegranates and the Fountain of Charles V. Progress was, however, extremely slow. Charles never occupied the palace, his son, Philip II, had no interest in it and it was not completed for hundreds of years.

The four exterior walls of the palace are similar in the lower half, different in the upper half. The lower half is of rusticated stone with bronze rings set in the stone between each window. It has an enormous solidity, more castle than palace, while the upper half has a rather lighter effect. The western façade, which is the principal frontage of the building, has two winged, reclining women above the main door, cherubs above the smaller doors to either side of it and Flemish warriors – reminders of Charles's origins – in the medallions above these doors. Directly above the lower medallions are two more depicting the labours of Hercules. The southern façade, which faces the Gate of Justice, is less elaborate, and the northern and eastern facades have few especially interesting features. As for the interior of the palace, the ground floor now houses the Museum of Hispanic-Muslim Art, the upper floor the Museum of Fine Arts. The former is particularly interesting in the sense that it contains a wealth of relics from the Alhambra's Muslim past.

In the centre of the palace, enclosed by its four wings, is a vast circular courtyard open to the elements and reminiscent of a bullring. Indeed, it is often claimed that, during its first two centuries of life, the palace was used only for entertainment, especially bullfighting. Around the courtyard are thirty-two Doric columns supporting a projecting gallery, and these are matched above the gallery by thirty-two Ionic columns which support the roof. Because of its vast size and proximity to the Alhambra's Muslim buildings, the Palace of Charles V has attracted both praise and criticism. Some consider it to be a Renaissance masterpiece, others that, in the context of the surrounding buildings, it is completely out of place. Undoubtedly, there is a jarring contrast between the light and airy palaces of the sultans and Machuca's weighty and imposing Renaissance structure, symbolic of Christian Spain's authority in the world in the sixteenth century. But the physical juxtaposition is quite illuminating in the sense that it illustrates perfectly, and in a single image, the clash of two very different cultures which, over a long period of time, played such an important part in Spanish history.

Philip II, son of Charles V, succeeded to the throne in 1556 but had no interest in the Alhambra or his father's palace, for he preferred to concentrate on the construction of the Escorial, his vast palace-monastery outside Madrid on which work began in 1563 and continued for twenty-one years. In 1590, eight years before Philip's death, parts of the Alhambra were, however, badly damaged by an explosion of gunpowder: notably, the Oratory of the Mexuar, the stained-glass windows of the Hall of the Ambassadors and the Hall of the Two Sisters, and the ceiling of the Hall of the Mozárabes. From time to time, earthquakes also posed a serious threat to the delicate structures of the palaces, and this meant, inevitably, that by the late sixteenth century the Alhambra had lost some of its original features.

When Charles II, a sickly individual and the last of the Hapsburg line, died in 1700, he had no heir, and the Spanish throne passed to the seventeen-year-old Philip V, duke of Anjou and the first in a long line of Bourbons to rule the country. His second wife, Elizabeth, whom he married after the death of his first wife in 1714, found the Alhambra enchanting, and she and Philip often stayed there in the royal apartments built many years earlier by Charles V. She particularly enjoyed the beauty and tranquillity of the Queen's Dressing Room, and it was in honour of the royal couple that a new baroque ceiling was installed in the Hall of the Mozárabes, replacing that damaged by the explosion of gunpowder. But if these were positive steps in repairing earlier damage, there was also a negative aspect to the way in which the Alhambra was run. During the time of Ferdinand and Isabella, the position of governor of the Alhambra had been given to the count of Tendilla and his successors. In 1700, however, the current governor, the marquis of Mondéjar, had opposed the

Bourbon claim to the Spanish throne and was therefore removed by Philip V on his accession. Mondéjar's reaction was to destroy the palace which had been his residence and which, situated near the gardens of the Partal, had been built by Yusuf III. According to some, this had been the most beautiful palace in the whole of the Alhambra.

Between 1700 and 1850 the condition of the Alhambra deteriorated a great deal, matching in that sense the obscurity and decline into which Spain had steadily slipped since its period of unequalled power in the sixteenth century. At one point the lovely Hall of the Two Sisters was used as a kind of factory for the manufacture of silk, while the various rooms of the Mexuar housed a donkey and sheep. In 1808 the invasion of Spain by the French led to the six-year Peninsular War which involved fierce resistance by the Spanish and savage recriminations by the French. The Alhambra at this time housed the French general, Sébastiani, and his staff, and parts of it were used to contain prisoners of war. Furthermore, Sébastiani set about decorating some of the rooms in a Parisian style which was distinctly at odds with the Moorish character of the building, and he also chopped down the elms in the Alhambra Wood which leads to the great Gateway of Justice. But the greatest damage was done when the French left the Alhambra in September 1812, for the departing soldiers used explosives to destroy eight of the towers, and more would have suffered the same fate had it not been for the intervention of José García, a crippled Spanish soldier who stayed behind and cut the fuses.

For more than fifty years after the end of the war, the Alhambra was in a ruinous state, as contemporary accounts indicate and as we shall see later on. The Tower of the Ladies, for example, was in an extremely poor condition, its great pool empty ever since the French invaders had damaged the water supply. The governors entrusted with looking after the building had long left it, for they preferred to live in the city, and the Spanish government made no money available for repairs. As a result of all this, poor and often disreputable people made the Alhambra their living quarters. Bats and owls flew through its once beautiful halls. Visitors were shown around by a ragged individual called Mateo Jiménez, who claimed to be a son of the Alhambra, and were introduced to Doña Antonia Jiménez, an aged spinster who acted as caretaker – something of a comedown from the counts of Tendilla. Other inhabitants at this time included invalid soldiers, whose job it was to guard those outer towers which sometimes served as prisons. In the 1830s prisoners in chains were in fact being used to convert part of the Alhambra into a storehouse for salted fish, and gunpowder, with all its inherent dangers, was stored in the Palace of Charles V. The extent to which the palaces were largely unsupervised is illustrated by the fact that visitors frequently chipped off tiles and the like as souvenirs, a far cry from the eagle-eyed watchfulness of today's attendants.[9]

In 1870 the fortunes of the Alhambra took a turn for the better when it became officially recognized as a national monument and resources were made available for its repair and restoration. Even so, accidents still occurred, and in 1890 the beautiful Courtyard of the Myrtles was damaged by fire. It was subsequently restored, as was the Tower of the Ladies, and ever since the work has continued, which frequently means that parts of the building are closed to visitors. For some, the process of restoration is seen as an attempt to make an ageing woman appear young, but it has to be said that throughout the twentieth century the work has been in the hands of experts drawing on thorough research. In any case, the Alhambra, like many other buildings of Muslim origin, has been subject to change through the centuries, be it at the hands of Muslim or Christian rulers, its governors, or its restorers. What cannot be denied is that, after so long a time, it once again looks magnificent and has regained its position as the finest example of Muslim architecture in western Europe.

The history of the Generalife is in some respects more confused and confusing than that of the palaces. As we have seen, this is the only garden to have survived from the many which covered the area around the Alhambra. In the opinion of some experts, it existed from as early as 1319, the date of the building at the northern end of the Courtyard of the Water Channel, which means that it predated the construction of the Palace of Comares and the Courtyard of the Lions. In general, the buildings around the water channel and the gardens have undergone many changes over the years, though the water channel itself, the building mentioned above and the Water Stairway are substantially what they were in times long past.[10]

Apart from the cathedral, there are, of course, many other buildings in Granada which bear witness to the transition from Islamic to Christian influence. To the west of the Alhambra and near the centre of the city is, for example, the Church of Santo Domingo, which was founded by Ferdinand and Isabella and built on land acquired from the mother of Boabdil, the last Muslim ruler of Granada. Across the River Genil, some 400 metres to the right of this church, is the Hermitage of San Sebastián whose horseshoe arch points to its previous existence as a Muslim oratory, and nearby is the Alcázar Genil, which contains the remnants of a fourteenth-century palace, also sold to Ferdinand and Isabella by Boabdil's mother. In the Plaza Nueva, at the beginning of the road which climbs to the Albaicín, the Church of Santa Ana has a main entrance which is Renaissance Plateresque in style, but its tower with its twin window divided by a single column suggests Moorish influence. And as well as this, of course, we have already seen in the previous chapter that in the Albaicín itself there are churches and convents which were constructed on the sites of mosques and which still retain some of their original architectural features.

Granada has a particular interest and fascination precisely because it was the last Muslim stronghold to fall to the Christians and has such strong associations with that crucial event. The point is well illustrated, indeed, by the juxtaposition in the city centre of the cathedral, where the bodies of the triumphant Catholic Kings lie, and, just a few metres to the south-east of it, the jumble of streets known as the Alcaicería where local goods can be bought. The word, of Arabic origin, means silk bazaar and points to the earlier existence of such a bazaar on this site. Even if the current buildings were constructed in the nineteenth century, they still have a remarkable fascination, as does Granada as a whole.

3

Foreign Travellers in Andalusia

While the Muslim heritage of Andalusia has exercised a constant fascination for visitors to the region, the accounts of foreign travellers, many of them distinguished writers, are extremely interesting, not merely in terms of their descriptive qualities, but also for the light they throw on the particular author and on the period in which they were written. There are relatively few accounts from the seventeenth century, but in the eighteenth and especially in the nineteenth century there were many more, for the number of foreign visitors greatly increased, and, by their very nature, their descriptions of their experiences, in many cases rather exotic, had the effect of attracting even more travellers. These individuals were, of course, usually well-to-do, and their journey through Spain was often part of the Grand Tour which took them to other countries. Their education and sophistication also meant that in many cases they arrived with certain prejudices and preconceptions which coloured their reaction to a country and a region which was very different from their own.

Early travellers, accustomed to comfortable surroundings, good food and considerable prosperity, complained of Spain's backwardness, poverty and ignorance, and in certain cases also revealed what we now regard as marked racial prejudice. Such was the attitude of the much travelled Scotsman, William Lithgow, who journeyed through Spain in 1620 and who, in *Rare Adventures and Painefull Peregrinations*, first published twelve years later, declared not only that the country was 'a masse of mountains, a barren ill-manured soyle', but also that 'the barbarian Moore, the Moorish Spaniard, the Turke and the Irishman are the least industrious and most sluggish livers under the Sunne'.[1] It was a view which some later writers would reiterate, but there were also those who, like the Welshman, James Howell, were much more enthused by their experience and who believed that the contribution of the Moors to their adopted land had been invaluable. Howell, a friend of Ben Jonson, was greatly attracted by the south of Spain, and in his *Instructions for Forreine Travel* and *Familiar Letters*, published in 1642 and 1645 respectively, he observed that 'since the expulsion of the Moors it [Spain] is also grown thinner and not so full of Corn; for those Moors would grub up Wheat out of the very tops of the craggy Hills'.[2]

The eighteenth century produced more visitors and similarly contrasting views. After the succession of the Bourbon Philip V and the much greater influence of French taste, there were many French writers who were scathing about Spain's backwardness, and there were also British individuals who shared that opinion and looked down on Andalusians in particular on account of their Moorish associations. Major William Dalrymple, for example, noted in his *Travels through Spain and Portugal in 1774*, published three years later, that the entrances to Spanish houses 'are the receptacles for any kind of filth, since the Spaniard performs the offices of nature behind the gate – a strong remnant of Moorish manners'. And he also agreed with the Basques, who, he observed, 'hold the Andalusians in contempt as being in immediate descent from the Moors'.[3] In contrast, Richard Twiss, in *Travels through Portugal and Spain in 1772 and 1773*, published in 1775, responded positively to Spanish inns and to the beauty of Andalusian women,[4] while Henry Swinburne, though regretting the disrepair into which the Alhambra had fallen, as well as the habitual drunkenness of its current governor, revealed his enthusiasm for Muslim architecture in *Travels through Spain in 1775 and 1776*, published in 1787.[5]

The nineteenth century saw both an influx of foreign travellers and a large number of informative and often fascinating descriptions of the attractions of Andalusia. In this context it is important to understand that, from the beginning of the century, closely following on from Napoleon's Egyptian campaign, many travellers and writers developed a strong interest in the Middle East and in all things which they considered oriental. It offered them a world which seemed exotic, mysterious and seductive, a far cry from the rationality, the Puritanism and the bourgeois mentality of western Europe. Spain, moreover, so close to Africa, occupied for centuries by the Moors and possessing a considerable gypsy and Jewish population, was at this time equated with the East and therefore figured prominently in the nineteenth-century cult of orientalism. It is this identification which largely explains the rhapsodic reaction of so many travellers when they found themselves in such places as the Alhambra.

The point can be illustrated perfectly in relation to the experiences of the French writer, François René de Chateaubriand, whose visit to the Middle East in 1806 ended with a journey to Spain and a visit to the Alhambra prior to his return home. Before setting out on his travels, Chateaubriand, though married, had met Nathalie de Noailles and, attracted as much to her as she was to him, had arranged to meet her in the course of his return journey through Spain. Their romantic association proved to be the inspiration for the novella, *The Adventures of the Last Abencerraje* (*Les Aventures du dernier Abencérage*), which Chateaubriand wrote in 1808–9 and which was published in 1826. The story, set in the sixteenth century, has for its two central characters Aben-Hamet, the last survivor of the Abencerraje family, and Blanca, the Spanish daughter of a noble family. They fall in love when Aben-Hamet travels from north Africa to Granada, the city of his ancestors, but their respective religions prove to be an insurmountable obstacle to their marriage. Aben-Hamet discovers too that Blanca and her brother are the last descendants of El Cid, Spain's national hero, whose wrongs against the Moors he has come to Spain to avenge. Unable to carry out this task because of his love of Blanca, and unable to marry her for religious reasons, Aben-Hamet returns to north Africa and the two lovers never meet again.

This romantic tale of impossible love is, of course, the association of Chateaubriand and Nathalie de Noailles channelled into fictional form, for Aben-Hamet and Blanca wander through the palaces of the Alhambra as the real-life lovers had also done, and at one point he writes her name on one of the walls of the Hall of the Two Sisters. The description of this incident has much of the overblown yet beautiful exoticism which we associate with the Romantics:

> As the moon rose, its fitful light spread through the empty halls and abandoned courts of the Alhambra. Its beams threw patterns on the grassy lawn, on the walls of the great rooms and their ancient tracery, on the arches of the courtyards, on the moving shadows of the water and the shrubs stirred by the breeze. A nightingale sang in a cypress-tree that grew through the dome of a ruined mosque, and the echoes repeated its sad song. By the light of the moon Aben-Hamet wrote the name of Blanca on the marble surface in the Hall of the Two Sisters, tracing it in Arabic so that the traveller might find one further mystery in this place of many mysteries …[6]

For Chateaubriand, the Alhambra, recreated in his imagination, was the perfect setting for a wonderful but impossible love that was the very opposite of the bourgeois marriage which had been arranged for him when he was twenty-four years of age and his bride was a mere seventeen.

The six-year Peninsular War, which began two years after Chateaubriand's visit, was a clear disincentive to foreign travellers, though there were some individuals who, having been involved in the war, produced accounts of their experiences, such as Major-General Lord Blayney, an Irish peer who was captured by the French in 1810 and imprisoned in the Alhambra. Four years later, in *Narrative of a Forced Journey through*

Spain and France as a Prisoner of War, he condemned the way in which General Sébastiani, as has been mentioned earlier, changed 'some of the apartments in the modern style: no proof of his good taste, for a Parisian salon or boudoir in a Moorish palace 500 years old is almost as absurd as dressing an antique statue in the costume of a modern *petit maître*'.[7]

Four years after the end of the war, George Ticknor, a young American who would later become a respected academic and Hispanist, spent six months in Spain as part of a Grand Tour. In the south of Spain he was particularly delighted by the Alhambra, for its crumbling condition and the sound of running water had a magical appeal, as did its 'light, luxurious style of Arabian architecture'. He concluded that 'the Alhambra is a name which will make my blood thrill if I live to the frosts of a century … a riotous tumultuous pleasure like a kind of sensual enjoyment'.[8]

The rhapsodic note suggested by Ticknor was even more pronounced in Victor Hugo's collection of poems, *Les Orientales*, published in 1829. In the preface to the collection, Hugo made the specific point that for him Spain was synonymous with the East:

> The colours of the Orient came to him [Hugo] as if of their own volition, and placed their imprint on all his thoughts, all his dreams; and his dreams and thoughts found themselves to be, almost without wishing it so, Hebraic, Turkish, Greek, Persian, Arabic, even Spanish, because Spain is still the Orient, Spain is half African, Africa is half Asiatic …[9]

In one of the collection's poems, 'Grenade', one of the stanzas specifically praises the Alhambra:

> The Alhambra! The Alhambra! Palace where the Genies
> Wove a golden dream, filled with harmony,
> Fortress of festooned and ruined towers
> Where night is full of magic syllables,
> Where moonlight through a thousand Arab arches
> Dapples the walls with white clover![10]

The significance of the Alhambra as exotic, escapist idyll could not be clearer, even if Hugo had never visited it, instead drawing his inspiration from books.

Amongst English-speaking travellers in the first half of the nineteenth century, there were two in particular whose writings undoubtedly put Andalusia on the map. The first of these was the American, Washington Irving, a New Yorker who had moved to England in 1815. Eleven years later he became assistant to the US consul in Madrid, but the position was less than demanding and allowed Irving to travel within Spain and to write about subjects which interested him. Granada, the Alhambra and the history of the Moors in Spain were his particular fascination, and in March 1828 he undertook an eight-day journey from Madrid, passing en route through Córdoba. The effect which Granada and the Alhambra had on him may be gauged by his reaction as they came into view:

> Granada, *bellísima* Granada! … we turned a promontory of the arid moun-
> tains of Elvira, and Granada, with its towers, its Alhambra, and its snowy
> mountains, burst upon our sight. The evening sun shone gloriously upon its
> red towers as we approached it, and gave a mellow tone to the rich scenery of
> the vega. It was like a magic glow which poetry and romance have shed over
> this enchanting place.[11]

On this occasion Irving stayed for only ten days, but the visit provided him with an opportunity to gather information for the book which he would publish four years later, and for which a longer stay in Granada in 1829 provided a further stimulus. Prior to this second visit, he spent much of his time in Seville, a city which he also loved and where his close friend, the Scottish painter David Wilkie, lived. In Seville, Irving wandered in the Alcázar, visited the famous tobacco factory, climbed to the top of the Giralda and spent much time in the cathedral:

> Visit it in the evening, when the last rays of the sun, or rather the last glimmer
> of the daylight, is shining through its painted windows. Visit it at night, when
> its various chapels are partially lighted up, its immense aisles are dimly illu-
> minated by their rows of silver lamps, and when mass is preparing amidst
> gleams of gold and clouds of incense at its high altar.[12]

However, his greater love was Granada, and so, in May 1829, accompanied by a Russian friend, Prince Dmitri Dolgoruki, he arrived there once again and obtained permission from the governor of the city to stay in the Alhambra itself where he would remain for four months. Initially, he lodged in the governor's former apartments above the Mexuar, from which he had a view over the Square of the Wells. Later he moved to the apartments constructed by Charles V. From one of the windows he was able to look onto the Garden of Lindaraja, from another across to the gardens of the Generalife. He often sat at night high up in the Queen's Dressing Room, and in the morning he frequently climbed to the top of the Tower of Comares in order to view the rest of the Alhambra, the city below and the sweep of the magnificent landscape around it. In the hot afternoons, he cooled down by swimming in the long pool of the Courtyard of the Myrtles. In 1832, Irving published an account of his stay in *The Alhambra*, the book which had been in his mind for some time and for which he had gathered information during his earlier stay in Granada. In 1851 he published a revised edition which incorporated additional material and which was a third longer than the original. It was a book which at the time enjoyed great success and has continued to do so ever since.

The Alhambra combines Irving's impressions of the palaces with tales and legends which he claims were told to him by others. When he arrived there in 1829, the complex had, as we have seen, fallen into a state of neglect, the governor had moved out to live in the city, and the rooms were occupied by individuals who were poor and often disreputable, as well as by visitors passing through. Having started to climb the Hill of Gomérez, Irving had reached the Gateway of the Pomegranates when he encountered 'a tall, meagre varlet, whose rusty-brown cloak was evidently intended to conceal the ragged state of his nether garments' (p. 33).[13] This individual, Mateo Jiménez by name, described himself as a 'son of the Alhambra', and offered to act as Irving's guide. Arriving at the Alhambra itself, Mateo then introduced him to 'a worthy old maiden dame called Doña Antonia Molina, but who, according to Spanish custom, went by the more neighbourly appellation of Tía Antonia (Aunt Antonia), who maintained the Moorish halls and gardens in order and showed them to strangers' (p. 36). In addition, Tía Antonia had a niece, 'a plump little black-eyed Andalusian damsel' (p. 36) called Dolores, whose job it was to conduct visitors through the palaces.

Irving also encountered many individuals who had made the Alhambra either their home or their playground. One such was

> a little old woman named María Antonia Sabonea, but who goes by the appellation of la Reina Coquina, or the Cockle-Queen. She is small enough to be a fairy, and a fairy she may be for aught I can find out, for no one seems to know her origin. Her habitation is in a kind of closet under the outer staircase of the palace ... (p. 47)

And then there was

> a portly old fellow with a bottle-nose, who goes about in a rusty garb with a cocked hat of oil-skin and a red cockade. He is one of the legitimate sons of the Alhambra, and has lived here all his life, filling various offices, such as deputy alguazil, sexton of the parochial church, and marker of a fives-court established at the foot of one of the towers. He is as poor as a rat, but as proud as he is ragged ... (pp. 47–8)

Many of these individuals were, then, rather bizarre, but so were some of the activities in which they indulged and which initially puzzled Irving as he observed 'a long lean fellow perched on the top of one of the towers, manoeuvring two or three fishing-rods, as though he were angling for the stars' (p. 49). When he later noticed other people doing the same thing, he realized that they were attempting to catch swallows and martlets, and that they had invented the art of angling in the sky.

As for the palaces, Irving did not neglect to describe their poor state. In the room which Tía Antonia used as 'parlor, kitchen and hall of audience … a rude fireplace has been made in modern times in one corner, the smoke from which has discoloured the walls, and almost obliterated the ancient arabesques' (p. 45). He noted that in general the Alhambra

> is in a rapid state of … transition. Whenever a tower falls to decay, it is seized upon by some tatterdemalion family, who become joint-tenants, with the bats and owls, of its gilded halls; and hang their rags, those standards of poverty, out of its windows and loopholes. (p. 47)

In general, as the above suggests, Irving's account of the Alhambra contained a great deal of information, providing a vivid picture of its present state, its current inhabitants, its former Muslim rulers and the history and development of the palaces. The following account of the Courtyard of the Myrtles, which he calls the Court of the Alberca, is a good example of his attention to detail:

> We found ourselves in a vast patio or court one hundred and fifty feet in length, upwards of eighty feet in breadth, paved with white marble, and decorated at each end with light Moorish peristyles, one of which supported an elegant gallery of fretted architecture. Along the mouldings of the cornices and on various parts of walls were escutcheons and ciphers, and cufic and Arabic characters in high relief, repeating the pious mottoes of the Moslem monarchs, the builders of the Alhambra, or extolling their grandeur and munificence. Along the centre of the court extended an immense basin or tank (estanque) a hundred and twenty-four feet in length, twenty-seven in breadth, and five in depth, receiving its water from two marble vases. Hence it is called the Court of the Alberca (from al Beerkah, the Arabic for a pond or a tank). Great numbers of goldfish were to be seen gleaming through the waters of the basin, and it was bordered by hedges of roses. (pp. 36–7)

From time to time, though, Irving allowed himself to be swept along by his imagination, and his descriptions of the Alhambra became decidedly 'poetic', as in the following passage:

> All was open, beautiful; everything called up pleasing and romantic fantasies; Lindaraxa once more walked in her garden; the gay chivalry of

Moslem Granada once more glittered about the Court of the Lions! Who can do justice to a moonlight night in such a climate and such a place? The temperature of a summer midnight in Andalusia is perfectly ethereal. We seem lifted up into a purer atmosphere; we feel a serenity of soul, a buoyancy of spirits, an elasticity of frame, which render mere existence happiness. But when moonlight is added to all this, the effect is like enchantment. Under its plastic sway the Alhambra seems to regain its pristine glories. Every rent and chasm of time; every mouldering tint and weather-stain is gone; the marble resumes its original whiteness; the long colonnades brighten in the moon-beams; the halls are illuminated with a softened radiance, – we tread the enchanted palace of an Arabian tale! …

Such is a faint picture of the moonlight nights I have passed loitering about the courts and halls of this most suggestive pile; 'feeding my fancy with sugared supposition', and enjoying that mixture of reverie and sensation which steal away existence in a southern climate; so that it has been almost morning before I have retired to bed, and been lulled to sleep by the falling waters of the fountain of Lindaraxa. (p. 69)

For all the factual nature of much of his account, then, Irving often surrendered to that exoticism so favoured by the Romantics, and this strongly colours too the stories and legends of the Muslim rulers and families which were woven into the narrative and which he claims were told to him by Mateo Jiménez and Tía Antonia. Many modern critics have derided and mocked Irving for his melancholy romanticism, his self-indulgence, and his languid style, but we have to remember that, in all these respects, Irving was very much a man of his time. Furthermore, he did more than anyone else in the nineteenth century to make the Alhambra one of *the* places to visit.

A more distinguished visitor was the future prime minister of Great Britain, Benjamin Disraeli, who in 1830 travelled for two months through Andalusia. An anglicized Jew, he was on his way to the Middle East, first visiting Spain because his Jewish ancestors had once lived there. Because of this, and also because he had recently suffered from severe depression, the bright sunshine and the historical associations of the south lifted his spirits. In letters to his sister he noted: 'There is a calm voluptuousness about life here that wonderfully accords with my disposition.' His reaction to the country was at times rhapsodic: 'Think of this romantic land covered with Moorish ruins and full of Murillo.' Visiting the Alcázar in Seville, he was enchanted: 'Ah that I could describe to you the wonders of the painted temples of Seville.' And he wished that he and his sister could visit the Alhambra together: 'Ah, that I could wander with you amid the fantastic and imaginative walls of the delicate Alhambra', which he described as 'the most delicate and fantastic creation that ever sprang up on a Summer night in a fairy tale'.[14] As for the Arabs who had once lived there, he admired them greatly, for under their rule the Jews had not been persecuted.

Another Englishman who wrote about Spain in much greater detail than Disraeli was Richard Ford, a High Tory of independent means. In 1830, accompanied by his wife Harriet, three small children and three female servants, he rented a house in the Plazuela de San Isidro in Seville, and in 1831 took his family to Granada where, like Irving, they lived in the Alhambra. Two years later, Ford explored the whole of Spain on horseback, and in 1844 published the result of his travels, the vast *Handbook for Travellers in Spain*, which ran to more than 1,000 pages. This first edition was soon withdrawn on account of some of its offensive observations on places which Ford had visited and people he had met. A second edition, with those observations excluded, was published a year later and proved to be a great success, and in 1846 he also published *Gatherings from Spain*, which included some of the introductory material originally intended for the *Handbook*.[15]

In the *Handbook* Ford described the south of Spain in the following way: 'The kingdom or province of Andalucía, in local position, climate, fertility, objects of interest, and facility of access, must take precedence over all others in Spain' (vol. 1, p. 220). And again:

> The soil … is most fertile, and the climate delicious; the land overflows with oil and wine. The vines of Xerez, the olives of Seville, and the fruits of Málaga, are unequalled. The yellow plains, girdled by the green sea, bask in the sunshine, like a topaz set around with emeralds. (vol. 1, p. 225)

Ford's enthusiasm about certain aspects of Andalusia did not, however, prevent him from criticizing others. Of the Andalusians, he concluded: 'Of all Spaniards the Andalucian is the greatest boaster; he brags chiefly of his courage and wealth. He ends in believing his own lie, and hence is always pleased with himself' (vol. 1, pp. 220–1). As well as this, he suggested that the Andalusian shared 'the besetting sins of the Oriental, his ignorance, indifference, procrastination, tempered by a religious resignation to Providence' (vol. 1, p. 221). Given such uncompromising comments, it is little wonder that some of the more offensive remarks of the first edition of the *Handbook* should have been omitted from the second.

When Ford passed through Córdoba, he was not impressed, for at this time it was in an extremely run-down state: 'Córdoba, seen from the distance, amid its olives and palm trees, and backed by the convent crowned sierra, has a truly Oriental look: inside all is decay' (vol. 1, p. 443). In the distant past, under the Muslims, it had prospered, but, as Lorca would suggest a century later, Christian rule led only to decline:

> Córdoba became the rival of Baghdad and Damascus, and was the centre of power and civilization in the West, and this at a time when weakness, ignorance and barbarism shrouded over the rest of Europe. It contained in the tenth century nearly a million inhabitants, 300 mosques, 900 baths, and 600 inns. It withered under the Spaniards; and is now a dirty, benighted, ill-provided, decaying place, with a population under 60,000, or, as some say, and probably correctly, 45,000. (vol. 1, p. 445)

Ford's description of the great Mezquita is, like much of his writing, rather factual, focusing on its length and width, the number of columns and entrances, the Roman origins of many of the columns and suchlike. Nevertheless, he was impressed by certain aspects of it: 'Some of the upper arches are beautifully interlaced like ribands; the pillars differ from each other in colour, diameter, and material …' (vol. 1, pp. 450–1). As for the construction of the cathedral within the Mezquita, he comments favourably on one or two aspects of its decoration, but criticizes the policy of Charles V in destroying Muslim monuments.

Seville, in contrast, was much loved and admired by Ford. He described it as 'the marvel of Andalucía', 'a purely Moorish city', 'a museum of Moorish antiquities' (vol. 1, pp. 365, 372, 373). As in the case of the Mezquita, Ford was drawn to the Moorish aspects of the Alcázar but detested modern alterations. He therefore praised 'the delicate arabesques, the pillar-divided windows, *ajimezes*, and the carved soffit' (vol. 1, p. 388). And again: 'Many of the doors, ceilings, and *Azulejos* are genuine Moorish … The hall of the ambassadors has a glorious *Media naranja* roof' (vol. 1, p. 389). On the other hand, 'the Spanish balconies and royal portraits mar the Moorish character: the baboon Bourbon heads are both an insult and injury' (vol. 1, p. 389). And similarly: 'This Alcazar was barbarously whitewashed in 1813, when much of the delicate painting and gilding was obliterated' (vol. 1, p. 389).

Despite his preference for Moorish buildings and objects, Ford greatly praised Seville's cathedral, describing it as 'the largest and finest in Spain' (vol. 1, p. 379). His account of it takes up some ten pages, in the course of which he takes the reader from one part of the building to another and provides a considerable amount of information about the size of chapels, the dates of completion, the number of windows and the architects and artists involved in the construction and decoration. Within this abundance of detail, his praise is, though, quite clear, as in the following examples.

Referring to the windows, he notes that 'the painted ones are amongst the finest in Spain' (vol. 1, p. 381). Again: 'The Gothic *Retablo* of the high altar, divided into 44 compartments, is unequalled' (vol. 1, p. 381). And he describes the effect on the individual of the interior of the building as a whole:

> the student will of course … visit the edifice at different times of the day and evening, in order to fully estimate the artistical changes and effects of light and shade. The interior is somewhat dark, but it is a gorgeous gloom, inspiring a religious sentiment, chastening, not chilling, solemn, not sad. (vol. 1, p. 387)

When the Fords arrived in Granada in 1831, they lived in the Alhambra in the governor's former apartments above the Mexuar, where Washington Irving had also lodged, and during a second visit they occupied the Tower of the Ladies, with its magnificent view of the Generalife and the Albaicín. Even so, Ford's first stay in the Alhambra occurred at a time when prisoners were being used to transform part of the building into a storehouse for salt fish – work which did little to preserve its original beauty or guarantee Ford's equanimity, disturbed as he often was by the sound of rattling chains. Indeed, he condemned the people of Granada for their neglect of the jewel in their midst, which he believed they regarded as 'little better than a *casa de ratones*, a rat's hole, which in truth they have endeavoured to make it by centuries of neglect' (vol. 2, p. 551). Little wonder, then, that he found parts of the Alhambra to be crumbling. The general neglect of the building was further illustrated by the fact that, although past explosions had caused serious damage, gunpowder was still being stored in the Palace of Charles V.

As we have already seen, Ford's descriptions of the places he visited were full of no-nonsense, factual information, and much more down-to-earth in that respect than Washington Irving's. His description of the view from the watchtower is fairly typical of his approach:

> Below lies Granada, belted with plantations; beyond expands the Vega, about 30 miles in length by 25 in width, and guarded like an Eden by a wall of mountains … The Vega is studded with villages and villas; every field has its battle, every rivulet its ballad. It is a scene for painters to sketch, and for poets to describe. To the l. rise the snowy Alpujarras, then the distant Sierra of Alhama, then the gorge of Loja in the distance, then the round mountain of Parapanda, which is the barometer of the Vega; for when its head is bonneted with mists, so surely does rain fall: 'Cuando Parapanda se pone la montera, lueve aunque Dios no lo quisiera.' Nearer Granada is the Sierra de Elvira, the site of the old Illiberis, and below the dark woods of the Soto de Roma.

To the r. is the rocky defile of Moclín, and the distant chains of Jaén. The Torre de la Vela was gutted by the French. It is so called because on this 'watchtower' is a silver-tongued bell, which, struck by the warder at certain times, is the primitive clock that gives notice to the irrigators below. It is heard on a still night even in Loja, 30 miles off ... (vol. 2, pp. 555–6)

There were times, on the other hand, when Ford's realistic and factual descriptions surrendered to the more rhapsodic style of Irving. When, for example, he arrived in the Alhambra, he wrote to his friend, the British Envoy Extraordinary in Madrid, Henry Unwin Addington, in the following manner:

Here we are, with the most delicious breezes from the snowy mountain above us, perfumed by a thousand groves and gardens of vine, orange and pom- egranate, carolled by nightingales, who daily and nightly sing in the dark grove ... all by the side of gushing streams and never-failing fountains.[16]

In particular, the onset of evening transformed the palaces into the stuff of legend:

But to understand the Alhambra, it must be lived in, and beheld in the semi- obscure evening, so beautiful of itself in the South, and when ravages are less apparent than when flouted by the gay day glare. On a stilly summer night all is again given up to the past and to the Moor; then, when the moon, Diana's bark of pearl, floats above it in the air like his crescent symbol, the tender beam heals the scars ... As we linger in the recesses of the windows, below lies Granada with its busy hum, and the light sparkles like stars on the obscure Albaicín, as if we were looking down on the reversed firmament ... Then in proportion as all here around is dead, do the fancy and imagination become alive. The halls and courts seem to expand into a larger size: the shadows of the cypresses on the walls assume the forms of the dusky Moor, revisiting his lost home in the glimpses of the moon, while the night winds, breathing through the unglazed windows and myrtles, rustle as his silken robes, or sigh like his lament over the profanation of the unclean infidel and destroyer. (vol. 2, pp. 570–1)

Thus, for all his down-to-earth and often trenchant comments on Spain and the Spaniards, Ford found the Alhambra irresistible. When he finally returned to England, he constructed a Moorish tower in the grounds of his large house near Exeter and terraced the gardens in Moorish style.

A contemporary of Ford, George Borrow went to Spain in 1835 on behalf of the British and Foreign Bible Association in order to arrange for the printing and selling of 5,000 copies of the New Testament in Spanish, and between 1836 and 1840 made three missionary tours in Spain and Portugal. He spent a good deal of time in Galicia, Extremadura and

Andalusia, and in the south was able to indulge his considerable interest in the gypsies. In *The Bible in Spain*, which was published in 1842 and which became Borrow's best-known book, he was, like many others, unimpressed by Córdoba, apart from its location:[17]

> Little can be said with respect to the town of Cordova, which is a mean, dark, gloomy place, full of narrow streets and alleys, without squares or public buildings worthy of attention, save and except its far-famed cathedral; its situation, however, is beautiful and picturesque. Before it runs the Guadalquivir, which, though in this part shallow and full of sandbanks, is still a delightful stream; whilst behind it rise the steep sides of the Sierra Morena, planted up to the top with olive groves. (p. 238)

As for the Mezquita, which in the above description Borrow calls the 'cathedral', he was, in contrast, full of praise:

> this is perhaps the most extraordinary place of worship in the world. It was originally, as is well known, a mosque, built in the brightest days of Arabian dominion in Spain. In shape it was quadrangular, with a low roof, supported by an infinity of small and delicately rounded marble pillars, many of which still remain, and present at first sight the appearance of a marble grove; the greater part, however, were removed when the Christians, after the expulsion of the Moslems, essayed to convert the mosque into a cathedral, which they effected in part by the erection of a dome, and by clearing an open space for a choir. As it at present exists, the temple appears to belong partly to Mahomet, and partly to the Nazarene; and though this jumbling together of massive Gothic architecture with the light and delicate style of the Arabians produces an effect somewhat bizarre, it still remains a magnificent and glorious edifice, and well calculated to excite feelings of awe and veneration within the bosom of those who enter it. (pp. 238–9)

Borrow's favourite city was clearly Seville, whose effect on him he described in the following way: 'Cold, cold must be the heart which can remain insensible to the beauties of this magic scene ... I have shed tears of rapture whilst I beheld it' (p. 658). There he rode his Arab horse, Sidi Habismilk, through the elm-covered road of Las Delicias, and there too he observed 'the black-eyed Andalusian dames and damsels, clad in their graceful silken *mantillas*' (p. 658). Although he found some of the city unattractive, 'the streets ... narrow, badly paved, and full of misery and beggary' (p. 659), he found the Moorish patios extremely attractive, for there 'are to be found shrubs, orange trees, and all kinds of flowers, and perhaps a small aviary, so that no situation can be conceived more delicious than to be here in the shade, hearkening to the song of the birds and the voice of the fountain ... Oft have I sighed that my fate did not permit me to reside in such an Eden for the rest of my days' (p. 659).

As for the city's important buildings and monuments, he described the Golden Tower in terms of 'a giant keeping watch … where the beams of the setting sun seem to be concentrated as in a focus, so that it appears built of pure gold' (p. 658). The Alcázar seemed to him a 'splendid specimen of Moorish architecture. It contains many magnificent halls, so called, which is in every respect more magnificent than the one within the Alhambra of Granada' (p. 216). And the cathedral was, for Borrow

> the most magnificent cathedral in all Spain … It is utterly impossible to wander through the long aisles, and to raise one's eyes to the richly inlaid roof, supported by colossal pillars, without experiencing sensations of sacred awe and deep astonishment … Notre Dame of Paris is a noble building, yet to him who has seen the Spanish cathedrals, and particularly this of Seville, it almost appears trivial and mean, more like a town-hall than a temple of the Eternal. (pp. 659–60)

Somewhat strangely, *The Bible in Spain* contains no information about Granada, apart from the reference to the Alhambra mentioned above and various allusions to the Moors of Granada during Borrow's visit to Tangier. Given his admiration for Muslim civilization, this is surprising, though it is explained by the fact that, for whatever reason, Granada did not form a part of Borrow's itinerary.

In 1840 the French writer, Théophile Gautier, travelled through Spain to Andalusia in search of the paradise which he had failed to find in France. The desolate landscape and the ugly towns of northern and central Spain seemed to him the outward reflection of his inner state, but all was transformed when he arrived in the south, where the sunlight on the mountains seemed to him the very same light that must have illuminated the Garden of Eden, and where he believed he had at last discovered his earthly paradise. He considered Córdoba to be the most African in appearance of any city in Spain, its streets completely un-European:

> Nothing about them recalls the manners and the customs of Europe. One walks between interminable chalk-coloured walls, with occasional windows trellised with bars and gratings, meeting nobody but a few evil-looking beggars, pious women muffled in black veils, or *majos* who ride past like lightning on their brown horses with white harness, striking showers of sparks from the cobblestones. If the Moors could return, they would not have to make any changes in order to settle here once again.[18]

In Seville, quite apart from the splendid monuments, he was attracted by the beauty of the women:

> The rapidity with which their fans open and close beneath their fingers, the flash of their glance, the self-assurance of their movements, the undulating

63

suppleness of their bodies, all this makes them unique. In England, France and Italy, you may find women with a more perfect and regular beauty, but surely you will never encounter prettier or saucier ones.[19]

And he concluded, too, that: 'in a *mantilla* a woman must be as ugly as the seven cardinal virtues not to look beautiful!'

It was, though, the Alhambra which was for Gautier the essence of paradise. He spent four days and nights there with a friend, Eugène Piot, the first two nights in the Courtyard of the Lions, the third in the Hall of the Two Sisters and the fourth in the Hall of the Abencerrajes. They were, he said, the most perfect nights of his life, though his emotional and spiritual pleasure in this environment did not prevent him from cooling his bottles of sherry in the fountain of the Courtyard of the Lions.

On his return to France, Gautier wrote two books inspired by his Spanish experience. The first, *Over the Mountains* (*Tra los montes*), later retitled *Journey Through Spain* (*Voyage en Espagne*), appeared in 1843, and the second, *Spain* (*Espagne*), in 1845. *Journey Through Spain* was a kind of travel guide in which Gautier sought to combine the personal quest described above with a desire to inform the French public about the nature of life in the Spanish peninsula. *Spain* consisted of forty-three poems inspired by the journey, some of them to do with the Alhambra. Thus, 'In the Moorish Alhambra' is in praise of the beauty of a young woman encountered in the Courtyard of the Lions:

> In the Moorish Alhambra,
> Beneath the slender arches,
> Where wild arabesques
> Entwine their branches,
> I wandered like a faithful knight,
> Forgetful of the Cegríes,
> The proud Abencerrajes,
> The beauty of these palaces,
> Just hoping for her smile.
>
> She said to me: 'See there
> The Courtyard of the Lions,
> The lovely Moorish patterns,
> The clear pools where one can bathe,
> The marble halls and columns.'
> 'No, neither flower nor marble,
> Nor any of these miracles!
> They matter not, it's you I wish to see.'
>
> 'Look there, beyond the mountains,
> See there the bright blue sky,

> The splendour of the Spanish sun,
> Before it sets and dies.'
> 'The beauty of your spirit
> Extinguishes its light.
> Against the blue horizon
> The sun is like the night,
> Compared with your eyes.'[20]

In another poem, 'The Sigh of the Moor', Gautier evoked the despair of Boabdil as he left Granada for the last time and, from the hill which has since been known as the Sigh of the Moor, el Suspiro del Moro, looked back at the Alhambra, from which he once ruled. And in 'The Laurel-Tree in the Generalife' he described the beauty of the tree and its effect on him in terms of a beautiful young girl.

Alexander Dumas, celebrated author of *The Count of Monte Cristo*, travelled to Spain in 1846, accompanied by his son, an Arab valet, three French artists, three trunks of clothes and six cases of rifles for protection. In the account of his journey, *From Paris to Cadiz*, he alluded to Spain as his 'longed-for country of Romance', described how in Seville he dressed as a *majo*, purchasing some exotic clothes, and, visiting Granada, compared the town to 'a sleepy maiden resting in the sunshine on a bed of moss and bracken, ringed round with cactus plants and aloes'. As for the gardens of the Generalife, he wrote ecstatically that 'nowhere in the world will you find in such a small expanse such fragrance, such freshness, such a multitude of windows, each opening on a corner of paradise'.[21] Like his fellow countrymen, Dumas was very much an orientalist.

During the second half of the nineteenth century, the number of foreign visitors to the south increased dramatically, many travelling by train. Such was William Clark, a fellow of Trinity College, Cambridge, who spent the summer of 1849 travelling in the peninsula and who, two years later, published *Gazpacho, or Summer Months in Spain*. When he visited the Alhambra, twenty years after Washington Irving, he discovered that Mateo Jiménez, Irving's guide, was still in residence. Clark found him to be 'a twaddling old fool' who consistently got his facts and dates wrong, and who, when pressed on such matters, quoted the authority of a certain 'Vasendon Eerveen'.[22] By this time there were other guides competing for business with Mateo, whose son had stabbed one of them for insulting his father. Quite clearly, the increasing popularity of the Alhambra brought its own problems, from rivalry among guides to attacks on visitors who were invariably well-to-do.

Matilda Betham-Edwards was undoubtedly a lady of means. Journeying to Spain in 1866, she believed that a woman should always travel in her 'best clothes and with half a dozen trunks at least. Luggage and good clothes ensure you good places, general civility, and an infinity of minor comforts.'[23] Two years later, she published *Through Spain to the Sahara*, in which she decried the way in which part of Córdoba's great mosque had been transformed into a cathedral. Even so, it remained for her a structure of great beauty:

> It is so vast, so solemn, so beautiful. You seem to be wandering at sunset time in a large and dusky forest, intersected by regular alleys of tall, stately palms. No matter in what direction you turn your face, northward, southward, eastward, westward, the same beautiful perspective meets your eye, file after file of marble and jasper columns supporting the double horse-shoe arch. Nothing can be more imposing, and at the same time more graceful than this arrangement of transverse aisles; and the interlaced arches, being delicately coloured in red and white, may not inaptly be compared to the foliage of a palmforest, flushed with the rays of the setting sun.

Having visited Granada and the Alhambra, she revealed her admiration for Moorish architecture and complained bitterly of the Spaniards' neglect of their great Moorish buildings:

> I confess that for me the Mahomedan phase, so graceful, so artistic, so beneficent as it was, surpasses in interest every other … To whom is she [Spain] indebted for her most sumptuous monuments, her most elegant arts, her most picturesque costumes, her most precious products? To the Moors. Who brought down the cool waters from the rocky prisons, turning whole wastes into sunny vineyards and gardens? The Moors … Who planted the orange tree and the palm, the fig and the olive? The Moors.[24]

Her lasting impression with regard to Andalusia's Muslim monuments was that the Spaniards 'do their best to defile them'.

In *Wanderings in Spain*, published in 1873, Augustus Hare described the discomfort of travel along Spanish roads, which jolted one to the bone, and, when one arrived at a particular destination, the deplorable state of Spanish inns. Visiting Granada's gypsy area, the Sacromonte, he found the inhabitants to be little better than savages, both in appearance and manner, and not to be trusted for a single moment. Even so, the Alhambra compensated for all earlier discomforts. It was for him 'the most beautiful place in the world'. Like Irving and Ford, he considered it to be best visited in the light of the moon or as evening descended, for then one could see 'the flood of purple and gold ebb on the plain'.[25]

During the twentieth century, visitors in the south included many famous writers of different kinds, of which one of the first was the sociologist, Havelock Ellis. In *The Soul of Spain*, published in 1908 and based on his travels a few years earlier, he described his stay in Seville and Granada, and noted of the Alhambra that it had become 'a carefully kept museum. Every year it grows more rejuvenated, and though the restoration is carried out with reverence, it is never beautiful to see in the aged the signs of artificial youth.'[26]

Much more interesting and substantial is the account provided by W. W. Collins in *Cathedral Cities of Spain*, which appeared in 1909, and which contained extremely attractive watercolour illustrations by the author. In Córdoba he encountered 'Decay and ruin at every turn', but felt that 'the rags, the squalor, and the ruin' were somehow 'picturesque'.[27] As were many others before him, Collins was overwhelmed by the interior of the Mezquita:

> Coming suddenly into the cool shade of its many pillared avenues, I felt as if transplanted into the silent depths of a great forest. In every direction I looked the trunks of huge trees apparently rose upwards in ordered array. The light here and there filtered through gaps on to the red-tiled floor, which only made the deception greater by its resemblance to the needles of a pine-wood or the dead leaves of autumn. (pp. 24–5)

At the same time, the sound of the organ reminded Collins that the Christians had converted part of the mosque into a cathedral, a transformation which, like previous visitors, he much deplored.

Collins regarded Seville as 'the most fascinating city in Spain' (p. 7) and was greatly impressed by both the cathedral and the Alcázar. Of the cathedral, he observed: 'The columns of the double aisles break up the two hundred and sixty feet of its width and add much to the solemn dignity of the vast interior, enhanced greatly by the height of the vaulting above the spectator' (p. 8). As for the Alcázar, he was delighted by its courtyards and gardens, in which 'The scent of orange blossom perfumes the air, the fountains splash and play, all is still … save the tinkle of the water and the cooing of the doves' (p. 14). Visiting the building's different rooms, he was impressed in particular by the Patio of the Maidens and by the Hall of the Ambassadors, describing the latter as the 'architectural gem of the Alcázar' (p. 15). His allusion to the complex as 'this fairy Palace, this flower from the East' (p. 15) illustrates to the full his sense of rapture.

In Granada, Collins encountered more beggars than in either Córdoba or Seville, but once more he described their 'disfigured humanity' as 'picturesque' (p. 36). The cathedral seemed to him 'the most imposing edifice of this style in Spain' (p. 38), the Royal Chapel 'of surpassing interest' (p. 39), but most impressive of all was, of course, the Alhambra. Devoting ten or so pages to a description of its various palaces, he concluded:

> The glamour of the East clings to every corner of the Alhambra, and the wonder of it all increased as I began to grow familiar with its courtyards and halls, the slender columns of its arcades, with their tracery and oft-repeated verses forming ornament and decoration, and the well thought-out balance of light and shade. What must it all have been like when the sedate Moor glided noiselessly through the cool corridors, or the clang of arms resounded through the now silent halls! It is difficult to imagine. (p. 54)

In many respects, Collins's reaction is reminiscent of that of Washington Irving almost a century earlier.

Another traveller, Edward Hutton, described his tour of Spanish cities in his *The Cities of Spain*, published in 1924. He was appalled by most of Córdoba, describing it as 'an image of desolation, tragic and lamentable. She is like a ruined sepulchre forgotten in the midst of the desert from which even the dead have stolen away.'[28] On the other hand, the experience of entering the Mezquita dispelled such feelings and inspired a sense of wonder:

> Ah, I forgot the city, I forgot the desolation, I forgot the dust that seems to have crumbled from innumerable civilizations as I wandered in that holy and sacred place; I lost myself in a new contemplation; I kissed the old voluptuous marbles; I touched the strange, precious inscriptions, and with my finger I traced the name of God. I remembered only beautiful things and joy, and in the worn and sacred Mihrab where the knees of so many who once cared for the soft sky have worn away the marble, I went softly, softly, because of them. (p. 194)

Only the cathedral in the middle of the Mezquita, the 'obscene Baroque Cathedral' (p. 194) succeeded in spoiling Hutton's appreciation of the beauty of Muslim architecture.

Granada evoked similar feelings. It was for Hutton 'a dead city, the colour of dust, shrunken and thirsty', while, above it, 'like a beautiful acropolis, the Alhambra rises among the woods, where there is always the sound of living waters, and where in springtime the nightingales sing all day from dawn till dusk, from sunset till morning' (p. 271). Within the Alhambra precinct, the Renaissance palace of Charles V was 'like a Vandal amid the flower-like work of the Arab, that architecture delicate and strong which it sought to humble by its mere size, its ridiculous seriousness, its immensity, its ignorant contempt' (p. 274). In contrast, the Muslim palaces inspired only admiration and contempt for those who conquered such a creative people: 'It [the Alhambra] yet remains perhaps the most lovely monument in Spain, certainly the most delightful, the most fascinating; the memorial of a people greater, after all, in every virtue of civilisation than those fierce fanatics who expelled them' (p. 275).

Having found both Córdoba and Granada to be wretched and impoverished cities, Hutton's reaction to Seville was very different indeed:

> That almost morbid impression of stillness and silence that the traveller finds everywhere in Córdoba remains with him to the very gates of Seville, where it vanishes before the curious smile, the languorous gaiety, the subtle, unsatisfied excitement of the greatest city in Andalusia. (p. 196)

Despite the fact that the streets were 'narrow and tortuous' (p. 197), Hutton found pleasure in 'the patios, cool in the fierce heat, where a fountain plays' (p. 199) and in the women 'more beautiful than flowers, in their summer dresses' (p. 200). Somewhat curiously, he provides no description of the cathedral, but a visit to the Alcázar inspired thoughts quite as fanciful as those experienced by Irving and Collins before him:

> As you enter room after room, court after court, patio after patio, full of silence and sunlight, you will almost hear the soft footsteps of some one who has but just gone out, leaving a faint trace of some presence in an inexplicable trouble on the threshold, a suggestion of scent in the air, the trembling of a curtain that has just felt the touch of a hand, a fading breath on the window-pane through which some one has glanced a moment before, a blossom fallen on the pathway, the fluttering of a leaf on a tree where some one has just plucked a fruit. And you remember that María Padilla often passed through these gardens, that under these very trees she trembled in the arms of her lover, that these cold pavements have felt the tenderness of her feet, this marble the wealth and sweetness of her body. (pp. 203–4)

The most curious twentieth-century travellers of all were probably those members of the British intelligentsia and the Bloomsbury set who at different times journeyed around Spain by train, bus and even mule. In 1920, Ralph Partridge, ex-officer and womanizer, Dora Carrington, a bisexual painter, and the homosexual Lytton Strachey, visited Seville, Córdoba and Granada, and also visited the writer and Hispanist, Gerald Brenan, in his house in the Alpujarras. In Córdoba, Strachey attended an evening Mass in the Mezquita and admired 'the pillars and arches of the antique mosque stretching away in every direction into far distant darkness … incredibly theatrical and romantic'. He was impressed too by the Alhambra, though he had certain reservations: 'Before long one observes picture-postcard elements, and the detail of the Alhambra is sheer Earls Court, but the general grandeur of situation and outline remain.'[29] This said, the final 50-kilometre trek to Gerald Brenan's house in the village of Yegen was done by mule, and Strachey, who suffered from piles, was in a state of collapse on arrival. It was an experience which evidently coloured his view of Spain, for when his friends, Leonard and Virginia Woolf, proposed a similar trip in 1923, Strachey warned them that 'Spain is absolute death'. As for Gerald Brenan, whom the Woolfs also visited, Seville was his favourite city, partly for reasons of pleasure. Visiting the Mezquita in Córdoba, he found the Christian addition weighty, massive and dispiriting, in complete contrast to the Muslim part of the building:

> A mosque is also a place for the contemplation of the Oneness of Allah. How can this better be done than by giving the eyes a maze of geometric patterns to brood over? The state aimed at is a sort of semi-trance. The mind contemplates the patterns, knows that they be unravelled and yet does not unravel them. It rests therefore on what it sees, and the delicate colour, the variations of light and shade add a sensuous tinge to the pleasure of certainty made visible.[30]

With regard to the Alhambra, Brenan was, for some strange reason, completely dismissive, describing it as a 'shoddy and bedraggled'.[31]

Later still, other well-known writers were to describe their experiences. The novelist Rose Macaulay drove alone through Spain in 1949, covering a distance of almost 6,400 kilometres, and in *The Fabled Shore* created a vivid picture of the Alhambra. In 1955, Laurie Lee, in *A Rose for Winter*, described his travels in Andalusia and saw the dreams of mathematicians in the elaborate decoration of the Alhambra's ceilings. But the most detailed accounts of Córdoba, Seville and Granada were provided by the travel writer, H. V. Morton, in *A Stranger in Spain*, published in 1955.[32] Visiting the Mezquita in Córdoba, he was 'carried away by enthusiasm' (p. 201). The striped red-and-white arches reminded him of 'an immense forest full of zebras' (p. 201), and he felt that he would have been 'happy in the Caliphate of Córdoba' (p. 202). As for the cathedral built inside the mosque, he concluded that nothing could be 'more emblematic of Andalusia, perhaps even of Spain, than to see this Christian jewel in its unlikely Moslem setting' (p. 203).

In Seville, Morton was duly impressed by the vast cathedral and, at first, by the Alcázar, but he felt that the latter soon became rather boring, for the delicate and intricate architecture went 'on and on like an endless

Arab anecdote, full of repetition, until you have the impression that the multiplication table has been set to music' (p. 203). The Alhambra was, though, a different story:

> The Court of the Lions is a thing of light, indeed of weightless beauty. I thought I should go there every day while I was in Granada. It has the look of something that has just alighted upon earth ... I felt like someone in a story who has passed through a door in a wall to find himself in some *gulistan* of Sa'di; for this is the country of djinn and wizard, the enchanted pavilion of Scheherazade ... (p. 213)

Although his style was more sober than that of many of his predecessors, Morton was evidently capable of surrendering to the same kind of rapture.

During the last fifty years there have been a number of other books which have focused on aspects of Andalusia, be it on the region as a whole, the great cities, the history of the Moors, or the Moorish monuments. Some of these are, of course, guidebooks, others are accounts of personal experiences. Mention should perhaps be made of *Spain*, by James (later Jan) Morris, published in 1964, in which the author concluded that the Muslim rulers had 'dug their roots deep ...' The interior of the Alhambra was not, however, to this writer's liking, though the building as a whole, seen from a distance, was:

> On the hill above the city there stands, of course, the Alhambra – foppish within, tremendous on the outside, especially if you pick out its red and golden walls through the lens of a distant telescope, and see it standing there beneath the Sierra Nevada like an illumination in a manuscript.[33]

As well as the foreign travellers who wrote about their experiences in Andalusia, there were also many artists, especially in the nineteenth century, who sketched or painted what they saw. Such was the cult of orientalism at that time that some of those artists who visited the Middle East chose to live there and adopted the local costume. They attempted to become, in effect, the figures they depicted in their sketches and paintings, opting for a way of life more exotic than that afforded them by their respective homelands.

In addition to writing the enormous *Handbook for Travellers in Spain*, Richard Ford produced an extensive pictorial record of his journeys through the peninsula. An essentially amateur artist, Ford had been surrounded by paintings from childhood, in particular by the landscapes of Richard Wilson, and he was also a great admirer of the work of Turner, as well as of the Spanish painters, Velázquez, Murillo and Zurbarán. As for his own artistic abilities, his earliest known efforts were

71

not particularly promising. In 1822 he published an edition of twelve of his etchings, none of which was of any real quality, but his talent undoubtedly flourished when he set out for his first trip to Spain in 1830. During this and his second visit of 1833, he completed more than 500 drawings, many depicting scenes in Seville and Granada. When he returned to England after the second visit, he had lessons with an accomplished landscape painter, John Gendall, and put this experience to good use when he came to paint the gouache and watercolour versions of his Spanish sketches. Although his drawings and paintings were never exhibited in his lifetime, some of them appeared in the form of rather poor engravings in various books, such as Lockhart's *Spanish Ballads*. In 1955 the Patronato of the Alhambra published most of Ford's Alhambra drawings in *Richard Ford, Granada, an Account Illustrated with Unpublished Original Drawings*. The text is in both Spanish and English.[34]

During his two stays in the Alhambra, Ford did drawings of all aspects of the building. One pencil drawing is entitled *Principal Entrance to the Alhambra by the Moorish Gate of Judgement*. The ancient fortress is depicted in *Alcazaba and the Torre de Siete Suelos, the Alhambra*, a drawing which Ford originally did in pencil but which he later reworked in gouache. As for the palaces, there is a pencil and wash drawing of the Courtyard of the Lions, *Patio de los Leones*, a *View of the Tocador de la Reina and Fallen Wall* in pencil and watercolour, and an atmospheric watercolour, *Sala de Comares, or Hall of the Ambassadors in the Alhambra, seen from the Tocador de la Reina*. During his stay in the Tower of the Ladies, he did a rather good pencil and wash picture of the building, then known as the Casa Sánchez. It reveals very clearly the decline into which the Alhambra had fallen. The pool contains no water – a consequence of the war against the French in the early part of the century.

There are, in addition, a number of more general views of the Alhambra, such as the pencil, pen and wash *View of the Alhambra and of the Sierra Nevada from the Top of the Tower of San Cristóbal and Overlooking the Albaicín*, and the pencil drawing, *View of the Generalife from the Alhambra*. But, if Richard Ford's drawings and paintings were numerous, mention must also be made of his wife, Harriet, for she produced interesting work in her own right. Her pencil and wash *The Patio of the Mexuar* is a good example of her artistic ability. It depicts an upper corner with elaborate wall decoration, stalactites and a wooden roof, is full of realistic detail, and reveals a fine sense of perspective, as does *Patio de los Leones from the Sala de Justicia*.

As for Seville, Ford did many pencil drawings, including *The Giralda Tower and Cathedral* and *Casa de Pilatos*, a view in pencil and pen entitled *Seville from the Cartuja* and a painting based on it. Similarly, a pencil drawing and a painting called *The Garden of the Alcázar* and a watercolour, *Murillo's House*. This pictorial record of Ford's stays in Seville and Granada is extremely interesting, and it reflects, of course, his deep and abiding fascination with the country.

Frederick Lewis (1805–76), a friend of Ford and a more accomplished artist, was a dedicated orientalist who frequently visited the Middle East and who, after a stay in Spain in 1833, settled in Cairo for ten years, dressed according to the local fashion. In the Alhambra he stayed with Ford and his wife in the Tower of the Ladies and made some fifty studies of different parts of the palaces. The outcome was his book, *Sketches and Drawings of the Alhambra*, which appeared in 1836 and which contained twenty-six lithographs. These were, of course, produced from work which Lewis had done on the spot, which included watercolours such as *Families Living and Working in the Tower of Comares* and *The Casa Sánchez in the Alhambra*. There were also more general views, including *View of the Alhambra and the Sierra Nevada from the Terrace of the Adarves,* and *Part of the Alhambra from the Alameda del Darro.*.

Lewis's enthusiasm for Spain was shared by the Scottish artist, David Roberts (1796–1864), who was also a great traveller and orientalist. He too visited the Middle East, which from 1838 became the almost constant subject of his painting, though, unlike Lewis, he did not choose to live there. His visit to Spain took place in 1833, the year in which Ford and Lewis, both friends of Roberts, were also there, but he failed to see them. Having travelled the considerable distance from Córdoba to Granada by mule, he stayed there for only three weeks, but so dazzled was he by the Alhambra that he found it difficult to decide which palace or courtyard he ought to sketch first. He wrote as follows to his sister, Lucy: 'The architecture is so peculiar and elaborate that it would take months to do it justice. Still, I hope by about the end of this month to have got much of the best of it; after which I intend going to Málaga.'[35] In particular, he enthused about the way in which the arrangement and dimensions of the buildings combined with natural light to produce the best effects in Islamic architecture.

After his return to England, Roberts worked on his sketches and drawings with a view to publication, and between 1835 and 1838 illustrated four of the highly popular series called *Landscape Annuals*, three of them devoted to Spain. In 1837 he also published his *Picturesque Sketches in Spain*, which twenty years later was still in great demand. A lithograph,

The Tower of the Comares in the Fortress of the Alhambra, vividly conveys the size and strength of the building, as does the wash drawing, *The Court of the Alberca.* The painting, *The Hall of the Abencerrajes,* contains all the wonderful arabesque detail of its walls, as well as the stalactites of its ceiling, the whole suffused in the golden light pouring through the windows in its roof.

Roberts also produced wonderful sketches and paintings of buildings in Córdoba and Seville. They include numerous pencil drawings and water-colours, such as *The Alcázar or Palace of the Moorish Kings, Chapel of Mahomed in the Mosque at Córdoba, Porch of an Ancient Mosque, Córdoba, Seville from the Cruz del Campo, The Giralda, Seville* and *Interior of Seville Cathedral.* And there are, as well, some very fine oil-paintings, including *The Moorish Tower at Seville, Called the Giralda* and *Interior of the Cathedral of Seville during the Ceremony of Corpus Christi.* It is noticeable, though, that Roberts often exaggerated the size and height of the buildings he drew or painted. In doing so, he clearly wished to emphasize both their grandeur and their sublime character.

Not unexpectedly, the Alhambra has always been of great interest to architects, and in this context it is important to mention the work of Owen Jones (1809–74), an architect and designer of Welsh descent who, in 1834, visited Granada in the company of the French Arabist, Jules Goury. They made a detailed architectural survey of the Alhambra's palaces and, although Goury died in the same year, Jones completed his work during a second visit in 1837. The results were published between 1842 and 1846 under the title, *Plans, Elevations, Sections and Details of the Alhambra.* Subsequently, Jones was involved, as superintendent of works, in the Great Exhibition of 1851, when the great glass structure known as the Crystal Palace was constructed in Hyde Park in order to display British craftsmanship. Three years later the structure was moved to Sydenham, in south London, and in one of its great courts Jones reproduced the Alhambra's Courtyard of the Lions, the Hall of Justice (the Hall of the Kings) and the Hall of the Abencerrajes. The limited space at Jones's disposal meant that the dimensions of the reproduction were not the same as those of the original, but his aim was to retain something of the general character of the original. As an introduction to the enterprise, he also published in 1854 *The Alhambra Court in the Crystal Palace,* a small but fascinating book in which he provided both a detailed account of his work in the real Alhambra and drawings and diagrams connected with that work. In 1856 Jones also published *The Grammar of Ornament,* in which he set out his views, heavily influenced by Islamic architecture and by his studies of the Alhambra, that ornamentation should be based on geometric pattern and should be both elaborate and abstract. In the years which followed, he designed the interiors of many important and fashionable houses, often introducing inlaid and carved work in Moorish style.

In the twentieth century, Andalusia's Muslim heritage continued to be a source of inspiration for English artists, though in general they are not as well known as some of those already mentioned. In some cases, they have illustrated books on Spain, as in the case of W. W. Collins's *Cathedral Cities of Spain,* beautifully illustrated by the author. The chapter on Córdoba contains lovely watercolours of the bell-tower, of the Mezquita seen from the distance and of the Courtyard of the Oranges. Similarly, the section on Seville has illustrations of the interior of the cathedral, a splendid representation of the Giralda and a luminous painting of the Patio of the Maidens in the Alcázar. In the chapter on Granada, the painting of the Courtyard of the Lions is, perhaps, less successful, but this is offset by a lovely picture of the gardens of the Generalife.

Edward Hutton's *The Cities of Spain* contains twenty-four colour illustrations by A. Wallace Rimington. Hutton's praise of the Mezquita in Córdoba is accompanied by an impressive painting of the Courtyard of the Oranges and the bell-tower. Somewhat strangely, there are no illustrations of the great buildings in Seville or Granada, but the chapter on Granada does contain a lovely watercolour of a typical Andalusian garden, another of a garden in the Alhambra and a third of houses in the Albaicín.

As well as English artists – and there were many more than those mentioned – the French also found Andalusia a rich source of inspiration. The somewhat exotically named Isidore Severin Justin Baron de Taylor (1789–1879), of English parentage but otherwise wholly French, was a soldier, diplomat, man of letters and artist. During his military career he was also director of the Théâtre-Français, where, in 1830, he produced Victor Hugo's *Hernani.* Between 1835 and 1837 he was in Spain, commissioned by Louis-Philippe to find paintings for the king's 'Galerie espagnole' in the Louvre. Spain subsequently occupied an important position in Taylor's written and illustrated work, one example of which was the three-volume *Voyage pittoresque en Espagne et en Portugal.* As well as this, Taylor completed various sketches of the Alhambra, and, with a view to publishing them, he sought the assistance of Asselineau, one of the most skilful illustrators of the time.

The book which stemmed from this collaboration was *L'Alhambra,* which contained a preface and nine full-page, beautifully coloured lithographs of different aspects of the palaces. Published in a limited edition, the book was little known in its time. The preface consists of an introductory historical account of the Alhambra and of the architectural features of its various rooms. The lithographs begin with *Porte de la Justice*, as if we are entering the Alhambra complex, and continue with illustrations of its different parts: *Cour de l'Alberca, Galerie de la Cour des Lions, Salle du Tribunal, Cour des Lions*, etc. In every case the detail is quite astonishing, but the beauty of the finished work depended, of course, on the skill of Asselineau as a lithographer and colourist. In this respect the lithographs have a wonderful delicacy, both in terms of the detail and the colouring. In *Cabinet des Infantes, Salle des Deux Soeurs*, for example, every detail of the ceiling, the walls and the tiles at their base is presented, but without ostentation, the whole delicately coloured in subdued yellows, reds and blues. As well as this, the sense of perspective creates a true feeling of depth as we are invited to look through archways and past columns into inner courtyards and patios. If, as Taylor observed, 'Nothing, even in the Orient, equals the elegance and beauty of this monument',[36] it can also be said that none of the nineteenth-century illustrations of the Alhambra equal his and Asselineau's in sheer quality.

Another Frenchman who was fascinated by the Alhambra was Philibert Joseph Girault de Prangey (1804–92). Born in Langres, he studied art at the École des Beaux Arts in Paris, travelled widely in Italy, Greece, Asia Minor, Palestine, Syria and Spain, and became fascinated by Islamic architecture and the oriental way of life in general. The titles of some of his books are sufficient indication of his interests: *Monuments Arabes et Moresques de Cordoue, Séville et Grenade*, published in 1836–9; *Essai sur l'Architecture des Arabes et des Mores en Espagne et en Barbarie*, published in 1841, and *Choix d'Ornaments Moresques à l'Alhambra*, undated.

De Prangey first visited Granada in 1832, three years before Taylor and one year after Richard Ford's first stay in the Alhambra. The result of this visit was his *Souvenirs de Grenade et de l'Alhambra,* published in Paris in 1837.[37] The book consists of introductory sections on Granada and its history, on the Alhambra and its various palaces, and on its architecture and colouring. This is then followed by detailed descriptions of the twenty-eight lithographs which illustrate the volume and by explanations of the architectural plans which appear at the end of it. The latter provide an accurate guide to the height and width of the different buildings, allowing the reader to see the size of one in relation to another. De Prangey's interest in the Alhambra was both architectural and artistic.

The technique of lithography had been introduced in 1798 and had quickly become established as an important form of book illustration. In the 1830s lithography, which involved printing from a design on stone, then developed into chromolithography, which consisted of printing from several stones, each with its own colour. Interested as he was in the colours of Islamic and Moorish architecture, the Alhambra proved to be an ideal subject for de Prangey.

His twenty-eight lithographs clearly offer more variety than the nine in Taylor's much smaller book. They include *Vue de Grenade et de la Sierra Névada*, *Porte de Jugement*, *Porte du Vin*, *Cour des Lions*, *Cabinet des Infantes*, *Cour de l'Alberca* – indeed, almost all aspects of the Alhambra. There are, too, lithographs of places outside the Alhambra: *Maison à l'Albaysin*, *Jardin du Convent de San-Domingo*, *Place Neuve à Grenade*, and *Côte des Moulins*. However, de Prangey's illustrations lack both the clarity and the delicacy of those by Asselineau, and the latter's colour tones are much more subtle. In general, de Prangey's colours are much darker than Asselineau's and they create a much more gloomy and oppressive effect rather than the light and airy feeling which the Alhambra possesses in reality.

A third Frenchman who travelled extensively in Spain was the great book illustrator and engraver, Gustave Doré (1832–83). Born in Strasbourg, he was financially independent and was therefore able to devote his life to travel and art. He illustrated the great masterpieces of world literature: Dante's *Divine Comedy* in 1861 and 1868; Cervantes's *Don Quixote* in 1866; and Ariosto's *Orlando Furioso* in 1879. Often described as a pseudo-romantic, Doré was a great visionary, as the bold and dramatic illustrations in these books suggest. As far as Spain is concerned, his engravings include several of Granada and the Alhambra: *The Darro River Flowing through Granada*, *Modern Christians in the Palaces of the Ancient Moorish Kings* and *Priests* and *'Majos' Admiring the Alhambra Vase*. Impressive in their detail, these engravings are more realistic than visionary. The first of them mentioned above vividly evokes crumbling buildings above the river and the towering mountains in the background. But Doré's realism could also have considerable wit and bite, of which the second is an excellent example. While his female companion looks around apprehensively, an elderly gentleman uses a hammer to prise a tile from the wall of one of the Alhambra's palaces, his eyes sheepishly turned towards the artist who has caught him in the act. The scene depicts, of course, the kind of vandalism to which the Alhambra was exposed in Doré's time.

As a direct result of the accounts of writers and the work of artists and architects, the Alhambra had, by the second half of the nineteenth century, become synonymous with glamour, and its name became applied to buildings in different parts of the world, in particular to those which specialized in entertainment. The Royal Panopticon of Science and Art in Leicester Square, London, became in 1858 the Alhambra Palace, a theatre decorated in Moorish style and providing popular entertainment, including music hall. It ended its life in 1936 and is now the Odeon cinema. Cinemas called either Granada or Alhambra are still to be found in many towns and cities in the United Kingdom, though their patrons are unlikely to be aware of the origin of the name – a far cry from its source but sufficient proof of the widespread influence of Muslim Spain.

Among the accounts and descriptions of the cities and monuments of southern Spain, those of the French Romantics – Chateaubriand, Hugo, Gautier, Dumas – as well as those of many English nineteenth-century writers, are particularly interesting. And so too is the work of artists such as David Roberts, Isidore Severin Justin Baron de Taylor, and Gustave Doré. One of the consequences of their writings and paintings, all marked by their rhapsodic and exotic character, was to provide the foreigner with an image of Andalusia which was exceedingly glamorous and which, in effect, became stereotypical, something which was also true, as we shall now see, of the foreigner's – and to some extent the Spaniard's – representation of flamenco.

4

Flamenco

Most people who have been to Spain will have seen a flamenco show, either in their hotel or on an organized visit to a *tablao*, a small theatre where every evening flamenco is performed for tourists, accompanied by the serving of sangría. In all probability the standard of performance will be mediocre, but very few, if any, of the audience will be aware of that, or indeed be able to distinguish one flamenco dance from another. Even so, everyone knows that flamenco is a form which is uniquely Spanish, and most people who see its performance respond as positively to its vibrant character as they do to the Moorish buildings of Andalusia. In some ways flamenco has a similar exoticism, but its origins are very different.

Around 800–900 AD, the people who later became known as Romanies and who probably lived in the Punjab in north-west India, emigrated to different parts of Asia, Europe and Africa, many of them eventually settling in Egypt. Another emigration took place some four to five hundred years later when Indian tribes also left their homeland, probably on account of persecution, and travelled west through the Balkans, Germany and France, finally arriving in north-east Spain, where documentary evidence discovered in Barcelona points to their presence there in the fifteenth century. At around this time, those tribes who had settled in Egypt many centuries earlier crossed the Straits of Gibraltar and landed in Andalusia, doubtless attracted by its climate and by the oriental culture of the region which made their assimilation much easier. This seems to have been facilitated too by the fact that the southern immigrants were less aloof than their northern counterparts, mixed more easily with the inhabitants of Andalusia, and were not unlike them in appearance. Because they had arrived from Egypt, the southern immigrants were known as *gitanos*, a shortened form of *egiptanos*, the Spanish word for Egyptians, and *gitanos* subsequently came to mean gypsies in general. Furthermore, although the tribes which had originally left India were admired and welcomed in other counties on account of their skills as horse-traders and weapon-makers, their descendants, clearly much changed from their ancestors, encountered a much harsher reality in the sense that from the outset they were regarded with fear and suspicion and, because of their vagabond ways, swarthy appearance and strange language, considered to be thieves, thugs, murderers and even associates of the devil. Between 1499 and 1783, therefore, laws were introduced which attempted to put an end to the gypsies' errant way of live by forcing them to settle into communities and to take up respectable forms of work, while any misdemeanour was severely punished.

Over a period of time gypsy communities, which were known as *gitanerías*, grew up in many Andalusian towns and cities, including Cádiz, Córdoba, Granada, El Puerto de Santa María and Seville. In addition, these communities served as a refuge for others – Jews, Moriscos, runaway slaves, escaped criminals – who were either persecuted or pursued by the law. Jews and Moriscos in particular had suffered religious persecution from the late fourteenth century, including torture, expulsion and even death. Because the gypsies, who claimed to be Christians, were not persecuted for religious reasons, those Jews and Moriscos who wished to remain in Spain clearly felt safer in the *gitanerías*. These therefore became a melting-pot for the underprivileged and the marginalized, and their common sense of persecution and its attendant trauma found an outlet in the form of songs which expressed their misfortune and misery.[1] This may, then, have been the context in which flamenco developed, but it is important to emphasize that at this early stage it was song, not dance, which was more important, and the word which was used to describe it was *gitano*, not *flamenco*. The word *flamenco* did not come into the language until much later. In the nineteenth century it was used to describe the gypsies themselves, *flamenco* deriving from the Latin *flama* (flame) and referring to the gypsies' flashy lifestyle. Later still, it was applied to their flashy music. As for *cante gitano* (gypsy song), it may have been sung by a single singer, a *cantaor*, who expressed both his own sense of injury and that of his listening audience. And, because the kind of people described above met in inns and taverns, the liberal consumption of alcohol would have given free rein to the expression of emotion.

As anyone who has heard a flamenco singer knows, the singing style is extremely rough and raw, so how was it that *cante gitano* acquired such an abrasive edge? Well before the sixteenth century there existed in Spain an extremely rich oral tradition of *romances*, short poems or ballads which were sung to a guitar or guitar-like accompaniment by blind men and women scratching a living, pedlars selling their wares and, of course, travelling gypsies. Later, in the more settled gypsy communities which developed in towns and cities and where a communal feeling of persecution and anguish was very strong, it seems clear that the ballads mentioned above came to be sung not in the gentle, lyrical style of old, but in a rough and aggressive manner which fully expressed these people's sense of rejection and their hostile reaction to it. Furthermore, as the largest outsider group in the communities which also included other unfortunates, the gypsies proved to be the most adept at appropriating and marketing the rough style of *cante gitano* which, by the late sixteenth century, was certainly associated with them in particular. Apart from the ballad tradition, however, *cante gitano* was also influenced by other musical forms which the gypsies encountered from the moment of their arrival in southern Spain. The Arabs and the Sephardic Jews both had advanced musical cultures. During the reign of Abd-ar-Rahman II, the ancient Indian system of notation had been introduced by the poet-singer Ziryab, who, as mentioned earlier, established a school of music and song. And of great importance too were the Jewish songs associated with the synagogues. In short, Indian, Muslim, Jewish and Christian religious and folk music all played their part in what we now call flamenco song.

Initially, the performance of *cante gitano* usually took place within gypsy communities, though singers were sometimes invited to perform outside them. As for the kind of songs which constituted *cante gitano*, suffice it to mention here its three broad categories: *cante grande* or *cante jondo* (deep song), which consists of the most serious and tragic songs; *cante intermedio*, which is usually less intense; and *cante chico*, which as *chico* suggests, is the lightest and most joyful. Within *cante grande*, the darkest and most emotional type of song is the *siguiriya*, which in performance was originally almost always sung by a man, was unaccompanied and dealt with such issues as love, betrayal, misfortune, or death:

Cuando yo me muera,	When I come to die,
Te pío un encargo,	I ask of you one favour,
que con las trenzas de tu pelo negro	that with the braids of your black hair
me marren las manos.	they tie my hands.

Together with the *siguiriya*, the *soleá* – the word is derived from *soledad* (solitude) – is also an important part of *cante grande*, though its mood is not always as dark. But the songs within this category certainly place the greatest demands on the singer's physical, vocal and emotional resources, and in the past were particularly suited to the sharp and piercing voice known as *afillá* (sharpened).[2]

The songs in the category *cante intermedio* vary from tragic to frivolous. The following *fandango* is an example of a much lighter mood:

A los racimos de uva	Your love is like
se parece tu querer;	bunches of grapes;
la frescura viene antes,	the freshness comes first,
la borrachera después.	drunkenness later.

As for *cante chico*, the mood is usually bright and cheerful:

Eres chiquita y bonita,	You are tiny and pretty,
eres como te quiero,	you are just as I want you,
eres una campanita	you are a small bell
en las manos de un platero.	in the hands of a silversmith.

During the first half of the nineteenth century, the great centres of flamenco song were the district of Triana in Seville, Cádiz, el Puerto de Santa María, Jerez, Puerto Real, La Isla de San Fernando and Sanlúcar, all towns and cities in south-western Andalusia. Córdoba and Granada were at this stage less important. Of the main centres, Triana, across the river from the area of Seville containing the cathedral, the Alcázar and the Golden Tower, was considered to be the crucible where ordinary and uninteresting musical material was transformed into the pure gold of flamenco. This was in the past a community of gypsy families from which many of the great flamenco singers emerged. Nowadays it is much changed, modern apartment blocks have replaced the older buildings and only a few gypsy families remain. A gypsy community also developed in the Santa María district of Cádiz, and yet another in the Santiago district of Jerez. Given the fact that all these towns were relatively close to each other and that the experience of their gypsy communities, in terms of victimization and oppression, was very similar, it is no coincidence that flamenco song should have developed in this part of Spain rather than in any other.

Although the first flamenco singers tended to remain in their communities, they often travelled from place to place, entertaining the workers on the estates of the aristocracy, singing in the great houses of the nobility, performing at wayside inns and taverns, or practising their art at fairs, baptisms, weddings and the like. They were not, however, professionals in the modern sense of the word, for many practised a different profession in their home town. As payment for their performances elsewhere, they were more likely to receive a meal and perhaps accommodation for the night. Even so, it is quite clear that the leading flamenco singers were highly regarded and proud of their status, as the following description of the nineteenth-century singer, El Planeta, suggests:

> His face was in no way unpleasant: oval shaped with dark, lively, intelligent eyes, a well-shaped nose, a wide mouth and regular white teeth. He had a

high forehead, plenty of hair, and a manner which spoke of a certain authority to which no one objected. All these things gave him the outward appearance of some wicked and difficult patriarch.[3]

In the early days of flamenco, dance and guitar accompaniment were of secondary importance and, as we shall see, came to prominence rather later. Historically, flamenco dance had its origins in India, for it evolved from the classical Indian dance forms of Katak, Kathakali and Bharata Natyam, all of which contain hand movements and footwork which we can recognize in flamenco. It seems likely that Hindu dancers had arrived in Spain as early as 500 BC. Their dances, which were of a religious nature, were later incorporated into the festivities of the Christian Church, and, when the Muslim invasion of Andalusia occurred in 711, they began to be performed in a much more secular way and were taken up by the Muslims themselves, for their dances were in certain respects very similar. Given the fact that Islam forbade a woman to draw attention to her feet and legs, much more emphasis was placed in the female dance on the movement of the hands, arms and upper body, a characteristic feature of early flamenco dance. When the gypsies came to Spain in the fifteenth century, then, there already existed there a form of dance with which they could easily identify. And, if we bear in mind too that the gypsy communities described earlier also contained Muslims, it is easy to understand how flamenco dance developed there. As for the guitar, its modern form emerged from two similar stringed instruments: the *kithara asiria*, which the Romans brought to Spain; and the *guitarra morisca*, which arrived with the Moors. But until the middle of the nineteenth century, the guitar, partly for traditional reasons, partly because it was expensive, was not used to accompany flamenco song.

In the second half of the nineteenth century flamenco began to be performed in locations outside the gypsy communities, in particular in what came to be known as the *cafés cantantes*.[4] The proprietors of ordinary cafés were quick to seize on the commercial potential of flamenco and therefore adapted their cafés for its performance. A stage would vary in size from small to fairly large, with a background of typical Andalusian scenes. The audience sat at tables. The lighting initially consisted of oil lamps, later of gaslight. A typical flamenco group consisted of one or more singers, two male dancers, three or four female dancers and a guitarist. The singer or singers, the most important individuals in the group, were splendidly dressed and sported a cravat or tie, a fine watch-chain, a walking stick and a colourful handkerchief. The other performers wore traditional costume: long dresses and shawls for the women, high-cut jackets and trousers for the men. As for the audience, it now began to embrace all social classes, so attractive did they find flamenco. In addition, foreign visitors flocked to the *cafés cantantes*, for the Spanish gypsy seemed to them the very embodiment of beauty and passion.

With the growth of the cafés, the character of flamenco also changed. The number of performers inevitably became greater, many became truly professional, and no longer were they all of true gypsy origin. As well as this, the flamenco songs which were so closely associated with the gypsies, such as the emotionally charged *siguiriya* and *soleá*, were now increasingly accompanied by other types of song which were part of Andalusian folklore. Again, flamenco song no longer reigned supreme, for flamenco dance gained in popularity, seemed more attractive and was well suited to the café environment.

Many of the key figures in this new stage of flamenco's development were associated with Seville. Perhaps the most important of all was Silverio Franconetti, who was born in Seville in 1831 and who in 1860 opened his own *café cantante*, the Café Silverio in the Calle del Rosario. It subsequently became the most famous establishment of its kind, attracting all the great flamenco singers and dancers of the time. Silverio himself was, as his name suggests, of Italian descent, not of gypsy origin, and in that respect representative of many of the new flamenco singers. Furthermore, although he loved to sing the older and purer kinds of flamenco song, such as the *siguiriya* and *soleá*, he soon realized that his clientele found the traditional style of singing harsh and austere, and that a more gentle, more musical quality would be welcome. Consequently, he introduced a softer style and the kind of vocal embellishments which were more characteristic of light opera. And, secondly, he incorporated typical Andalusian folksongs into traditional flamenco, thereby broadening the repertoire as well as softening the sound.

The *cafés cantantes*, as has been mentioned earlier, also witnessed the growing importance of flamenco dance. Like flamenco song, it falls into three categories: *baile grande*, which consists of the slower and most serious dances; *baile intermedio*, which can still be serious but is lighter in general; and *baile chico*, which is characterized by joyful and lively dances. All three types of dance can be performed by either men or women, and mixed dancing is also common.[5]

In both *baile grande* and *baile intermedio* the male dancer, the *bailaor*, holds his body straight, while the arms are curved. The emphasis in the dance is very much on the legs and on footwork, and the overall impression is one of dignity, manliness and passion. In the case of the female

The Courtyard of the Water Channel in the Generalife. Copyright: Eleri Thomas.

The Courtyard of the Myrtles, described by Washington Irving.
Copyright: Eleri Thomas.

The Albaicín in Granada. Copyright: Mark Liddington.

A forest of arches and columns: the Mezquita in Córdoba. Copyright: Visual&Written SL/Alamy.

Flamenco passion. Copyright: Daniel H. Bailey/Alamy.

Carmen: the prettified image. Copyright: Photos 12/Alamy.

Blood and sand: the drama of the bullfight. Copyright: LOOK Die Bildagentur der Fotografen GmbH/Alamy.

The Giralda in Seville.

dancer, the *bailaora*, the emphasis in both *baile grande* and *baile intermedio* is less on the legs and feet than on the movements of the upper body, arms and hands. The hands are used to make graceful circular movements and the arms are raised to form an elegant curve, but the emphasis on feet and legs is much smaller, for the *bailaora* moves very little off a given spot and stamping of the feet is rare. In contrast, *baile chico*, which is much more exuberant, involves a good deal of footwork. Flamenco dance, especially in its slower and more serious forms, is also a largely solo activity whose successful execution depends on the inner, emotional resources of the dancer, in complete contrast to classical ballet, which requires precise technique and athleticism. This means in turn that the latter dance form needs large performance spaces and youthful exponents, while flamenco dance can be performed in very small areas and by much older dancers, some into their seventies and eighties.

In the early days of the *cafés cantantes*, most of the dancers were of gypsy origin, and their technique was fairly limited in relation to that of their successors. As time passed, however, the repertoire became more extensive and technique more ambitious and polished. An example of this was Antonio el de Bilbao, who, despite his name, was born in Seville around 1880, and who, by the early 1900s, became famous in the *cafés cantantes* for his fast and brilliant footwork. On one occasion in Seville, he is reported to have performed a twenty-minute *zapateado* (foot stamping), an exhausting item, to the total astonishment of the onlookers. As for the female dancers of the latter part of the nineteenth century, Juana Vargas la Macarrona, born in Jerez around 1860, was already dancing at the Café Silverio in Seville at the age of sixteen, as was Rosario Monje la Mejorana, who was born in Cádiz around 1862. Their technique was clearly more sophisticated than that of their predecessors, but even so they employed little footwork, focusing instead on the movements of hands, arms and the upper body.

The character of the female dance was described rather well, if somewhat romantically, by Edward Hutton when he visited the Café de Novedades in Seville in the early 1920s:

> The dancer stands before her fellows who are seated in a semicircle behind her; she wears a long dress that falls in folds to the ground. After a time, while some sing intermittently, some now and then play a guitar, some beat time with their hands and stamp with their feet, she begins to dance to the maddening thunder of the castanets. It is a dance of the body, of the arms, of the head, in which the feet have almost no active part. At first she stands there like a flower that is almost overcome by the sun, sleepy and full of

languor; her arms seem like the long stalks of the water-lilies that float in the pools. Suddenly she trembles, something seems to have towered in her heart and to be about to burst into blossom. Her whole body is shaken in ecstasy; wave after wave of emotion, of pure energy, as it were, sweeps over her limbs.[6]

In the context of Hutton's description, it is worth pointing out that, even from as early as the seventeenth century, in, for example, Cervantes's short story, *The Little Gypsy Girl*, the gypsy had been portrayed as an idealized and exotic figure. It was an image which, as in their descriptions of the monuments and cities of southern Spain, the French Romantics further emphasized, as indeed did other foreigners such as George Borrow in his *The Zincali: An Account of the Gypsies of Spain*, published in 1841. Furthermore, as the preceding description of the flamenco singer, El Planeta, indicates, it was an image which flamenco singers and dancers themselves encouraged, precisely because they well knew what paying customers, foreigners and well-to-do Spaniards alike required.

Just as flamenco dance flourished in conjunction with the growing popularity of the *cafés cantantes*, so the first truly professional guitarists began to appear. Prior to this, flamenco song had usually been performed unaccompanied, and even when the guitar was involved the guitarist was little more than an accompanist. In the *cafés*, even though they still accompanied the singers and dancers, fierce competition among them meant that many guitarists improved their technique to the point where there became stars in their own right. Such was Francisco Díaz, who was born in the province of Córdoba in 1855 and who was known profession-ally as Paco Lucena. Having commenced his career in the *cafés cantantes* in Málaga, he later moved to the Café Silverio in Seville where he gave solo performances. Capable of introducing his knowledge of the classical guitar into his performance of flamenco, he is said to have astonished audience with his skill, which included playing with a gloved left hand.

As well as Paco Lucena, two guitarists who in the early part of their career played in the *cafés* and whose brilliance transformed them into acknowledged virtuosi of their instrument, were Javier Molina and Ramón Montoya. Molina performed both in the Café Silverio and in the Café Burrero, a similar Sevillian establishment. Montoya, like Paco Lucena, possessed a considerable knowledge of the classical guitar, intro-duced classical elements into his flamenco playing and, more than any of his contemporaries, took the flamenco guitar into the modern period.

If the district of Triana in Seville played a crucial part in the evolution of flamenco, it is important too to recognize the significance of the area of

Granada known as the Sacromonte, mentioned briefly in chapter 1. The road which leads to it begins just after the Casa del Chapiz in the Albaicín. Along this road, the Camino del Sacromonte, and to the left are the caves which for centuries housed the gypsy community of Granada. Much modernized nowadays, there are streets of caves nicely furnished and hardly a single one without a television, but since torrential rains in 1962 caused many of the caves to collapse, fewer gypsy families continue to live there. Flamenco performances for tourists are the source of much of the inhabitants' income, but they are generally of inferior quality, a mere shadow of the past when the Sacromonte contained many more gypsy families and produced great singers, dancers and guitarists.

A good idea of what the Sacromonte was like in the past may be formed from Paco Sevilla's *Queen of the Gypsies*, an account of the life of the great flamenco dancer, Carmen Amaya. In the mid-1920s, when she was about thirteen years old, Carmen accompanied her aunt, the dancer Juana la Faroana, on a visit to Granada. There they visited their relatives in the Sacromonte:

> A crisscross of narrow paths branched out in all directions, leading ever upward on a hillside honeycombed with cave dwellings. Each cave had been carved out of the dry, rocky soil and, in the majority of them, doorways and windows appeared in the walls that sealed the openings. The front of the caves were whitewashed, making them stand out like bleached stains in the huge clusters of prickly pear and spiked aloe cactus … Some caves, hidden in immense cactus thickets, served as taverns, while others were host to tourists looking for authentic dance and music. Further up the hill, poorer caves might consist of only two or three rooms – the living room, a bedroom, and perhaps a room for the animals … At night, the Sacred Mountain became a volcano of flaming furnaces as gypsy men pounded hot iron into ornate utensils and decorative gratings in their smoke blackened smithies.[7]

Here, on her first visit to this gypsy community, Carmen met the extended family of Amayas, almost all of them skilled in different aspects of flamenco and, in that sense, typical of the many families who lived on the mountain.

Another stage in the evolution of flamenco saw the gradual decline of the *cafés cantantes* in the early twentieth century and its movement into other locations, as well as its increasing commercialization. A significant figure in this process was Antonio Chacón, born in Jerez in 1869. Although he was well versed in the older and purer forms of flamenco song, such as the *siguiriya*, his rather sweet and melodious voice prevented him from exploiting the full potential of *cante grande*. He therefore specialized in the less harsh songs of *cante intermedio*, and in addition smoothed out their rough and often ungrammatical gypsy language, replacing it with grammatically correct Spanish. Again, although Chacón at first sang in the *cafés*, he later performed in theatre shows of a popular nature, in elegant establishments attended by the aristocracy, at country houses and on numerous occasions at the Royal Palace in Madrid. At the height of his career, he was the undisputed king of flamenco, as well as the best paid. But his popularization of flamenco song also weakened it, for people began to regard the traditional songs of *cante grande* as crude and primitive, thereby hastening their decline.[8]

Another retrograde step concerned the increasing popularity at more or less the same time of what was known as *ópera flamenca* which, as its name suggests, owed something to opera.[9] Because its aim was commercial, performances usually took place in large venues, including bullrings. The difference between this form of entertainment and the flamenco of the past may be gauged by the fact that an orchestra was now involved in place of the guitar. As for flamenco songs, they merely formed part of a dramatic story, and the older forms were abandoned in favour of those which were lighter and regarded as more pleasing. Singers also formed companies and took their shows from town to town. Voices were well trained, clear and in some cases falsetto. And, finally, because *ópera flamenca* became such a money-spinner, many singers who specialized in the older and more traditional forms jumped on the bandwagon.

The truth of this is illustrated by the composition in 1926 of a company which contained many of the outstanding exponents of the older forms of flamenco: the guitarists Ramón Montoya, Javier Molina, Luis Yance and Niño Ricardo; the great dancer Juana la Macarrona; and the singers El Cojo de Málaga, Manuel Centeno and Pastora Pavón La Niña de los Peines. The company performed in many of the large towns and cities of Andalusia in theatres and bullrings, locations as far removed as possible from the intimate settings of the gypsy communities and the *cafés*. As far as the motivation of such individuals is concerned, it would be charitable to suggest that they were interested in undertaking something new, but more realistic to believe that financial gain was the greater stimulus. At all events, the degree to which flamenco was becoming progressively watered down and fundamentally changed may be measured by the way in which the repertoire of one of the stars of *ópera flamenca*, Miguel Sampedro Montero Angelillo, consisted entirely of *cante chico* forms, and these sung in a falsetto voice.

The process was one which also affected flamenco dance. First, the number and range of dances increased greatly, and rhythms which in the past had been the exclusive domain of flamenco song, as in the case of the *siguiriya*, were adapted to dance, this now becoming a *baile por siguiriyas*. Castanets were also introduced, even though purists considered that they inhibited hand and arm movements and were therefore alien to the true spirit of flamenco. As for the female dance, in which foot and leg movements had originally played little part, much more intricate and elaborate footwork became common, and some female dancers even began to wear male costume – trousers and jacket – instead of the traditional dress with its flounced train. Finally, the creation of large flamenco companies of the kind mentioned above led to the introduction of the *ballet español* or *ballet flamenco*. This was in effect a mixture of classical, regional and flamenco dance style performed by classical dancers who were also able to perform a refined form of flamenco. It became immensely popular and, of course, hastened the decline of the traditional dance forms.

All these changes can be seen in the work of particular male and female dancers who gained an international reputation. One of the best-known male dancers was Antonio Ruiz Soler, born in Seville in 1922 and known worldwide as Antonio. Although he was an accomplished flamenco performer, his training had been in classical dance, which he introduced into much of his work. He also adapted to dance the rhythm of the older flamenco songs, as in the case of the *martinete*, once sung in the blacksmiths' forges and which now became the *baile por martinete*. And he was also one of the first flamenco dancers to engage in mixed dancing, for he and his partner, Florencia Pérez Padilla, commonly known as Rosario, danced all over the world until 1952, when they formed separate companies.

Two famous female dancers of the time, Antonia Mercé la Argentina and Encarnación López la Argentinita, were closely associated with the *ballet español*. The former specialized in the more refined, classical kind of dance, and she also used castanets, something of which the old school of dancers would thoroughly have disapproved. One of the highlights of La Argentinita's career was the stage show performed in 1933, *Las calles de Cádiz* (*The Steets of Cadiz*). Set in the gypsy community of Santa María in Cádiz, the cast included the great flamenco dancer mentioned earlier, Juana la Macarrona, who was by that time in her seventies. This highly successful show illustrated perfectly the way in which flamenco had moved into theatrical spectacle, though it has to be said that in this case the transition was achieved with integrity and good taste. As well as these dancers, mention has to be made of Carmen Amaya, alluded to earlier in relation to the Sacromonte, for, although she preserved certain elements of the female dance, she also introduced the fast and complex footwork previously associated with male dancers, and she frequently wore the short jacket, shirt and trousers which up to then had been a male preserve.

Concern with what was considered by the purists to be the decline of flamenco, and of the *cante grande* tradition in particular, led in 1922 to the Festival of Deep Song in Granada, a notable event which involved the celebrated composer Manuel de Falla and Federico García Lorca, soon to become the greatest Spanish poet-playwright of the twentieth century. Fearing for the future of *cante grande*, the intellectuals and creative artists of Granada proposed in 1921 that a competition should take place in which performers from the whole of Andalusia could participate. Prior to the competition, Falla produced an essay, "'Deep song". Primitive Andalusian song', in which he made a clear distinction between the older kinds of song, such as the *siguiriya*, which had originally come from India, and the more modern songs which, as we have seen, were introduced later. Not long afterwards, in February 1922, Lorca delivered a lecture on the same theme at the Arts Club in Granada in which he also defined the character of 'deep song' in highly expressive language and offered numerous examples of its intensity.[10]

As far as the festival was concerned, it had been decided that only non-professional singers would be allowed to compete, and for four months or so prior to the event Lorca and the painter, Manuel Ángeles Ortiz, scoured taverns and caves in search of amateur performers who were familiar with the traditions of *cante grande*. The competition finally took place over several days, commencing on 13 June, in the Square of the Wells in the Alhambra, and its judges included Antonio Chacón and the guitarist, Andrés Segovia. John B. Trend, a friend of Falla and future professor of Spanish at the University of Cambridge, described the occasion in the following way:

> The stage itself had been erected under the trees which line the rusty red walls of the Alcazaba and the Tower of Homage. Behind the little, tiled well-house was a low wall on the edge of a precipice, with the stream of the Darro clattering over the stones at the bottom; while, on the hill opposite, the dark gardens and greenish white walls of the dimly lighted Albaicín seemed as if they were part of a gigantic tapestry curtain which might have been hung from the tall trees which stood at the corners. At the back of the audience was the noble but unfinished palace of Charles V, while the Alhambra lay hid in the darkness behind ... The singing suggested once again that primitive Andalusian song is a secular counterpart to plain-song; at any rate the melodies of *cante jondo* are made of much the same material as some of the

Gregorian melodies of the Church; while the wailing Ay! or Leli, leli! with which many of them began, had a definitely Oriental suggestion. A cold analysis can give little idea of the musical effect, the passionate exaltation of the singing, the profound tragedy of the words, and the sheer beauty of style of the whole performance. The songs were not curious and interesting survivals from an Oriental past, but living pieces of music charged with every emotion which tradition, memory, surroundings and pure musical beauty could give them.[11]

The contest produced two prizewinners: Diego Bermúdez Cañete, nicknamed 'El Tenazas' ('Pincers'), and Manolito Ortega. Diego Bermúdez, who was sixty-eight years old and a practised exponent of 'deep song', had apparently walked the 130 or so kilometres from Puente Genil in the province of Córdoba. On the first day of the competition, it is said that he began by singing two *siguiriyas* extremely movingly and was loudly applauded. On the second day he was less effective, having drunk too much alcohol during the previous evening, but he was awarded a prize for his performance on the first day. The other prizewinner, Manolito Ortega, was only twelve years old, but, as Manolo Caracol, he would later become one of the truly great singers of 'deep song'. Born in 1909 into a family steeped in the traditions of flamenco and bullfighting, and which contained among its members the legendary bullfighter, Joselito, his success in the Granada contest marked the beginning of a brilliant career in which he would sing all over Spain and often in the presence of aristocrats and famous politicians of the time. As for Diego Bermúdez, he subsequently participated in several flamenco shows, but his experience was short lived and he died in poverty in Puente Genil in 1933.[12]

For all the effort that went into it, the Granada competition failed to produce positive results. Above all, it has been suggested, the organizers made a fundamental error in restricting entry to amateur singers and leaving the greatest exponents of 'deep song' on the sidelines, some of them forming the jury. For that reason the standard of performance was not very high, with the exception of Manolito Ortega, and he, as has been noted, came from a line of professional singers, which merely drew attention to the poor quality of the amateurs. The view has also been put forward that, in searching for the older and pure form of 'deep song', the intellectuals of Granada were indulging in mere fantasy, for that had been fundamentally changed by modern developments in flamenco. This second argument, though, carries less weight than the first, for there were still many great exponents of *cante grande* and still more to come in the years ahead.

While the movement of flamenco into the *cafés cantantes* and then the theatres had changed its character, a much more savage blow was inflicted by the outbreak of the Civil War in the summer of 1936 and by the Franco dictatorship which followed it. For many years after the cessation of hostilities, the Franco regime viewed flamenco as an example of a colourful Spain which could be used not simply to entertain foreigners who might not be sympathetic to the dictatorship but also to suggest that the atrocities of the war were things of the past. Young women in polka-dot costumes, performing poor quality flamenco dance in towns, cities and coastal resorts, therefore became a kind of propaganda tool for tourists, whereby flamenco – as well as the bullfight and religious festivals – was glorified as an example of Spain's 'national' culture. This, moreover, had the effect of promoting abroad yet another stereotyped image of Spain and Andalusia, which differed somewhat from the exoticism of the Romantics by placing greater emphasis on the folkloric. In many respects this image has survived to the present day and continues to inhabit the imagination of the foreign visitor.

Given the above, it is quite amazing that from around 1950 flamenco should have risen, phoenix-like, from the ashes of its demise. The renaissance was due in part to Spanish flamenco companies which toured outside Spain and whose performances, often of very high quality, inspired foreign enthusiasts to visit the country in search of flamenco in its proper environment. The effect of this was that many of the older performers, who had retired in despair, were rediscovered. In addition, many of the great singers began to record anthologies of flamenco song, so that the pure forms of *cante grande*, for example, were made known to a new and enthusiastic public. Again, from the mid-1950s flamenco night clubs, known as *tablaos* and dedicated to the performance of traditional flamenco, began to open in Spanish cities – La Zambra in Madrid opened in 1954. And, finally, flamenco festivals, such as the First Festival of 'Deep Song' in Córdoba in 1956, started to take place on a regular basis, thereby giving further impetus to the renaissance.

There were, of course, a number of key figures who played a leading part in the rebirth of flamenco. As we have already seen, Manolito Ortega, otherwise known as Manolo Caracol, had been a prizewinner in the Granada festival of 1922. Subsequently, he became an important figure in the flamenco renaissance, a magnificent singer whose voice was reminiscent of the old-style gypsy performers and which, according to one commentator, seemed 'to capture with incomparable accuracy and intensity the socially disrupted world of the Andalusia-gypsy race and the suffering of the Andalusian people throughout the centuries'. Even more influential was Antonio Mairena, a singer who was mainly based in Seville and who was also an educator. Not only did he rescue many of the older types of flamenco song from virtual oblivion, he also, through his writings, informed his readers of the history and development of flamenco and, as a leading organizer of important festivals, brought to public attention some of the great singers and dancers of the past. Of the younger generation of singers who have promoted the older forms of 'deep song', it is worth mentioning three, not least for their colourful nicknames: Antonio Fernández Díaz, better known as Fosforito, was born in Puente Genil in 1932; Antonio Nuñez, known as Chocolate, in Jerez in 1931; and Fernando Fernández Monje, colourfully known as Terremoto (Earthquake), in Jerez in 1934. The latter combined a typically rough and piercing gypsy voice with a rather childlike nature. Having won an important prize on one occasion, he demanded that it be much larger, 'like Real Madrid's European Cup'.[13]

While these and other singers were deeply involved in the regeneration of *cante grande*, there were others, somewhat younger, who, like some of those who performed in the *cafés cantantes*, moved in a different direction. A leading light in this respect was José Monje Cruz, better known as Camarón de la Isla, who was born in 1950 in La Isla de San Fernando, Cádiz. Although he knew and respected the older forms of flamenco song, Camarón adapted his singing to more modern and softer styles of music, bridging the old and the new and becoming enormously popular in the process. Similarly, Enrique Morente, born in Granada in 1942, knew, sang and recorded the older songs at the beginning of his career, but subsequently he has adapted the work of poets as well as literary episodes to flamenco music. They are innovations which have not been welcomed by the lovers of old-style flamenco.

During the last fifty years or so, flamenco dance has been largely dominated by women such as Rosita Durán, Lucerito Tena, Luisa Maravilla, Micaela Flores Amaya La Chunga, Cristina Hoyos, Blanca del Rey, Manuela Vargas, Merche Esmeralda, Manuela Carrasco and, most recently, Sara Baras and Eva Yerbabuena. Many of these women have succeeded in combining the best features of the older forms of dances with the new, thereby respecting tradition but appealing to contemporary taste. The best-known, as far as worldwide audiences are concerned, is Cristina Hoyos, who was born in Seville in 1946 and who was taught by Seville's leading flamenco dance teacher, Enrique el Cojo. She perfected her art in Spain's most prestigious *tablaos*, and in 1969 joined the company of

Antonio Gades as principal dancer. In 1974 she appeared opposite Gades in the flamenco-dance stage version of Lorca's *Blood Wedding*, and seven years later in the film of that name directed by Carlos Saura. Two years later, Saura completed his even better-known film, *Carmen*, in which Cristina Hoyos played a dance teacher, and followed it up in 1985 with *Love the Magician*, based on the Manuel de Falla ballet, in which Hoyos also appeared. As well as this, she has taken her various dance companies all over the world. In the mid-1980s she danced in her own version of *Carmen*; in 1989 she choreographed and performed in *Flamenco Dreams*, which later came to London. And in 1992 she both danced at the opening and closing ceremonies of the Olympic Games in Barcelona and also performed in *Yerma and the Flamenco Spirit*, again based on a Lorca play. In many respects, the modern shows presented by flamenco dance companies are reminiscent of the movement of flamenco into the theatres in the early part of the twentieth century, and, as we shall see later, they have been much criticized by flamenco purists.

Of the male dancers of the last forty years or so, the best known is probably Antonio Gades, not least because of his roles in the three Saura films mentioned above. Born in 1936 in Elda, Alicante, he acquired during his late teens and early twenties a sound knowledge of flamenco, regional dance and classical ballet, and, as far as flamenco was concerned, resolved to rid it of the flamboyance which he regarded as detrimental to its character. Having performed in his own stage version of *Blood Wedding* in 1974, he became, four years later, director of the Spanish National Ballet and, not long afterwards, began the collaboration with Carlos Saura which produced the three flamenco films. As well as this, he toured internationally his stage version of *Carmen*, created a free-dance version of Falla's *Love the Magician*, which he called *Fuego*, and also adapted to flamenco dance Lope de Vega's famous seventeenth-century play *Fuente Ovejuna*. As far as the character of his own performance is concerned, Gades succeeded in bringing to flamenco the strength and simplicity which he believed it should possess, but his involvement in stage shows and films has also led purists to question the extent to which they can be regarded as genuine flamenco.[14]

One of the main criticisms has been that such performances, carefully rehearsed and extremely well choreographed, lack the feeling and spontaneity which true flamenco demands. In response to this, Gades has observed that his art, far from being something which he approached with studied calculation, has been 'the medium which has offered me the possibility of self-expression, which has provided me with the same degree of expression as a painter has with his paint'.[15] In short, the discipline with which Gades and his company performed in no way excluded the passion which flamenco dance at its best demands, and much the same can be said of other companies who have toured the world in recent years. *Flamenco Dreams*, presented by the Ballet Cristina Hoyos, consisted of a series of dances which covered all three categories of *baile grande*, *baile intermedio* and *baile chico* and included a *siguiriya*, *farruca*, *bambera*, *tango*, *alegría*, *taranto*, *soleá*, and *bulería*. In other words, due homage was paid to the considerable range of flamenco dance, but, equally importantly, each dance was performed with the emotional depth or lightness which it required, the whole drawing the audience into the extremes of darkness and sunlight so characteristic of the flamenco experience. Similarly, the company of Paco Peña has toured the world in the last decade. Born in Córdoba in 1942, he formed the Paco Peña Flamenco Company in 1970. In the relatively recent stage show, *Art and Passion*, as in Cristina Hoyos's *Flamenco Dreams*, traditional flamenco dances were much to the fore: a *martinete*, a *soleá*, a *tientos*, a *zapateado* and a *granaina* constituted the serious dances, *bulerías*, *tangos* and a *garrotín* the lighter and more exuberant ones, all dazzlingly performed. There can be no doubt then that, in the case of companies of quality and integrity, traditional flamenco is in safe hands. Indeed, these stage shows are quite unlike those of the 1920s and 1930s, when flamenco was seriously diminished in stature by the introduction of popular, non-flamenco elements. On the other hand, although a contemporary dancer such as Joaquín Cortés has also brought flamenco to the attention of an international audience, he has introduced into his programmes elements which are much more to do with the world of 'pop' and 'celebrity'. While they appeal to a young audience, they undoubtedly compare unfavourably with the work of the internationally known flamenco artists described above. Cortes's methods were all too clear in his recent stage show, *Gypsy Passion*, in which two large video screens, an amplified band and costumes more suited to the catwalk of a fashion show were sufficient indication of his desire to relocate flamenco within the garish and highly commercial world of the pop concert – a relocation which seems distinctly at odds with the raw passion of flamenco performance at its best.

The second half of the twentieth century has also produced some magnificent guitarists. Melchor de Marchena, born in the town of Marchena, near Seville, in 1913, was one of the old school, a virtuoso who nevertheless imbued his playing with intense emotion, and who, for many years, accompanied Manolo Caracol at his establishment, Los Cañasteros, in Madrid. Agustín Castellón, better known as Sabicas, born in 1913 in Pamplona, was also a great virtuoso, as well as an accompanist. His mastery of the instrument was second to none, though his technical skill has been thought by some to have detracted from the emotional intensity of his playing. And a third master of the guitar is the internationally acclaimed Paco de Lucía, who was born in Algeciras in 1947. Unlike Marchena and Sabicas, he has sought to take flamenco in a new direction.

In 1961, when he was only fourteen, Paco de Lucía was awarded first prize for amateur guitarists at the Jerez de la Frontera flamenco competition. Subsequently, he made his name, in particular through his association with Camarón de la Isla, with whom he made a number of recordings while still in his teens. At this stage in his career, he was very largely an accompanist of traditional flamenco song, but his later work has involved a good deal of experimentation with other musical traditions, especially jazz and Brazilian music, which he has adapted to flamenco. In other words, Paco de Lucía, who nowadays appears in all the great concert halls of the world, is one of those artists who has sought to expand the boundaries of traditional flamenco, though it has to be said that he has done so with great integrity.

A similar attempt at innovation has been attempted over the last twenty-five years by other individuals and groups, and in this process the centre of activity has often involved Madrid rather than Andalusia. This is explained by the fact that during the 1960s and 1970s high unemployment in the south of Spain led many people, including families of gypsy origin, to move away to the capital in search of jobs and greater prosperity. Consequently, many of the younger flamenco musicians of today have grown up there and, while respecting the traditions of flamenco, have also been influenced both by their city environment and by more cosmopolitan kinds of music. The group called La Barbería del Sur consists, for example, of three individuals of gypsy origin in which the guitarist, David Amaya, is the son of the flamenco dancer, La Tati, and his father is the nephew of the great Carmen Amaya. David Amaya and his fellow musicians have a background, therefore, which is steeped in the traditional forms of flamenco, but their music, as in the case of their album of 1995, *Knock Us Down If You Can*, also draws on samba, salsa and heavy metal. Another group, Ketama, contains four young men, all born in Madrid, whose families are from Granada and Jerez. Although they too have a traditional flamenco background, their instruments include electric guitar, synthesizers and drums, and their music has elements of pop, reggae, rock and Latin American. Furthermore, Ketama has collaborated with other musicians who are specialists in particular instruments such as the eight-string African harp and the double bass.

Other contemporary groups also experiment with different musical styles and employ a variety of non-flamenco instruments. Amalgama, for instance, mixes flamenco, jazz and Indian music. The jazz pianist, Chano Domínguez, combines jazz, rock and flamenco rhythms. And Faín Dueñas, the founder of the group Radio Tarifa, has a thorough knowledge not only of the electric guitar but also of Arabic, Moroccan and Turkish stringed instuments. To some extent, experimentation of this kind can also be seen in contemporary flamenco companies. Quite recently, the company led by Sara Baras appeared at Sadler's Wells. It consisted of male and female dancers, flamenco singers and guitarists. The dances were also of the more traditional kind and extremely well performed, but the musical instruments included a violin, whose sound is far removed from the percussive nature of the stamping of feet, the clapping of hands and the beating of sticks on the floor. Indeed, the introduction of instruments such as flute, harp and violin produces a much blander, softer sound than that required to communicate the real emotional depth of flamenco song and dance. It may seem more pleasing to a mass audience, but it is far removed from the authentic flamenco sound.

5

Carmen

Carmen is undoubtedly the literary character most closely associated with Seville, largely, of course, as a result of Bizet's opera. Other fictional characters and operas are also connected with the city, notably Mozart's *Don Giovanni* and Rossini's *The Barber of Seville*, but it is Carmen, the dark, passionate, seductive, sensual *femme fatale*, universal temptress, who lingers in the imagination. Today's visitor to Seville will see, some 300 metres to the south of the cathedral, a large building which is part of the university but which was formerly the Royal Tobacco Factory (the Real Fábrica de Tabacos) where, in the famous story, Carmen was employed. Built in the middle of the eighteenth century, this huge building, some 250 metres long by 180 wide, housed the working quarters on the upper of its two levels. In the nineteenth century, at the height of its success, it employed 10,000 women and, until 1965, continued to produce cigars, cigarettes and snuff. Little more than 500 metres away, to the north and near the river, is the Maestranza bullring, the Plaza de Toros de la Maestranza, where Bizet's bullfighter, Escamillo, practises his art, and where Carmen is stabbed to death by her jealous and abandoned lover, Don José. Seville, then, is the backcloth to much of Carmen's story, though Córdoba figures too in the earliest version, while the mountainous area around Ronda, south-east of Seville, where Carmen and Don José join a band of smugglers, is also important. And, finally, of course, Carmen is a gypsy who loves dancing.

Needless to say, the nineteenth-century versions of Carmen corresponded to the stereotyped and fanciful image of the gypsy which we have already seen in the accounts and descriptions of foreign visitors to Spain, and could not be further removed from the reality of the civilized, controlled and well-educated bourgeois women with whom many of the writers of that time came into contact. Bizet's opera is by far the best-known nineteenth-century version of the Carmen story, its music immediately recognizable, but the original tale had been created thirty years earlier, in 1845, by another Frenchman, Prosper Mérimée. Eleven years before this, Mérimée had been appointed to the position of inspector general of historic monuments, in which capacity he wrote a great deal on archaeology and architecture, as well as on history, but he was also an enthusiastic writer of short narratives who based his stories both on what he had read and on personal experience. His first visit to Spain occurred in 1830, when his father, a painter, teacher and researcher, sent him to gather information about museums. During the six months of his visit, he travelled the length and breadth of the country, compiling the information which his father required, becoming ever more fascinated by the ordinary people and encountering too some extremely colourful and unusual individuals. On one occasion he was strung up from a tree by a former guerrilla lieutenant who was convinced that Mérimée was a spy; on another he drank wine from a goatskin with a convict on parole; and he met too a group of ferocious-looking men whom he believed to be bandits but who, to his great disappointment, turned out to be local farmers.[1]

As far as the initial inspiration for Carmen was concerned, it seems that it stemmed from this first visit, for in his *Lettres d'Espagne* Mérimée described how at an inn he had been served by a dark-skinned girl called Carmencita. Secondly, it was also around this time that he encountered a middle-aged aristocrat, Don Cipriano Guzmán Palafox y Portocarrero, count of Teba, and, as a result of that meeting, his wife, Manuela. Furthermore, four years later, the count inherited a sizeable fortune and the title of count of Montijo, and in 1835 the countess moved to Paris with her two daughters, which meant that Mérimée maintained with her the friendship that had begun in Spain. Quite clearly, the countess supplied him with information and stories about the country. He admitted, for example, that Don José's role in the story was based on an anecdote recounted by the countess fifteen years earlier.

Mérimée's version is relatively straightforward.[2] As the narrator, he describes in chapter 1 how, during historical researches in Andalusia, he encounters and shares food and a cigar with a fierce-looking young man with whom he then travels to an inn and whose name turns out to be Don José. Mérimée's guide subsequently tells him that Don José is a notorious bandit with a price on his head, and that he intends to inform the authorities. Warned of his possible capture, Don José then makes his escape and Mérimée travels on to Córdoba, where, in chapter 2, he meets a beautiful young gypsy girl who has been bathing in the Guadalquivir and whose name, she reveals, is Carmen. Mérimée accompanies her to her house, where she proceeds to tell his fortune, but they are interrupted by the appearance of Don José, who, angered by the presence of another man, obliges him to leave the house and the city. When Mérimée later returns to

Córdoba, he learns that Don José is in prison, and when he visits him, Don José recounts the circumstances which have led to his arrest, the description of which takes up chapter 3.

While serving as a sergeant in the army, Don José had been stationed in Seville. On guard duty outside the tobacco factory, minding his own business, his attention was drawn to a young, extremely sexy gypsy girl by whom he was immediately fascinated, so different was she from any other girl he had known. When, not long afterwards, a quarrel broke out in the tobacco factory in which the same girl knifed another woman, Don José was called upon to take her to the guardhouse and then to the prison. On the way there, however, he allowed Carmen to escape, for which he was himself demoted and imprisoned for a month. When he was free again and serving as a common private, he encountered Carmen once more, became involved in a sword fight with a lieutenant and, having killed him, was obliged to desert the army, joining up instead with Carmen's smuggler friends in the hills near Ronda. There they were joined by García, a brutal individual who, Don José discovered, was Carmen's husband. Later, he killed García after a card game and spent some time with Carmen, but she, as unreliable and as flirtatious as ever, became involved with Lucas, a picador. Increasingly upset by Carmen's repeated affairs, Don José suggested that they go away and live together, but she refused, telling him that she no longer loved him. Driven to desperation, he stabbed her to death, buried her body, travelled to Córdoba and gave himself up.

Published in 1845, Mérimée's *Carmen* belongs to the same period as the writings on Spain of Théophile Gautier and therefore, as we have seen, to a time when, in France especially, orientalism and a taste for the exotic were very strong.[3] In this respect Spain was, for many writers of that era, as well as for the reading public, a mysterious and picturesque land of passionate women, gypsies, bandits, smugglers, bullfighters, guitars, castanets, tambourines, magic and superstition. When, therefore, in chapter 1, Mérimée first encounters Don José, he describes him as a strongly built young man, tanned by the sun, and there is the strong possibility that he is a bandit of the kind which foreign writers and travellers believed to be so prevalent in the south of Spain. This early example of the exotic is then reinforced by Mérimée's discovery that Don José is not in fact an Andalusian but a Basque – in short, from a region in the far north of Spain which was itself regarded as unfamiliar and mysterious.

Carmen is, of course, the epitome of the exotic: the beautiful, volatile gypsy girl at the opposite extreme from the sophisticated and cultured French bourgeois young women with whom Mérimée was familiar. When

he first meets her, she has just emerged from the Guadalquivir where, after
dark,

> women undress and enter the water, making a terrible noise with their
> shrieking and laughing … These vague white shapes against the dark blue of
> the water stimulate poetic minds, and, if one uses one's imagination, it is not
> too difficult to envisage them as Diana and her nymphs as they bathe. (p.
> 119)

In reality, of course, such an episode would have been most unlikely. As
for Carmen herself, her beauty may not have been perfect but it was
certainly both strange and wild:

> Her skin, which by the way was extremely smooth, was almost the colour of
> copper. Her eyes were slanting but beautifully shaped; her lips were a little
> thick but well defined, and revealed teeth that were whiter than blanched
> almonds. Her hair, a little on the coarse side, was long and lustrous, black but
> with hints of blue, like the wing of a crow. To avoid too long a wearisome
> description, let me say that in short every defect was balanced by a virtue
> which contrast enhanced more strongly. She possessed a strange, wild
> beauty. And if her face amazed one at first, it was a face that was unforget-
> table. Her eyes especially had an expression that was voluptuous and fierce,
> and which I have not seen since in any other human being. (p. 121)

Later on, when Don José recounts his first meeting with her, he describes
her in a manner which reveals his immediate fascination and which epito-
mizes the widely held view of the exotic gypsy:

> She wore a very short red skirt and displayed a pair of white silk stockings
> with more than one hole, and small red morocco shoes that were tied with
> vivid red ribbons. She had thrown back her mantilla to reveal her shoulders,
> and in the opening of her blouse she had a large bunch of acacia flowers.
> Between her teeth she held another acacia, and, as she advanced, she moved
> her hips like a filly from some Córdoba stable. In my part of the country,
> people would cross themselves if they saw a woman dressed like that. In
> Seville the men offered up some bold compliment on her looks, and she
> responded with a sidelong glance, her hands on her hips, as impudent as the
> true gypsy she was. (p. 127)

While the characters of Mérimée's story are presented in a vivid and
colourful manner, their passions and emotions are also extremely volatile.
No sooner has Don José set eyes on Carmen, than he feels as if a bullet has
struck him. When other men flirt with her, he is driven to distraction: 'I
was tempted to rush into the patio and bury my sword in the bellies of all
those whippersnappers who were flirting with her. My anguish lasted for

at least an hour' (p. 134). When he and Carmen quarrel, he leaves in a rage and weeps bitter tears. When a lieutenant offends him, he kills him. Later, he kills Carmen's husband, García, in a dispute over cards. And, finally, when she tells him that she no longer loves him, he is driven to distraction, pleads with her, weeps, loses control and stabs her to death. As for Carmen herself, Don José observes that her 'moods were like the weather in our country. When the sun shines brightest, a storm in the mountains is never so near' (p. 139). At times she is sweetness itself, at times as hard as nails, abandoning Don José as the whim takes her. She heartlessly mocks his jealousy, manipulates him, takes advantage of other men's attraction to her, refuses to belong to any one man and rejects Don José's threats, defiant to the end: '"No, no, no!" she said, stamping her foot; and she tore from her finger the ring I had given her and threw it into the undergrowth.' Similarly, her husband, García, is a man who is quick to violence: 'With his dark skin and his even darker soul, he was the most evil scoundrel I have ever met' (p. 143). He has no hesitation in attacking and even killing anyone who crosses him.

The characters, events and passions of Mérimée's story are, then, heightened in a way which corresponds to the image which his readers, particularly in Parisian bourgeois circles, would have had of Spain, with its gypsies and its bandits, and which was part and parcel of the exotic. But his particular achievement was also to place the exotic elements of the story within a realistic framework which made them that much more credible. In this respect, we need only look at Don José's account to Mérimée of the tobacco factory in Seville where he first encounters Carmen:

> You see, señor, there are four or five hundred women working in that factory. They are the ones who roll the cigars in a large hall which no male can enter without a permit from the local magistrate, for the simple reason that the women, especially the young women, wear very little when it's hot. When they go back to work after their meal, lots of young men watch them passing by, and they make all sorts of comments. (pp. 126–7)

And just afterwards he describes what he saw when, informed of a fight between two women, he entered the building:

> Imagine it, señor. I went into the hall and was faced by three hundred women dressed in shifts and little else, all of them screaming, yelling, gesticulating, and making such a racket that you couldn't have heard God's thunder. On one side one of the women lay on her back, covered in blood, with a cross on her face carved by two strokes of a knife. Opposite the victim, who was being attended by the best of the group, I saw Carmen held by five or six of the women. (p. 128)

The authenticity of Mérimée's description of the tobacco factory may be gauged by reference to the account provided by Théophile Gautier, who, on this occasion at least, appears to have cast aside his Romantic inspiration:

> Most of them [the women] were young, and some of them were very attractive. They were dressed in an extremely careless manner, which allowed us to appreciate their charms to the full. Some of them had the bold swagger of a cavalry officer and held the stump of a cigar firmly fixed in the corner of the mouth, while others – oh, let my muse come to my assistance! – chewed away like ancient mariners, for they are all permitted to have as much tobacco as they wish while on the premises.[4]

Again, Mérimée describes Carmen dancing in a manner which is largely realistic:

> In her hand she held a Basque tambourine. There were two other gypsy women with her, one young and one old. An old woman always accompanies the gypsy girls, and there was an old man too, another gypsy, who played a guitar for the girls to dance … Everyone was in the patio, and, despite the crowd of people, I could see almost everything through the gate. From time to time I had a glimpse of Carmen's head as she leaped in the air with her tambourine. (p. 133)

There is, then, a relatively realistic and authentic framework to the story of Carmen which invests the more exotic and extreme events and the heightened and often violent passions contained within it with an aura of credibility.

In the end, however, there is much more to Mérimée's story than local colour, for he succeeded in creating in Carmen a character who already possessed an altogether deeper-seated fascination. Throughout the narrative, Don José alludes to her in terms of the devil, increasingly so as he becomes more and more beguiled by her wiles. She thus has a dark and mysterious allure which he finds irresistible and which he has previously experienced in no other woman. Beautiful, unpredictable, passionate, mysterious, Carmen is the kind of woman men dream of, fantasize about, but probably hope they will never meet. As far as Don José is concerned, he is an essentially good man who faces temptation, fails to resist it and is destroyed. In that context, Mérimée's *Carmen* embodies the universal struggle between good and evil.

Bizet's famous opera *Carmen* received its first performance in March 1875 at the Opéra-Comique in Paris, thirty years after the publication of Mérimée's story. By and large it was a failure. The reaction of the audience, if not overtly hostile, was generally unenthusiastic and unappreciative. As far as the reviews in the press were concerned, the overall opinion seems to have been that Mérimée's *Carmen* was too sensational and obscene to form the basis of a staged work, while in the performance of the opera, Célestine Galli-Marié, in the role of Carmen, acted the part in far too provocative a manner, employing gestures and movements that were the 'very incarnation of vice'.[5] As well as this, many of the music critics chastized the opera for a lack of both melody and drama – a strange reaction, given that so many of its melodies stick in the memory and there is so much dramatic incident – and suggested too that the music was too loud, frequently overwhelming the voices. Subsequently, of course, Bizet's *Carmen* has become one of the best-loved and most frequently performed operas in the entire operatic repertoire. Most people recognize Bizet's music, but few will have ever heard of Mérimée.

Although critical reaction to the premiere had drawn attention to the scandalous nature of Bizet's story, the truth of the matter is that the operatic version is far less extreme than Mérimée's original. Bizet had been commissioned to write an opera for the Opéra-Comique by its two directors, but the opera house was essentially a 'family' theatre in which no opera had previously been performed which had prostitutes, thieves and murderers among its characters and which ended with a murder on stage. From the outset, then, doubts were expressed about the suitability of *Carmen* for this particular opera house, and there were therefore unavoidable constraints upon what Bizet's librettists might be able to include in their adaptation of the Mérimée story. Meilhac and Halévy were both successful popular dramatists who were apprehensive about offending public taste, and when they began to work on Mérimée's original, they at once suggested modifications aimed at toning down its more violent and scandalous elements. Bizet, it seems, tried to resist their suggestions, but there can be no doubt that in the end the libretto became a rather paler reflection of the Mérimée story.

In the original, Don José is undoubtedly a more violent and passionate character. As a result of his obsession with Carmen, he kills first a lieutenant, then Carmen's husband García and finally Carmen herself, while in the opera only Carmen dies at his hands. In support of the librettists' changes in this respect, it has been suggested that the single murder is more effective than a series of deaths, but Mérimée's purpose was clearly to show how those deaths point, step by step, to the disintegration of Don José's character as the result of his passion for Carmen. Even if opera requires compression and simplification, there is in the presentation of

Don José a dilution of Mérimée's tale which is evident in many other aspects of the opera.

One of its more sentimental features concerns the introduction of Micaela, the young woman from Don José's home town in the Basque country with whom he had been in love prior to his encounter with Carmen. She appears in the opera on several occasions, attempting to win Don José back, as well as bringing him news from home. Quite clearly, Micaela functions in the opera as a foil to Carmen, her fair hair symbolic of her innocence and purity in contrast to the dark-haired Carmen's dangerous volatility. In general, she is rather too good to be true, and a note of cloying sentimentality is introduced when she appeals to Don José to return home in order to see his sick mother. But without doubt this good girl who seeks to put him on the straight and narrow once again would have been clutched to many a bourgeois bosom at the Opéra-Comique in 1875.

Bizet's bullfighter, Escamillo – the more common Spanish word for 'bullfighter' is, incidentally, not 'toreador' but 'torero' – is based on Mérimée's Lucas, but in the opera the role is considerably enlarged. In the earlier story Lucas is not a bullfighter but a 'picador', one of the men on horseback who softens up the bull with his lance in preparation for the bullfighter's intervention and final dispatch of the wounded animal. He therefore has a far less glamorous role, he appears only briefly towards the end of the narrative and the bullfight in which he is involved takes place in Córdoba, not Seville. Bizet's Escamillo is much more attractive, appears on three occasions and takes part in the bullfight not in Córdoba but in the much more famous Maestranza bullring in Seville. In short, the much greater prominence afforded to Escamillo makes him a clear rival to Don José, and the relationship of the central characters to each other becomes much more that of an eternal triangle, emphasized further by the fact that Carmen's husband, murdered by Don José in the original version, is no longer present.

Bizet's Carmen, unlike Micaela, was, of course, a new type of operatic heroine, if she can be so described. Previously, the heroines of nineteenth-century French opera had been largely pure and innocent, and to suggest that she should not be so was unheard of. The spectacle of Carmen proceeding to tempt Don José on stage was therefore quite shocking, as reaction to the premiere indicates. But, if this was so, Bizet's character is undoubtedly a toned-down version of Mérimée's for, while she is lively, capricious and teasing, she lacks the sheer earthiness and volatility of the original, whom her creator had described as fierce and voluptuous and compared to the devil. Far from extending the possibilities of her character, Bizet and his librettists actually reduced them and thereby diminished her appeal to the imagination. If it is true to say of myth and legend that, as in the case of Don Juan, Faust and several others, they are capable of reworking and constant reinterpretation at a deeper level, this cannot be said of Bizet's *Carmen*, which offers nothing new in terms of its story and its characters. Even so, Carmen herself remains in essence the exotic figure of the gypsy portrayed by the French Romantics in general, and Bizet undoubtedly embodied in her the sexual passion and the rebellious streak which education, religion and the need for social approval had largely obliterated in the middle and upper-class French woman.

As far as the music of *Carmen* is concerned, the nineteenth-century cult of orientalism also played an important part. In order to create a musical sound which evoked the exoticism of the Middle East, of which, as we have seen, Spain was considered to be a part, nineteenth-century composers employed particular instruments, such as the flute, the triangle, the harp, the guitar and the tambourine, and evocative rhythms, especially dance rhythms, to suggest a world both alluring and seductive.[6] This is precisely what Bizet did in *Carmen*. His aim was not to imitate Spanish music but to create a musical effect that, for the French audiences of the day, corresponded to their image of Spain. Indeed, unlike Mérimée, who knew Spain well, Bizet never went there.

The music of *Carmen* reveals, in fact, very little direct Spanish influence. Carmen's first appearance in act 1 is distinguished by her seductive singing of the 'Habanera', in which she compares love to a bird that is free and which no man will tame. The source of this beautiful song was, in fact, a song called 'El Arreglito' (The Arrangement), by the Spanish-American composer, Sebastián Yradier, but Yradier's compositions were themselves only adaptations of genuine folk songs which he polished and refined for performance in the *salons* of the day. Furthermore, Bizet based his 'Habanera' not on a published version of Yradier's composition, but on his memory of having heard it sung. And, as well as this, the tradition to which the song belonged was not Spanish but the Negro music of Cuba. In other words, the gypsy girl of Bizet's opera is initially identified by music which may well suggest her seductive and teasing qualities but which is in no way connected with Andalusia.[7]

Apart from this, there are only two other examples in the entire opera of music which was derived from Spanish sources but which was also substantially modified. The first is the music between acts 3 and 4. It is based on an Andalusian song known as a *polo*, which Manuel García is known to have sung in Madrid in 1804 and which Bizet discovered in a collection published in Paris in 1872. Even so, García's method had been to transform traditional folk songs in his own way and Bizet, in adapting this particular song, clearly went a stage further. While traces of flamenco 'deep song' remain, one has only to listen to genuine Andalusian music in order to appreciate how different it is from Bizet's. The second example occurs in act 1. This is the occasion when Carmen defies Zuniga with the words 'Tra, la, la, la, la, la, la, la.' Originally a satirical song on Spanish hairstyles, deriving from Ciudad Real, south of Madrid, Bizet once more modified it, notably by changing the rhythm from 3–4 to 6–8.

Genuine Spanish influence on the music of *Carmen* is, then, very limited, and the opera is truly French, not Spanish. Furthermore, it was conceived in a largely conservative atmosphere that was bound to stifle the daring of Mérimée's original story. As a character, Carmen herself is less wild and capricious and, although elements which are at the very core of Spanish and, in particular, Andalusian culture – the gypsy background, dance, the bullfight – have been woven into the fabric of the opera, the result may be described as a 'paella' prepared from a French recipe. For a taste of the real thing, it is necessary to turn to a version of *Carmen* created by a Spaniard.

As we have seen, Carlos Saura's film was premiered in 1983. It became a huge success and was subsequently nominated for an Oscar in the Best Foreign Film category. As for Mérimée's and Bizet's treatment of the story, there is no doubt where Saura's sympathies lay:

> The opera *Carmen* is in a sense a betrayal of Mérimée's story … The 'local colour' derives from Bizet, not from Mérimée, and perhaps mainly from the librettists, Meilhac and Halévy … They realized how risky it was to put on stage a woman who is a thief, witch, whore, and almost a murderess … a woman, moreover, who mocks conventional morality and adopts an attitude to life which borders on anarchism … I believe that the opera has eliminated the violence and sensuality, the mystery, and even the justification for a form of behaviour which in Mérimée is perfectly comprehensible and does not need to be justified. Carmen is what she is. Carmen is not a conventional woman, for she symbolises freedom, although that freedom may demand that she sacrifices others, steal, or prostitute herself …[8]

Even so, Saura realized that Bizet's music is so well known that it was important to use some of it as a point of reference. But, having made this decision, he then relocated it to Spain in two important ways: first, the music is often altered and given a new rhythm; and, secondly, it is invariably placed firmly within the context of Spanish dance. In both cases, moreover, that context is flamenco, the importance of which Saura emphasized very strongly. His purpose was to discover the essential elements of Carmen in his country's roots, and to do so through flamenco dance and song. Dance was to be the protagonist, with rhythm, music and movement much to the fore. It seems highly appropriate that Carmen, associated with Seville, should be reinterpreted in terms of a dance form which is so fundamentally Andalusian and of which Seville is traditionally such an important centre.

The film begins with three sequences in which the importance of flamenco is immediately emphasized. In the first of these, a group of female dancers are put through a series of flamenco steps by Antonio, the director of a flamenco dance company. The second sequence consists of the film's titles accompanied by Bizet's orchestral music set against engravings of flamenco dance. The third sequence then takes place once more in the rehearsal room where the dancers again practise a flamenco routine. In other words, Bizet's music is placed between two flamenco sequences and is already given secondary importance. Furthermore, the key elements of flamenco dance are strongly emphasized. The rhythm is now created by the typically percussive sound of feet and clicking fingers. And, as far as dance movement is concerned, we note the slow, sinuous advance of the female dancers, the upright posture of body and head and the graceful movement of hands and arms. Flamenco thus evokes the woman who is beautiful, tantalizing, sensual, but also dignified and disdainful – in short, the essence of Carmen herself. It is important to note too that the dancers wear casual modern clothes. This anticipates Saura's intention to update and contemporize the Carmen story, and to bridge the gap between the past and the present, between fiction and reality.[9]

In the process of adapting Bizet's *Carmen* to the flamenco tradition, a key moment occurs when Antonio is seen listening to a tape of the well-known *seguidilla* from the end of act 1 of the opera. The famous flamenco guitarist, Paco de Lucía, begins to adapt Bizet's music to the requirements of the guitar, thereby replacing a full-size orchestra with a single instrument, and furthermore adapting the slower rhythm of the original music to the quicker rhythm of flamenco dance. Clapping, another essential ingredient of flamenco, is also introduced, and in its new form the *seguidilla* is rehearsed by the female dancers in a sequence which once more emphasizes the graceful movements of hands and arms. At the end of the sequence, Mérimée's description of Carmen is introduced by Antonio, who is still in the process of finding a dancer suited to the part: 'Carmen had a wild and strange beauty ... her lips full and well-shaped ... Gypsy eyes, wolf eyes' (Mérimée, p. 121). In other words, Saura, through Antonio, opts for Mérimée's more fiery portrayal of the young woman.

Having so far failed to find his Carmen, Antonio decides, appropriately, to attend a flamenco dance school in Seville, where he finally discovers her in one of the dance classes. The two vital ingredients in this new version of the story are thus brought together: first, the art of flamenco; secondly, the beauty and character of the dancer chosen to play Carmen. With regard to the first point, the flamenco teacher, Magdalena, instructs her pupils in the movement and posture required of the female dancer: 'Arms up ... slowly ... like an eagle's wings ... The breasts like a bull's horns but warm and soft ... The head up, the posture princely.' As to the second point, the dancer, whose name is also Carmen, is dark-skinned, has large, attractive eyes, full lips and a shapely figure, corresponding closely to Mérimée's description of her.

While these early sequences return the Carmen story to Spain and to the flamenco tradition in particular, the rest of the film focuses on four key episodes, each of which is distinguished by strong flamenco elements: the incident in the tobacco factory when Carmen stabs a fellow worker; Carmen's tempting of Don José; Don José's murder of Carmen's husband; and the final bullfight sequence which ends with Carmen's death. The tobacco factory scene is undoubtedly one of the film's highlights and once again follows Mérimée in its emphasis on violence, in complete contrast to Bizet, who omitted the incident completely. The film sequence begins with four gypsy women seated at a table. There is nothing pretty about them. Reminiscent of some of Goya's paintings, these are women of the people and of the south, and when they begin to sing, their voices are harsh, in complete contrast to the pleasant harmonies of Bizet's opera. Here, then, all glossiness is stripped away, but at the same time this raw material is transformed into art, and the entire sequence is organized and constructed in a way which builds step by step to its inevitable conclusion. Together with their singing, the four women establish the rhythmic pulse of the scene by beating on the table – a variation on flamenco clapping – and the song is then taken up by the entire company. Movement is introduced as Carmen and one of the other women express their hostility in an expressive dance routine in which they circle, threaten and confront each other, and this is then developed into a much more complex sequence in which the interplay of bodies and the hammering of feet create an enormous vitality which ends in Carmen's stabbing her rival. Throughout the scene, we are made to feel the atmosphere of the tobacco factory and the raw passion of the characters, yet this is achieved, as is so often the case in flamenco dance, by means of the most marked discipline and control.

In the sequence depicting Carmen's tempting of Don José, Saura retains Bizet's 'Habanera', but the scene now takes place not in public but in private, and Bizet's music is used as an accompaniment to flamenco dance which, in a highly ritualistic manner, expresses the male–female relationship. Initially, Don José is passive, seated on a chair as Carmen, the provocative and teasing temptress, advances slowly towards him. In the second part of the sequence, she draws him after her, and he, awakened from his earlier lack of interest, performs a short and aggressive dance which proclaims his masculinity. Finally, she leads him around the table until they come together in a passionate embrace. In contrast to the raw and violent emotions of the episode in the tobacco factory, this episode is much more delicate and reveals the capacity of flamenco dance to express, through body language and in an external and observable way, the interior landscape of feeling and emotion. Furthermore, through its economy and stylization, it succeeds here, as elsewhere, in raising an individual and a particular incident to a higher, more universal and poetic level, for the Carmen–Don José relationship suggests the timeless and enduring tug-of-war between the sexes.

In the opera, Bizet had omitted Don José's murder of Carmen's husband, García, an incident to which Mérimée had given prominence. In the film, Saura both retained and expanded the episode, and, as well as this, placed it fully in the context of flamenco dance. The absence of instrumental and vocal accompaniment means that everything is reduced to pure movement, and the men's use of sticks rather than knives, together with the sound of their feet, create that insistent, percussive sound which is both dramatic and an essential element of flamenco. The sequence is cleverly paced throughout, from the way in which the two men initially weigh each other up, to their slow circling and their sudden, rushing assaults. The dignified posture of the two men and the austere and bare background against which the fight takes place also endows the sequence with a strongly ritualistic quality which, stripping away the tinsel of Bizet's opera, projects a powerful and universal image of male conflict for possession of the female.

The bullfight in the famous bullring in Seville forms the background to the climax of Bizet's opera, while the 'toreador' theme associated with Escamillo is probably one of the most familiar pieces in the whole of music. In characteristic fashion, Saura replaced it with genuine Spanish and flamenco elements. The film sequence begins with the bullfighter preparing himself in front of a mirror and practising some passes with his cape. There then follows a dance performed by the entire company in which the music is the very Spanish 'pasodoble', which also evokes the jaunty, brash music that introduces the bullfight and therefore emphasizes the very unauthentic nature of the 'toreador' theme. Subsequently, the bullfighter dances with Carmen, after which he and his companions perform a short defiant dance in which clapping, stamping and singing all play their part. Observing Don José's jealousy, the company launches into a powerful flamenco song about jealousy and treachery, Don José drags Carmen away and stabs her.

While Saura's version of *Carmen* relocates the story to Spain by placing it firmly in the traditions of flamenco, he also updates it in a quite startling way by blurring the distinction between the characters in the story itself and the dancers who play them. Antonio, the director of the dance company, therefore becomes as infatuated with his female lead, Carmen, as does Don José with the fictional Carmen; and the edges are similarly blurred between the 'real' Carmen's husband, José Fernández, and the fictional Carmen's husband, García, as well as between the 'real' and the fictional bullfighter. Antonio's growing involvement with the dancer, her flirtations with others and Antonio's increasing jealousy run parallel with the dancers' performance of the traditional story and, in terms of the film's unfolding, are so closely interwoven that there are moments when the two threads are virtually indistinguishable. In short, the film has an extra and very telling dimension which exists neither in Mérimée nor in Bizet, and whose effect is to rework the original fiction in late twentieth-century terms, creating in the character of Carmen a modern, liberated woman.

Not long after he has chosen the young woman to undertake the role of the fictional Carmen, Antonio begins to become obsessed with her on a personal level, his experience therefore forming a parallel with that of Don José. She, moreover, proves to be as fickle towards all men as was her fictional counterpart, and it is not long before she is attracted to another man. When Antonio finds them together, a bitter exchange follows in which she declares her independence of all admirers: 'Let go of me! … I'm free! I'll do what I want!' Later, as we have seen, she flirts with the dancer who plays the bullfighter in precisely the way that the fictional Carmen does with Escamillo in the opera, and the consequences for her and for Antonio are the same, so that the film's climax is a total fusion of fiction and reality. And, as well as this, the dancer Carmen has a husband, José Fernández, a drug dealer who is a late twentieth-century equivalent of Mérimée's García.

Saura's interweaving of fiction and reality works on two important levels. First, as far as Spanish society since the beginning of the 1980s is concerned, the modern, liberated woman, like the fictional Carmen, has undermined traditional attitudes both social and moral. In the past, the Spanish male, as in many other countries, has been able to 'have his cake and eat it'. The feminist movement, challenging traditional male supremacy, has therefore come as an unpleasant surprise and a source of consternation to men who find themselves obliged to accept and adapt to a new situation. After many centuries, Don Juan is compelled to yield the centre of the stage to Carmen, a situation which not only brings about a reversal of roles, but which is also full of tension and explosive possibilities. It is this process which Saura presents so effectively in reworking the traditional story for a modern audience. And, secondly, the theme of the modern, liberated woman has a resonance which goes far beyond its Spanish context. In effect, moving beyond both Mérimée and Bizet, Saura has revealed how the traditional Carmen story, like so many myths and legends, can be reinterpreted and updated in a way that has meaning for a different age. And, even if elements of the exotic can still be found in the traditional part of Saura's story, his transference of the role to a modern woman who shares the traditional character's passion and independence of mind goes much of the way to stripping away the old stereotype.

Saura's *Carmen* is undoubtedly a very striking and important film. Quite apart from the relevance of his updating of the story, he has brilliantly incorporated it into the flamenco tradition and thereby returned it to its Spanish roots. The film has a vibrancy, a visual quality and a feel which are typically Spanish and Andalusian. Anyone who is interested in the south of Spain should make every effort to see it.

6

The Bullfight

It is safe to say that, in general, the British have an intense dislike of the bullfight, though many would support fox-hunting. This aversion stems in part from the fact that they tend to think of bullfighting as a sport, while the truth of the matter is that it is much more a ritual which, though changing with the passage of time, is deeply embedded in the past. It is a ritual in which the killing of the bull is an essential element – in Portugal the bull is not put to death in the ring – and one for which the country has developed the finest arenas: in Andalusia the bullring at Ronda is the oldest in Spain, the Plaza de Toros de la Maestranza in Seville one of the finest and most famous. The drama of the bullfight has also inspired the creative energies of some of the most celebrated Spanish artists and writers. Goya was an aficionado, as numerous paintings suggest. So was Picasso, and García Lorca, the greatest Spanish poet-dramatist of the twentieth century, eloquently mourned the death of one of Spain's best-known bullfighters in his *Lament for Ignacio Sánchez Mejías*.

The bulls of Andalusia, as well as the ritual killing of a bull, are thought by many to have their origin in the ancient world. An early myth concerned the tenth labour of Hercules, which consisted of capturing the red cattle of King Geryon from the island of Erytheia, near present-day Gibraltar. In order to achieve his objective, Hercules succeeded in killing Geryon, seized the cattle and on his homeward journey passed through Tartessus, a region which is now Andalusia, and where bulls of a similar colouring are to be found. A second link between the bullfight and the ancient world has to do with the worship of the Great Mother-Goddess, which was practised in early times throughout the Mediterranean. This worship was accompanied by a myth in which the Mother-Goddess had a son or a husband who, in the form of an animal, very often a bull, was sacrificed annually in order to guarantee the cycle of the seasons and the continuity of Nature. As well as this, spectacles involving bulls were common in Roman times, not least in the amphitheatres of Seville, Córdoba and Cádiz. And the Celtiberian people also developed the hunting of cattle into something rather different when, in what is now

Andalusia, they held games in which men displayed both skill and bravery before killing the wild beast with an axe or a lance. Subsequently, the Moors, inhabiting Spain, and especially the south, for such a long period of time, developed further the art of the bullfight.[1]

For García Lorca the modern bullfight was the living proof of the connection between Andalusia and ancient civilization, 'the living spectacle of the ancient world in which are to be found the classical essences of the most artistic peoples in the world'.[2] In his lecture, 'Play and theory of the duende', he compared the smile of a contemporary bullfighter, Ignacio Espeleta, to that of Arganthonius, a king of the ancient region of Tartessus.[3] He argued too that the bullfight, as well as being highly poetic, contained the vitality and passion of the classical world: 'It is as if the "duende" [inspiration] of the classical world has come together in this perfect celebration.'[4] Furthermore, Lorca saw the bullfighter as the equivalent of the priest of ancient times, 'the cruel minister … his sword no less than the direct descendant of the sacrificial knife',[5] while the killing of the bull paralleled the ancient sacrificial rite. The element of sacrifice, part of a 'religious mystery' also evoked for Lorca the Catholic Mass, for if the death of the bull reminds us of the ancient sacrifice to a pagan god, so the sacrament symbolizes the death of Christ as a sacrifice to ensure the salvation of men and women. For many creative artists, then, the bullfight was and continues to be much more than a colourful spectacle or entertainment. It is a meaningful drama, a ritual, a tragic action in which are contained the most powerful and basic emotions of human life.

The modern art of bullfighting was established by Pedro Romero, who was born in Ronda in 1754. Prior to this and after the expulsion of the Moors from Spain, bullfighting was the province of noblemen on horseback, as the following account, written by Edward Hyde in 1650, makes clear:

> The toreadors enter, all persons of quality richly clad, and upon the best horses in Spain, every one attended by eight or ten more lackeys, all clinkant with gold and silver, who carry the spears which their masters are to use against the bulls … The persons on horseback have all cloaks folded up upon their left shoulder, the least disorder of which, much more the letting it fall, is a very great disgrace; and in that grave order they march to the place where the King sits, and after they have made their reverences, they place themselves at a good distance from one another, and expect the bull.[6]

During one of these bullfights, it seems that Pedro Romero's grandfather, Francisco, entered the bullring when one of the aristocrats had been thrown from his horse and began to distract the bull with his hat. This was the origin of the bullfighter confronting the bull on foot. Subsequently, Pedro Romero introduced the passes and moves, as well as the red cape, the *muleta*, which characterize the bullfight today. In the impressive bull-ring at Ronda, opened in 1785 as the popularity of the bullfight grew, Romero is said to have killed more than 5,000 bulls and to have practised his art into his eighties. Nowadays, in the museum which forms part of the building, one can gain some idea of the history of the bullfight and see the 'suit of lights', the 'traje de luces', worn by Pedro Romero. There are also photographs of two famous foreign aficionados: Orson Welles and Ernest Hemingway. Welles's ashes are, in fact, buried on the estate of Ronda's most famous modern bullfighter, Antonio Ordóñez, not far from the bull-ring.[7]

The bullring itself consists of a large sand-covered circle surrounded by a red wooden fence which is just over 120 centimetres high and known as the *barrera*. Between the *barrera* and the first row of seats is a narrow passageway which runs around the whole of the ring and which accommodates a variety of individuals: bullfighters who are not in the ring, assistants of various kinds, policemen, vendors of food and drink, carpenters ready to repair the *barrera*, doctors and sometimes photographers. The seating area ascends in circular rows from behind the *barrera* and is uncovered, while further up are the gallery and the boxes, which are covered and which are therefore more expensive. The largest bullrings in Spain can accommodate as many as 20,000 spectators, while those in the small towns have seating for around 1,500. Because the bullfight takes place during the afternoon – the season lasts from March until November, weather permitting – different parts of the seated area will be exposed to the sun at different times as it moves from east to west. The seats which are in the shade for the entire bullfight are called *sombra*; those that are initially in the sun but later in the shade are called *sol y sombra*; and the seats that are permanently in the sun and which are therefore the cheapest are designated *sol*. One of the most important individuals connected with the bullfight is the president, who occupies a box opposite the enclosure from which the bull is released into the arena and who tries to ensure that the strict rules which control bullfighting are upheld. In some respects the president is not unlike an emperor in a Roman amphitheatre, for he it is who issues the instruction to release each bull by placing a white handkerchief on the edge of his box. On rare occasions, when a bull has shown extraordinary courage, its life is spared by the display of a green handkerchief. As for the length of a bullfight, six bulls are killed in the course of an afternoon. Each bull is in the ring for approximately twenty minutes, but the time taken up by other associated occurrences means that the entire spectacle lasts for three hours or so.

The bullfight begins when the president has entered his box. He waves his handkerchief to signal the beginning of the event, a trumpet sounds and two mounted men known as *alguaciles*, 'constables', gallop across the arena, bow before him, and gallop back to their starting point. They then lead out the parade of the bullfighters to the accompaniment of music: at the front, three *matadores*, each of whom will fight two bulls; behind them their assistants, the *banderilleros* and the *picadores* in order of seniority; and, at the rear, the muleteers and mules which, after each fight, will drag the dead bull from the ring. When the *matadores* have acknowledged the president by bowing and removing their black hats or *monteras*, the procession breaks up, the bullfighters remove their heavy capes and the president gives the signal for the first bull to be released into the ring. A moment of high tension succeeds an opening sequence of great ceremony and theatricality.

The fighting bull is a fearsome spectacle, a wild beast of solid muscle and sinew weighing half a ton, bred for the fight, afraid of nothing and so strong it has been known to force a train to stop. After charging into the arena, it looks around and, seeing some movement near the *barrera*, sometimes hurls itself at the wooden planking. It is capable of ripping out with one toss of its head a whole section of planking, 120 centimetres in height. The first glimpse of this dangerous creature is enough to send a ripple of apprehension through the spectators, as well as a sigh of relief that they are not in the *matador*'s shoes.

When the bull is released into the ring, the first person to appear is one of the *banderilleros*. Holding a large yellow and magenta cape, he provokes the bull into charging and then moves quickly backwards in zig-zag fashion. This manoeuvre is intended to reveal whether the bull prefers to attack to the right or the left and is carefully observed by the *matador* from behind the *barrera*. When the *banderillero* has completed the exercise, the *matador* himself emerges and engages the bull in a series of slow and elegant passes with the cape which are known as *verónicas*: the *matador* stands quite still, moves the cape ahead of the bull's horns and has him pass extremely close to his body – a ballet-like but dangerous series of moves which teach the bull to follow the cape and reveal the *matador*'s domination of the animal. They are then completed with a *media verónica*, a half pass in which the sudden swirl of the cape abruptly stops the bull's charge and the *matador* turns his back on him. The *verónica* derives its name, interestingly enough, from St Veronica, who wiped Christ's face with a cloth and who is normally represented holding the cloth by its two upper corners, just as the *matador* holds the cape for these particular passes.

After these initial stages, designed to reveal the characteristics of the bull's attack, the bullfight then takes the form of three parts or *tercios*, rather like the three acts of a play.[8] The first *tercio* is known as the *suerte de varas*, the 'trial of the lances', and involves the *picadores*, mounted and armed with long lances, or *pics*, with metal heads. In this part of the bullfight the *picador* confronts the bull and, as it charges the horse, is supposed to drive the point of the lance into the bull's enormously tough neck muscle in order to tire it, as well as to test its bravery. If the bull proves to be brave, it will attack more than once and, according to the regulations, receive three thrusts of the lance. But in many ways this part of the bullfight can be the most upsetting and unsatisfactory – the latter for the true aficionado, the former for those who have a love of horses. The *picador* is in general poorly paid, the least glamorous of those involved in the actual bullfight, and is often the least skilled. A good *picador* will be able to prevent the bull reaching the horse by hitting the target with the lance, holding the bull off and turning the horse so that the bull passes by. A clumsy and incompetent *picador* will wait too long, perhaps miss the target and allow the bull to hit the horse. In this case, even though the horse is protected by a mattress-like covering, it will be thrown to the ground, together with its rider. And, if the bull's horns happen to get underneath the protective covering, the horse will inevitably be seriously injured and maybe killed. The horses are, in any case, often old and of poor quality, and unfit for the work required of them. Furthermore, the horse contractors who provide the horses for the *picadores* have been known to use the same horses time and time again, even though they may have been injured in the bullring, and, because the *picadores* are so poorly paid, to have given them a little extra money as an incentive to use them. If in the course of this first part of the bullfight the horse and the *picador* are thrown to the ground, the bull is usually distracted by one of the *matadores*, but the *picador* will not escape the whistling and jeering of the spectators. He is on occasion the most hated figure in the bullring. Indeed, the clumsiness of the *picador* is often accentuated in this part of the bullfight by the activities of the *matador* who, between the confrontations involving the *picador* and the bull, will take the bull away from the horse with a series of skilful manoeuvres with the cape.

The second act or *tercio* of the bullfight is much more elegant and involves the *banderilleros*. Their task is to run across the arena towards the bull and, as the bull charges and lowers his head, to plant two darts with barbed points into the bull's neck, thereby arousing the animal from the fatigue caused by the confrontation with the *picador*. Very often the *banderillero* runs towards the bull at an angle, puts his feet together at the vital moment, places the *banderillas* and pivots past the horns. Alternatively, he may make a quarter-circle movement in front of the charging bull, or he may choose to stand still, swaying away from the horns and driving in the *banderillas* as the bull passes by. There are various other ways of planting them, but, whatever way is chosen, the *banderillero* is always accompanied in the ring by two other men, usually by a *matador* who stands in the centre, and another *banderillero* who takes up a position to the rear of the bull. Each has a cape, and the purpose is that, as the bull turns to pursue the *banderillero* who has placed the *banderillas*, he will see a cape and be distracted.

The placing of the *banderillas* is of considerable importance. First, they should be placed behind the bull's neck, should be close together, and should not be placed where they will interfere with the *matador*'s final sword thrust. Again, they should not be driven in too deeply, for in that case they would not hang loose, as is the desired aim, but stand up straight and, as a consequence, prove an obstacle to the *matador*'s work with the cape in the final stages of the fight. The intention is not, in effect, to cause the bull pain, but to tire him in preparation for this final stage, and to that end the *banderillas* should merely pierce the hide, not inflict a painful wound. This second stage of the bullfight is, at its best, marked by elegance and skill and is clearly the stage which most foreigners can appreciate most easily. The sound of trumpets brings it to an end and announces the beginning of the final act.

The third part of the bullfight involves the *faena*, the 'job' or 'task' whereby the *matador* is required to perform a number of passes with the bull before dispatching it with a single thrust of his sword. In order to effect the passes, the *matador*, on foot, is armed with the *muleta*, a heart-shaped scarlet cloth which is folded over and held in place along a tapered wooden stick, and the *estoque*, a sword of about 75 centimetres in length, curved downwards at the tip in order to allow successful penetration of the bull's neck muscle. The *muleta* is usually held in the left hand, the *estoque* in the right, and the *faena* begins with a series of passes in which the *matador* sets out to tire the bull further and, in the process, to display his own skill and courage. The principal passes are those known as the *ayudados*, the *natural* and the *pase de pecho*. In the case of the *ayudados* – the verb *ayudar* means 'to help' – the point of the sword is introduced into the cloth of the *muleta* and so 'helps' to make the cloth wider. Both hands are therefore used, and the *muleta* either passes above the bull's horns – an *ayudado por alto* – or below the bull's muzzle – an *ayudado por bajo*. As for the *natural*, it is, when performed well, the most elegant but also the most dangerous of passes. Holding the *muleta* in the left hand, the *matador* faces the bull, incites him and, as he charges, sways on the spot, his feet still, pivoting in a quarter circle and taking the bull past him with a slow movement of the cape. A flick of the cloth will, more often than not, stop the bull suddenly, a movement which twists its spine and helps to tire it further. If it does not stop, but turns and charges the *matador* again, he will perform a *pase de pecho*, a 'chest pass', which means that, as the bull attacks him not from in front but from behind or from the side, the *matador* has to react quickly, using the *muleta* to allow the bull to pass very close to his chest. Quite clearly, in order to execute these extremely risky passes, the *matador* requires coolness, judgement, dexterity and courage. If he displays all these qualities, his confrontation with the bull will provide a spectacle of true beauty; if not, it will be the opposite and will invite the hostility of the onlookers.

By the time the *matador* has completed his work with the *muleta*, he will know how tired the bull has become and whether or not it is the right time to dispatch the animal with the sword. If the bull is to be killed instantly, its head must be lowered and the sword must enter between the shoulder blades. The blade is not long enough to reach the heart, but if it enters cleanly between the shoulder blades and avoids both the vertebrae and the ribs, it cuts the aorta and death is immediate. If, on the other hand, it strikes bone, the sword will bounce off and the *matador* will have to try again, probably to the disapproval of the crowd. But the difficulty of the kill should not be underestimated. In order to attempt it, the *matador* holds the *muleta* in his left hand, raising it to see if the bull follows it with his eyes, and, if he does so, lowers it so that the head is also lowered. He will then stand sideways on to the bull and, holding the sword in his right hand, sight along it towards the animal's head. Because the bull is still some metres in front of him and the distance between the muzzle and the shoulder blades is not insignificant, the *matador* may launch himself forward and drive the sword in over the horns. On the other hand, the bull may move forward, charging the lowered *muleta*. When the *matador* moves in on the bull, it is called a *volapie*, which literally means 'flying foot'. When the bull moves forward towards the *muleta*, it is called killing *recibiendo* or 'receiving'. In either case, if the bull raises his head, the danger to the *matador* is obvious. Of the two methods of dispatching the bull, killing *recibiendo* means that, at a given moment, man and bull are one, as if joined. It has been described as the moment of supreme beauty in the bullfight.

At the end of a successful performance, the *matador* will be rewarded by the president with one of the bull's ears – two if he has been outstanding. Rather like modern-day footballers or athletes, he will then complete a circuit of the arena, accompanied by his *banderilleros*, and, if the spectators are enthusiastic and appreciative, they will shower him with gifts. The successful bullfighter is undoubtedly a glamorous and highly paid star.

Among the great bullfighters of the twentieth century, Juan Belmonte, José Gómez Ortega, better known as Joselito, Manuel Rodríguez, otherwise known as Manolete, and Luis Miguel Dominguín, have become legends. Juan Belmonte was born in 1892 and grew up in Seville, in the district of Triana. As a consequence of his relatively small stature and no great strength, Belmonte preferred to stay much closer to the bull than *matadores* had done in the past, standing erect and almost motionless. Previously, bullfighters had resorted to footwork in order to avoid the bull's charge, but Belmonte developed instead an unparalleled use of the *muleta*, keeping it low and using the arms rather than the legs. When Belmonte fought, there was always, therefore, a sense of imminent danger, and he was usually gored several times during a season – in one particular season he was gored twelve times – but these experiences in no way diminished his courage or his appetite for the fight. In 1919, Belmonte created a record by appearing in 109 bullfights in a single season. Unlike many other bullfighters, however, he never placed the *banderillas*, mainly because he could not run swiftly. When, after a long career, he finally retired, he devoted himself to raising fighting bulls on his estate in Utrera, some 30 kilometres south-east of Seville.

Joselito, born in 1895 in the town of Gelves, came from a family of bullfighters and was the youngest man ever, at the age of seventeen, to receive the title of *matador*. A close contemporary and rival of Belmonte, his style was very similar but his physique was very different. Stronger and much more of an athlete than Belmonte, he appeared to do everything with much greater ease, again working very close to the bull but doing so with apparently less risk. During an eight-year career he killed 1,557 bulls and, before 1920, was gored badly only three times. His athleticism also meant that, unlike Belmonte, he was one of the very best *banderilleros*, which in turn made him more of an all-round bullfighter. But, despite his great skill and the ease with which he worked the bulls, things went very wrong on 16 May 1920. On the previous day he had fought in Madrid and had been whistled at and heckled by the crowd, many no doubt the supporters of another bullfighter. The following day he fought in Talavera de la Reina, some 120 kilometres to the south-west of Madrid, and was fatally gored. The horn entered the lower part of his intestines, he was immediately taken to the nearby medical room, but died of shock while the doctors were working on the wound. For eight years Joselito and Belmonte had achieved great things, creating what was, in effect, a golden age of bullfighting. Joselito's death led to Belmonte's retirement, but he later returned to the arena and continued his career for another fifteen years.

Manolete – full name Manuel Laureano Rodríguez Sánchez – was born in Córdoba in 1917, the son of a bullfighter, and is generally regarded as the true successor to Belmonte and Joselito. By the age of seventeen he had become a professional bullfighter and had already become known for his characteristic style. This consisted of an upright stance, side on to the bull and barely any movement of the feet. As well as this, Manolete largely dispensed with the passes with the cape which usually characterized the earlier part of the bullfight and concentrated instead on the final stage, taking maximum risks and allowing the horns of the bull to pass by his clothing as closely as possible. One of the great stars of bullfighting, he appeared in all the great Spanish bullrings, and in 1945 fought as well in Mexico, Peru, Venezuela and Colombia. Two years later, on 28 August, he appeared in the bullring at Linares in Andalusia before 10,000 spectators, on this occasion confronting the fierce Miura bulls. Facing the fifth bull, which was called Islero, Manolete prepared for the kill, drove in the sword, but in doing so was gored in his right thigh as the bull moved forward. He was taken at once to the infirmary where the doctors succeeded in stopping the bleeding, operated on the leg and gave him several blood transfusions. But within an hour he was dead. At the age of thirty, one of the two great bullfighters of his time had taken one risk too many.

Manolete's greatest rival was Luis Miguel Dominguín, who was born in Madrid in 1926. He was the son of the bullfighter, Domingo Dominguín, and his two brothers, Pepe and Domingo, also became bullfighters. He first appeared in the bullring when he was only twelve years of age and became a full professional when he was eighteen, appearing, like Manolete, in all the famous Spanish bullrings. Indeed, on the very afternoon when Manolete was killed in the ring at Linares, Dominguín shared top billing with him. But, unlike Manolete, he survived many fights, retired in 1973 at the age of forty-seven and died in 1996 at the age of seventy. Otherwise, Dominguín had an extremely glamorous life, particularly where women were concerned. Having married Lucía Bosé in 1955, an affair with a cousin led to a scandal and the end of the marriage in 1968. In 1982 he abandoned Pilia Bravo in favour of Rosario Primo de Rivera, whom he married in 1987. But apart from his marriages, Dominguín had relationships with many celebrated film stars and women of considerable social standing, including Ava Gardner, Lana Turner, Rita Hayworth and Lauren Bacall. His colourful life illustrates perfectly the wealth and the fame which a successful bullfighter could achieve, assuming, of course, that he survived the bulls.

Bullfighters have frequently been associated with flamenco and flamenco performers with the bullfight. As we have seen earlier, both activities are combined in Carlos Saura's *Carmen* when, in the film's final sequences, Antonio and the bullfighter challenge each other not by engaging in fisticuffs but by performing a short and aggressive flamenco dance. Furthermore, when Antonio kills Carmen, his knife brings to mind the bullfighter's sword and the killing takes places on a sand-coloured floor which is rather reminiscent of the bullring. But if this is the case in what is, after all, a piece of fiction, the relationship between bullfighting and flamenco can also be seen in reality.[9] In many cases, gypsy families produced sons and daughters who, driven both by their particular talent and by the hope of financial reward, became bullfighters or flamenco performers, or indeed both. Aurelio Sellés, born in 1887 into a gypsy family in Cádiz, became a *novillero*, an apprentice bullfighter, and initially regarded bullfighting as his true love, but he subsequently became a *cantaor*, a flamenco singer. Similarly, Juan Sánchez Valencia el Estampío, born around 1880 to a poor gypsy family in Jerez, tried his hand at bullfighting but then became a highly accomplished and successful flamenco dancer in the *cafés cantantes*. His training as a bullfighter influenced his movement in dance, and some of his dances were based on his experiences in the bullring. Again, if we consider the case of Pastora Imperio, who was born in Seville in 1890, we can see clearly the way in which, within families, bullfighting and flamenco were closely interwoven. She, one of the truly great dancers of the time, was the daughter of a bullfighter's tailor and became the wife of Rafael El Gallo, the bullfighter brother of the famous Joselito. Their mother, moreover, was the flamenco dancer, Gabriela Ortega, and the family also had among its members the flamenco singers, El Planeta, Curro Dulce, Enrique Ortega and Carlota Ortega. The great flamenco singer Manolo Caracol was also a relative, and so, by marriage to Joselito and Rafael El Gallo's sister, was Ignacio Sánchez Mejías, the subject of Lorca's poem, *Lament for Ignacio Sánchez Mejías*, quoted subsequently.

Sánchez Mejías is a particularly interesting individual, not only because his death in the bullring was the inspiration for Lorca's famous poem, but also because he had a deep love of the arts which was clearly unusual in a bullfighter. As far as bullfighting was concerned, he was for a time a *banderillero* for Juan Belmonte, Rafael El Gallo and Joselito. He was confirmed as a professional *matador* in April 1920, at the age of twenty-nine and barely a month before the death of his brother-in-law, Joselito, in the bullring at Talavera de la Reina. Two and a half years later he retired, but made a comeback in 1924, only to retire once more three years later. A second comeback took place in 1934, when he was forty-three, and in July and early August of that year he took part in a number of bullfights in different Spanish cities. On 11 August he took the place in the bullring at Manzanares of another bullfighter, Domingo Ortega, who had been injured in a car crash. While attempting a special pass which involved sitting on the barrier step, he was gored by his first bull, Granadino, and was immediately taken to the neighbouring infirmary. Aware of the poor medical facilities, he had given instructions that, if he were to be injured, he should be taken to a hospital in Madrid, but the ambulance was late in arriving and, in the course of its return journey, broke down. The injured bullfighter finally reached the hospital eight hours or so after he had been gored, by which time he already had a high fever. Despite blood transfusions, gangrene soon set in and the end became inevitable. He died on Monday 13 August, at 9.45 in the morning.[10]

Quite apart from bullfighting, Sánchez Mejías had a considerable interest in flamenco dance and song. During his marriage to Joselito's sister, he had a ten-year affair with Encarnación López, La Argentinita, one of Spain's leading flamenco dancers. In this context he took a leading part in 1931, before his second comeback to the bullring, in setting up a company of Andalusian performers led by her. Prior to this, in 1927 he organized and financed the visit to Seville of a number of contemporary poets, including Lorca, in connection with the tricentenary celebrations for the great seventeenth-century Spanish poet, Luis de Góngora. Indeed, Sánchez Mejías was a personal friend of many of the leading Spanish poets of the 1920s and 1930s and was himself the author of three plays, of which *Sinrazón* (Without Reason) was performed in 1928 at the Teatro Calderón, one of Madrid's leading theatres. He was, then, a cultivated individual for whom bullfighting was merely a part of his life, but today he is best remembered as the bullfighter whose death was the inspiration for Lorca's great elegy, which begins:

> At five in the afternoon.
> It was exactly five in the afternoon.
> A small child brought the white sheet
> *At five in the afternoon.*
> A basket of lime ready
> *At five in the afternoon.*
> The rest was death and only death
> *At five in the afternoon.*[11]

While bullfighters were often connected with flamenco singers and dancers, and these with bullfighters, the links between the two activities can also be seen to go much deeper. Like the flamenco performer, the bullfighter is a participant in a powerful drama which, at bottom, is a struggle between man and beast, between the rational and the irrational. In this confrontation the bull is the embodiment of the instinctive forces manifest in the natural world, its black colour suggestive of the threat which man, in the shape of the bullfighter, is obliged to face. This conflict, furthermore, is something which is suggested very clearly in many a flamenco song, especially in those which belong to the *cante grande* variety:

> Una noche e trueno　　　　　One stormy night
> yo pensé morí,　　　　　　　I thought I would die,
> como tenía una sombra negra　because a black shadow
> ensima de mí.　　　　　　　hung over me.

The struggle is the same, be it man against the bull or man against fate.

This clash between reason and instinct is also suggested by the contrast in the bullring between light and shadow, *sol* and *sombra*. While, as we have seen, this division is linked to the price of tickets and therefore has a practical basis, it is not too fanciful to see its metaphorical implications, and these are present too in the stark contrast between the black bull and the colourfully dressed bullfighter, whose costume is known, significantly, as the 'suit of lights'. Furthermore, just as the flamenco singer often expresses and embodies in his singing the emotional experiences of his audience, so the bullfighter is the centre of attention and the personification of the fluctuating emotions of the watching spectators. The initial charge of the bull into the ring immediately creates a sense of fear, the danger inherent in this fierce beast suggestive of the dangers which face us at some point in our everyday lives. As, in the course of the bullfight, the bull comes close to the man, our sense of apprehension is increased, and the final stages, in which the bullfighter is entirely alone in the face of his powerful, if weakened adversary, that sense of danger is even greater. On the other hand, the death of the bull brings with it an enormous sense of relief which can fairly be compared to the catharsis or purging of the emotions at the end of a Greek tragedy, or indeed of a flamenco performance.

The bullfight may also be compared to flamenco song and dance in terms of its stylization and theatricality. In the performance of flamenco song, the singer gives particular emphasis to certain words and phrases, employs repetitions and introduces pauses in order to create a dramatic effect. It is a stylization which in flamenco dance has its equivalent in the precise movements of arms, body and feet, and in the staccato drumming of feet on the floor, as well as in the structure of the dance as it moves towards its climax. As we have seen, the bullfight has its dramatic structure too as it unfolds in three stages. The first stage, which involves the bullfighter's assistants and the *picadores*, sets the scene. In the second stage, in which the *banderilleros* run swiftly across the arena and place the darts in the bull's neck, there is a quickening of the rhythm, a lightness which is in marked contrast to the final stage, the tense and dramatic confrontation between the bull and the bullfighter, at the end of which, as in a tragic play, one of the participants has to die. While foreigners may continue to label the bullfight as a sport, it is quite clear that its structure and stylization mark it out as a great ritual.

The bullfight also contains other elements which link it to flamenco dance in particular. In terms of colour, blacks and reds stand out: black in the bull and in the male dancer's waistcoat and trousers; red in the bullfighter's cape and suit, and, quite often, in the female dancer's costume. Again, in a mixed dance the male is often reminiscent of the bull in the strong and aggressive nature of his movement, while the female, not unlike the bullfighter, obliges him to slip past her, her swirling skirt echoing the bullfighter's cape. In the Ballet Rambert's dance-drama, *Cruel Garden*, based on the life and death of Lorca, he is presented as the bullfighter, while the bull embodies malevolence, fury, blind hatred and fate. In short, elements of the bullfight and of dance are brilliantly interwoven.

A final element which connects the bullfight and flamenco is what the Spanish call 'duende', which is difficult to translate into English but which roughly means an inspirational power which drives the bullfighter and the flamenco singer or dancer to produce an exceptional performance. In his lecture entitled 'Play and theory of the duende', Lorca described 'duende' as 'spontaneous creation' fired by a 'mysterious power', and observed: 'The duende is at his most impressive in the bullfight.'[12] In this respect, if the bullfighter is to achieve a performance of genuine artistry and beauty, it is not sufficient for him to be merely brave. He must also be driven by that force which, as in the case of the flamenco artist, climbs up inside him, 'from the soles of his feet', and takes control of his very being. Lorca believed that an inspirational power of this kind was present in the best bullfighting performances of Belmonte and Joselito.

Foreign travellers to Spain, including some of those mentioned in chapter 3, have expressed their opinions on and reaction to bullfighting. Richard Ford, in *Handbook for Travellers in Spain*, wrote in some detail about this subject, as he did about everything Spanish. Like many British visitors, he was appalled by the spectacle of the horses ridden by the *picadores* and exposed to the most fearful injuries:

> This is one *blot* of the bull-fight: no Englishman or lover of the noble horse can witness his tortures without disgust; ... the eyes of these poor animals, who will not face the bull, are often bound with a handkerchief like criminals about to be executed; thus they await blindfold the fatal gore which is to end their life of misery ... The bull often tosses horse and rider in one ruin; and when the victims fall on the ground, exhausts his rage on his prostrate enemies ... It is, in truth, a piteous, nay, disgusting sight to see the poor dying horses treading out their entrails.[13]

In general, however, Ford defended the bullfight as something ingrained in the Spanish way of life, and criticized those foreigners who claim to be appalled by what they consider to be its cruelty:

> In England, no sympathy is shown for *game* – fish, flesh, or fowl. They are preserved to be destroyed, to afford *sport*, the end of which is death: the amusement is the *playing* the salmon, the *fine run*, as the prolongation of animal torture is termed in the tender vocabulary of the chase. At all events, in Spain horses and bulls are killed, and not left to die the lingering death of the poor wounded hare in countless *battues*.[14]

Around the same time, the marquis of Londonderry, attending a bullfight in Seville, revealed his prejudices when he concluded that, because aristocrats were no longer participants, the whole occasion had become debased:

> But now that the whole has sunk into a mere exhibition of hired combatants, men of a very low caste in society, instead of the chiefs and heroes of former days, and that the noble war-steed of olden times has given way to the wretched and miserable hacks that alone are now brought forward, the

126

harness and trappings of the horses, and the decorations of the picadors, matadors, and banderilleros – in short, the whole display being deteriorated to a mere paltry show, the spectacle is anything but ennobling, and affords no better idea of the former glories that illustrated it, than the processions and tinsel glitter of a booth at the fair gives of a royal pageant in its reality.[15]

Edward Hutton, devoting a whole chapter to the bullfight in *The Cities of Spain* in 1924, came down hard on those foreigners who support blood sports but condemn the bullfight:[16]

> It is not that I hate bull-fighting less, but that I hate hypocrisy and stupidity more, so that it is difficult for me not to doubt the sanity or the honesty of him who defends pheasant-shooting, for instance, but condemns the Spanish sport. (p. 209)

Attending a bullfight in Seville, Hutton provides a colourful account of the preliminaries:

> The Corrida itself is certainly one of the sights of the world. The great amphitheatre, half in shadow, is full of people in every sort of splendid costume. Above is the soft sky, below, as in Rome of old, the golden sand of the arena, and everywhere around you the people of Seville. Before you, on the sunny side of the arena, thousands upon thousands of poor folk, splendid in many colours, with yellow, red, green, and crimson handkerchiefs, parasols, mantillas embroidered with flowers. On the shady side thousands and again thousands in every sort of costume, the white mantilla predominating among the women, though it is overwhelmed by the innumerable sombreros of the men. Everywhere the *aguadores,* with their great jars and jingling glasses, push their way through the multitude, selling water; all sorts of merchants crying oranges, newspapers, fans, strange kinds of shellfish, and pictures of the toreros, elbow their way through the crowd; but over all is the immense inarticulate voice of the people, joyful with laughter, uncertain and high with excitement, full of expectation. (p. 213)

As for the bullfight itself, Hutton found the spectacle of horses, attacked, wounded and, in one case, killed by the bull, quite disgusting; the participation of the *banderilleros* rather less so; and the final killing of the bull by the *matador* skilful but difficult to watch. Indeed, after the killing of the first of the six bulls, he left the arena 'without reluctance', unable to stomach any more.

The writer Kate O'Brien attended a bullfight in Santander in 1936 and, like Hutton, found it upsetting, but she was able to appreciate many of its elements:

> Bravery, grace and self-control; the cunning of cape and sword against incalculable force; sunlight and the hovering of death; comedies and tragedies of

character; tinny music timing an old and tricky ritual; crazy courage and sickening failure and the serenity of great matadors curving in peril among monstrous horns.[17]

In *A Stranger in Spain*, published in 1955, H. V. Morton, like Edward Hutton before him, described in some detail his visit to a bullfight in Seville. His description is extremely vivid and largely dispassionate, though one feels his sympathy for the old and pathetic horses, one of which is grotesquely injured. As for his reaction to the bullfight in general, he notes that it is something with which the Spanish have grown up and which foreigners, including the English, cannot possibly understand:

> No one brought up on the works of Beatrix Potter can understand, much less appreciate, a bull-fight, and nothing can ever be done about it. The ceremonial slaughter of an animal with all the attendant blood-thirsty formalities does not seem cruel to a Spaniard, at least to those who have grown up with bull-fighting. What those Spaniards would say who had never seen a *corrida* until they had reached the age of thirty is another matter.[18]

Kenneth Tynan, the theatre critic, was someone for whom the three-act drama of the bullfight had a considerable appeal. In August 1971 he attended a bullfight in the famous bullring at Ronda where the main attraction was the great *matador*, Antonio Ordóñez. For Tynan the true drama and intensity of the bullfight could be realized only when the bull and the man were as one, a fusion which was clearly achieved on that particular afternoon:

> The fight unfolds in an atmosphere of intoxication, with Antonio the cool centre of the tumult. As with all great displays in the ring, it's as if bull and man were both drawing on the same profound source of energy – animal impulse compressed and canalised into deliberate beauty. The cape slowly billowing, the bull surging with it, never less and seldom more than a foot from its folds; the whole making an image like a great ship under a sail. At this level bullfighting temporarily heals the rift, dissolves the tension, between reason and instinct, intellect and passion. The animal, by the end, is part of us. We no longer regard it as an alien force, outrageous in its violence, at all costs to be vanquished. Beneath an apparent contradiction – the bull's power versus the man's intelligence – we perceive a deeper harmony.[19]

In comparison with the reactions of others, Tynan's may seem rather fanciful, but it well illustrates the range of feeling which the bullfight is capable of inspiring in different individuals.

Nowadays the bullfight is by no means as popular with Spaniards as it has been in the past. During the Civil War, many fighting bulls were killed either for their meat or for motives of revenge on their owners. After the war, moreover, steps were taken to minimize the danger which the bull posed for the bullfighter: the horns were made less sharp and bullfighters began to adopt a sideways-on rather than a full-on position in front of the animal. And, again, from the 1950s bullfighting came to be governed by a small group of impresarios who employed bullfighters who were past their prime and encouraged the breeding of bulls which were far less fierce than they had been even a decade earlier. From a moral point of view, there is also increasing opposition within Spain to the ritual killing of bulls. Football, even if players' wages are an affront to any normal moral values, is obviously less cruel and less dangerous to those on the field of play.

7

Religious Fervour

> Through the narrow street there come
> Strange unicorns.
> From what field,
> From what mythological forest?
> Closer still,
> They seem astronomers.
> Fantastic Merlins
> And the Ecce Homo,
> Enchanted Durandarte,
> Frenzied Orlando.[1]

In this poem, 'Procession', Lorca captures beautifully the strangeness, the mystery and the emotional intensity that characterize the Holy Week processions as they make their way slowly through the streets of the cities, towns and villages of Spain. To the foreign visitor, the strange figures in long cloaks and tall, pointed hoods must indeed seem like unicorns, astronomers, fantastic magicians, or indeed members of the Ku Klux Klan. In front of them are the huge floats borne on the backs and shoulders of tired and sweating men, their skin in many cases rubbed raw by the weight of their burden, and on the floats, lavishly decorated, are the images of the crucified Christ or his grieving mother, Mary. Heavy and ominous drumbeats accompany the snail-like procession, stopping when the weary float-bearers need to rest and gather their strength. As they move on once more, the drums thunder, shrill trumpets pierce the air, the crowd applauds and, if the procession stops beneath a balcony in a city like Seville, a flamenco singer may launch into the anguished flamenco song known as a *saeta*. Good Friday to Easter Monday, the period embracing the agony of Christ and his resurrection, is an occasion when, especially in Andalusia, high emotion, spectacle and theatricality come together in a form which is unique to Spain.

Religious feeling, often not far removed from fanaticism, was, of course, an integral part of the Spanish experience from the time of the Christian occupation of Granada in 1492. As we have seen in chapter 2, an increasingly rigorous policy was adopted by Ferdinand and Isabella against Muslims and Jews. It continued through the subsequent reigns of Charles V and Philip II during Spain's so-called Golden Age, and from the time of Ferdinand and Isabella the notorious Inquisition set itself the task of ruthlessly eradicating all non-Catholics. The Golden Age, which embraced the sixteenth and seventeenth centuries, was, significantly, the era of the great cathedrals, of Spanish mysticism and of painters, much of whose work had a strong religious bent. In short, the religious feeling evident in the activities of Holy Week is the modern expression of something deeply rooted in Spanish history.

No one embodied such feeling more strongly than Philip II, arguably the Spanish monarch most familiar to us, and nothing expressed it more powerfully than the palace-monastery of El Escorial, which he had constructed outside Madrid and to which any visitor to the capital should pay a visit. Made of granite and built over a period of twenty-one years between 1563 and 1584, this massive and austere building, from which Philip ruled his vast empire, perfectly expresses the puritanical and intensely religious character of the man. He had intended the building to function as both administrative centre and monastery in which his life was virtually that of a monk. Although he was an astute politician, religious zeal guided his personal life and provided his consolation in difficult times. In the Escorial itself, his rooms were simply furnished, and from his bedroom he was able to see into the church where Mass was regularly celebrated. At the very end of the seventeenth century, the Hapsburg dynasty came to an end with the death of the sickly Charles II and the Spanish throne passed to the Bourbons. Nothing illustrates better the spirituality of Philip II and the materialism of the French than the difference in the Escorial between the austere quarters of the Spanish king and the luxury of those occupied by his French successors.[2]

The religious values embraced by Philip were, of course, reflected in many other aspects of his reign. Within Spain itself, he concerned himself with rooting out heretics, be they Protestants, Jews or Muslims, which meant in turn that the Inquisition, established by Philip's grandfather, became extremely powerful. On 25 September 1559, for example, sixteen Protestants were burnt at the stake in Seville in the first auto-da-fé. In the following years other heretics were burned both in the south and the north of the country, Philip himself attending an auto-da-fé where he witnessed the burning alive of an Italian nobleman, Don Carlos de Seso, leader of the Protestant group in Valladolid. The Moriscos – Muslims who professed to be Christians but who often continued to practise their own faith – became a particular target and, as we have seen earlier, were subjected to highly repressive measures, ending in a decree for their expulsion from the country in 1582. As far as foreign policy was concerned, Spain played a leading part in the formation of the Holy League, a combined operation involving Spain, Venice and the papacy and designed to confront the increasing danger presented by the Turks in the Mediterranean. It ended with a glorious Catholic victory over the Turkish navy in the Bay of Lepanto in 1571. Again, the religious battle continued against a different opponent in northern Europe where Protestantism was on the increase, not least in the Netherlands, where William of Nassau, prince of Orange, was resolved to free the country from Spanish occupation. And then, of course, there was Protestant England, which Philip dreamed of turning into a Catholic country in order to fulfil his ambition of ruling a united Catholic Europe. Quite clearly, this was an age when religion and politics were interwoven to the point where it is often difficult to decide which was the more important factor, but there can be no doubt that the age of Philip II bore the imprint of his own religious character more than any other.[3]

In this context, the building of Spain's great cathedrals bore witness to religious fervour. Dating from well before the age of Philip II, they provide evidence of the crusading spirit which fired the Reconquest, and no Spanish cathedral illustrates this better than that of Santiago de Compostela in the north-west. It occupies the site where the bones of Santiago, or St James, are said to have been discovered as early as 829, and where, in consequence, a church was built. In 977 it was destroyed by al-Mansur, ruler of Córdoba at that time, but the cathedral then rose in its place, the work being completed in 1188. Although the association of St James with the cathedral is undoubtedly untrue – he was actually beheaded in Jerusalem – it has fired the imagination of Christians through the ages, and in the eleventh and twelfth centuries more than half a million pilgrims annually undertook the pilgrimage to Santiago along the roads through France and northern Spain. Another aspect of the legend of St James has him appearing on horseback, fighting alongside the Christians during the Reconquest in as many as forty battles, urging them on and personally slaughtering hordes of Muslims. Quite clearly, the stories surrounding St James and Compostela were a matter of faith for thousands of Christians and typical in that sense of the religious spirit which is still to be seen in the Holy Week processions.[4]

The great Spanish cathedrals are, in a way, an indication of the slow but relentless advance of the Reconquest. Burgos, some 450 kilometres south-east of Santiago, is, of course, associated with El Cid, second in importance only to St James in terms of his heroic exploits against the Moors, and it also boasts a magnificent cathedral, founded in 1221. Further south again, Toledo, recaptured from the Moors by Alfonso VI, with the help of El Cid, in 1085, possesses one of the finest cathedrals in the whole of Spain, the construction of which lasted from 1227 until 1493. In Andalusia, as we have already seen, the Christian ousting of the Muslims led in turn to the construction of the cathedral within the Mezquita in Córdoba, and in Seville to the building on the site of a former mosque of one of the largest cathedrals in the world. In every case, these buildings celebrate the might and spirituality of the Christian faith. The Gothic style of many of them – Burgos and Toledo are good examples – emphasizes weight, solidity and grandeur, while their soaring interiors and spires reach up to heaven in a manner which inspires the believer to direct his or her thoughts to God.

No one directed their thoughts to God more than the mystics of the sixteenth century, in particular St Teresa of Ávila and St John of the Cross, both of whom were significantly associated with the strongly religious age of Philip II.[5] Born in Ávila, to the north-west of Madrid, in 1515, St Teresa became a Carmelite nun in 1534 and devoted her life to the reform of the Carmelite Order. Although she had received little formal education, she wrote a number of books in which she sought to explain to her readers the nature of the spiritual life and, in particular, the mystic experience whereby the soul achieves perfect union with God. In *The Interior Castle*, for example, she describes the seven rooms of the castle of the soul and the way in which the soul passes through each room until, in the seventh, its journey culminates in union with God. Because this intense experience is so difficult to communicate to the ordinary reader, she frequently employed everyday images to do so: the garden which flourishes when it is properly watered, or prayer which feeds the soul as a spring feeds the soil.

St John of the Cross, real name Juan de Yepes, was also born in the province of Ávila, in 1542, and was closely associated with St Teresa. Like her he entered the Carmelite Order and set about reforming it. Much better educated – he graduated at the famous University of Salamanca – he was one of the great poets of the sixteenth century and also wrote detailed prose commentaries on his poems, all of which sought to communicate the mystical experience. As in the case of St Teresa, St John resorted to metaphors and images which are common to the experience of most people in order to help them understand the nature of the soul's union with God. In his finest poem, 'Dark Night', this is therefore described in terms of a young woman leaving her silent house at night in order to meet her lover:

> One dark night,
> Inflamed by love's desire,
> Oh, happy fate!
> I left unseen,
> My house in silence.[6]

Her only guide is a light which burns in her heart, and this leads her through the darkness to her lover in whose presence her own existence is forgotten. Quite clearly, the poem has a strongly erotic character, but St John's purpose is purely to suggest the intense rapture and urgency of the mystic experience, which in another poem, 'Song of the Living Flame of Love', is evoked in phrases as passionate as 'Oh, delicate hand! Oh, gentle touch!', each of them suggestive of an intimate sexual experience. Indeed, one is often inclined to wonder if those religious figures who flogged themselves in order to punish the flesh and sharpen the spirit did not simultaneously, if unintentionally, experience a degree of sexual excitement.

The religious intensity of the mystical experience finds its expression too in the luminous, flame-like figures of the greatest religious painter of the Golden Age: Domenicos Theotocopoulos. Better known as El Greco, he was born on the Greek island of Crete in 1540 or 1541, and was therefore a contemporary of St John of the Cross. After periods in Venice, where he was a pupil of Titian, and then Rome, he arrived in Toledo in 1576 or 1577, at the age of thirty-six and remained there for the rest of his life. Toledo at the time was the great cultural and ecclesiastical centre of Spain, and El Greco was clearly inspired by it. During his first two years there, he was commissioned to produce paintings for the Church of Santo Domingo and for the cathedral, and in them we can see already the hallmarks of his style. In the church, *The Assumption of the Virgin*, *The Trinity*, and *The Resurrection* are characterized by their elongated, soaring figures, as is *The 'Espolio'* (*The Disrobing of Christ*) on the High Altar of the sacristy of the cathedral. If anything, the figures in El Greco's paintings became even leaner and longer as his style developed over the years. In this respect the two men in *St Francis and St Andrew*, completed some twenty years after El Greco's arrival in Toledo, are unnaturally tall and slender, while *The Immaculate Conception*, painted more than ten years later in the artist's final manner, portrays the Virgin and the angels who surround her as soaring, ethereal figures floating above the earth and gazing upwards towards a white dove. As well as this, light plays a vital part in El Greco's painting. In *The Adoration of the Shepherds*, painted at more or less the same time as *St Francis and St Andrew*, the figures are lit as if on a stage, but the effect is to suggest too that they are illuminated from within, as is the case in many other paintings. In addition, El Greco painted faces which suggest a greater concern with the next world than with this: faces that are lean, almost feverish, as in fasting or illness, and whose eyes are turned away from the earth and towards heaven. Indeed, in his religious paintings in general, it is as if the world is insignificant, for it often occupies the lowest part of a picture, while the figures move ever upwards and away from it. And again, as in the poems of St John of the Cross, human beings are in El Greco's paintings in the midst of darkness but on a journey towards everlasting light. Given the spirituality of this artist's work, it comes as something of a surprise to discover that, although it was revered by many influential people of the time, the ascetic and highly religious Philip II was not one of them. He much preferred the paintings of Titian.[7]

Apart from El Greco, many of the great painters of the Golden Age, all of whom painted religious subjects, were, as mentioned earlier, either from Seville or were associated with it. The oldest artist in the so-called Seville school of painting was Francisco de Zurbarán, who was born in the small town of Fuente de Cantos, in Extremadura, in 1598, but who spent most of his life in Seville.[8] A very different kind of painter from El Greco, he nevertheless embodied the religious spirit of his time in the sense that he constantly carried out commissions for monasteries and churches. The subjects of his paintings clearly illustrate the nature of this aspect of his work: *St Thomas Aquinas visiting St Bonaventure*, *The Death of St Bonaventure*, *The Cloaked Madonna*, and *The Miracle of St Hugo* which were all completed for religious organizations in Seville itself. As for his style, it has none of the febrile character of El Greco's work, but, even so, it is distinguished by a soberness and a severity which marks out Zurbarán as a fine example of seventeenth-century Spanish asceticism. It has been said of him that no one ever created such austerity, spirituality, or grandeur out of a monk's white cowl, and no one ever avoided the subject's inherent monotony with such success.

The account of Seville cathedral in chapter 2 suggests the importance of another painter closely associated with the city. Born in 1618, Bartolomé Esteban Murillo spent his entire life in Seville except for a couple of years in Madrid. Like Zurbarán, he was constantly in demand for religious paintings and undertook important commissions for churches, monasteries and, in particular, Seville cathedral. It has been said of

Murillo that he painted for the simple devout man in the street and that in his time he was the most sought-after painter in Seville. Clearly a pious individual, he was highly skilled in narrative painting, as his many pictures of scenes from the scriptures and from the lives of saints suggest. *St Isabel of Hungary Attending the Sick*, undertaken for the church attached to the Hospital de la Caridad in Seville, is a fine example, and it illustrates too Murillo's sensitivity to female beauty. This latter quality is to be seen too in his depiction of the Virgin, as in *The Virgin of the Rosary* and *Mater Dolorosa*, both in the Prado. But, if Murillo was one of the most popular and skilled painters of his day, his work lacks the impact and the power of El Greco, and its sentimentality is often rather cloying.

Juan de Valdés Leal, born in Seville in 1622, illustrates in certain respects the more dramatic and theatrical aspect of Spanish religious painting in the seventeenth century. Mention has been made already of the two paintings, *In the Blink of an Eye* and *No More, No Less*, which are to be found in the Hospital de la Caridad in Seville. In comparison with the Murillo paintings in the same building, they have a sensational effect. Indeed, on observing them, Murillo once said that they could only be viewed if one stuffed one's fingers up one's nose in order to avoid the stench of the decomposition they depict. In his portrayal of the vanity of the world, Valdés Leal was the equivalent of seventeenth-century writers such as Francisco de Quevedo, one of whose poems ends with the characteristic refrain: 'The glories of this world / Attract with their brightness, reward us in smoke.' On the other hand, Valdés Leal painted many less sensational subjects, such as *The Assumption of the Virgin*, *Christ Bearing the Cross* and the altarpiece for the Carmelites of Córdoba which contains imposing representations of the prophets. His pessimism was therefore combined with a religious idealism; both of these were highly characteristic of a time in Spanish history when the fortunes of the nation were in steady decline.

Alonso Cano, born in Granada in 1601, devoted most of his energies to painting altarpieces and religious scenes. One of his various paintings of the Immaculate Conception can be seen in the oratory of Granada cathedral, his *Seven Mysteries of the Virgin* in the main chapel. Standing somewhere between Zurbarán and Murillo in terms of his style, Cano was a fine colourist whose paintings contain a strong sense of drama, as his *Dead Christ Supported by the Angel*, now in the Prado, suggests.

Strangely enough, Diego Rodríguez de Silva y Velázquez, born in Seville in 1599 and, along with El Greco, one of the greatest painters of Spain's Golden Age, is not primarily associated with religious subjects. At the age of twenty-four he became painter to the Spanish Court, and much of his work consisted therefore of brilliant portraits of royalty and the aristocracy, and of historical and mythological subjects. Of the relatively few religious paintings, *Coronation of the Virgin*, now in the Prado, suggests that Velázquez was less interested in religious feeling than in the beauty and dignity of the figures of the Virgin, God and Christ, as well as in the ceremonial nature of the scene. El Greco's similar painting of the same episode suggests the inner feelings of the same individuals. Velázquez's figures are essentially portraits.

While paintings of religious subjects fill Spain's cathedrals, churches, monasteries, convents and charitable organizations, the same can be said of statues and images, in particular of Christ and the Virgin Mary.[9] These were subjects which were repeated endlessly as early as the twelfth and thirteenth centuries, most of the simple and expressive images carved from wood which was then finished in polychrome. In the second half of the thirteenth century, wood began to be replaced by stone, and the interiors of churches and cathedrals were filled with sculptures of such subjects as the Crucifixion, the Descent from the Cross and the Virgin Mary. By the sixteenth century the same subjects prevailed, but the influence of the Renaissance meant that materials were more varied – marble was used as well as stone – and the carved figures were much more natural in appearance. A century later, Alfonso Cano, mentioned above for his painting, created extremely beautiful statues of the Virgin both in Seville and in Granada. By the eighteenth century, sculptors were fashioning images in the more elaborate style of rococo; among these Francisco Salzillo specialized in making images, notable for their pathos, for the Holy Week processions. Subsequently, of course, the religious emphasis has been much less than that which prevailed in the Spain of the Reconquest and the Golden Age, and painters and sculptors have moved in very different directions. But, even if religious fervour in Spain is less than it was, the Holy Week processions continue to display a powerful release of devotion and atonement for one's sins.

The Holy Week processions developed in association with organizations known as *cofradías*, brotherhoods, which, from the seventeenth century, were engaged in charitable work designed to assist the poor and the sick. In some cases they ran hospitals and rented out spaces for theatrical performances, the income from which enabled them to continue their philanthropic activities. As well as this, each brotherhood was, and still is, responsible for one of the processions which passes through the streets of towns and cities between Good Friday and Easter Monday. In

Seville, for example, where the most spectacular processions take place and which number from forty to fifty in the course of the four days, each brotherhood has its own religious images, and the capes and hoods of those who remind us of the Ku Klux Klan are in its own distinctive colours. Each procession sets out from the church with which it is associated and wends its snail-like way to the cathedral, where its receives a blessing before commencing the return journey, the whole exercise taking up to ten hours. At the head of the procession is a band, behind it the various floats. The first of these presents an episode from the Passion of Christ, the second contains an image of the Virgin, the grieving mother following her crucified son. The lower part of the float on which the images are borne is enclosed by brocade in order to conceal the individuals who carry them. Alongside and behind the floats are the members of the brotherhood, some carrying heavy crosses and with chains around their ankles.[10]

In the Seville processions the scenes from the Crucifixion and the images of the Virgin are particularly impressive. The former are highly realistic to the point of being gruesome, and in this respect two images of Christ stand out: the *Santo Cristo de la Expiración*, which comes from the Capilla del Patrocinio in Triana and which was made as long ago as 1682 by the sculptor, Francisco Antonio Gijón; and the *Jesús del Gran Poder*, from the Church of San Lorenzo and the work of Juan de Mesa. As for the images of the Virgin, they are both beautiful and lavishly decorated. In some cases their tears are made of pearl, jewels cover the throat and hands, the velvet or brocade gowns are encrusted with gold, and around them are an abundance of white carnations and candles. One of the most popular Virgins is the *Virgen de la Esperanza*, which comes from the Capilla de los Marineros in the district of Triana, and another is the image known as the *Virgen de la Esperanza Macarena*, which is housed in the basilica in the Macarena district of the city.

As the above suggests, the cult of the Virgin Mary occupies a prime position in Spanish religious life in general, and in the *Handbook for Travellers in Spain* Richard Ford noted that, during Holy Week in Seville, he observed certain processions which were dedicated entirely to the Virgin and which were designed specifically to promote the notion of the 'sinless' Mary. They took place at nightfall, when long lines of men, women and children made their way through the narrow streets,

> headed by devotees, who carry richly chased lamps, *farolas*, on staves. The parish priest follows, bearing the glittering banner of gold and velvet, the *Sin Pecado* [Without Sin], on which the Virgin is embroidered; as soon as the

cortège passes by, the candles in the balconies are put out: thus, while all before is one glare of light, all behind is dark, and it seems as if the banner of the Virgin casts glory and effulgence before her, like the fire-pillar which preceded the Israelites in the desert.[11]

The extremely elaborate nature of the Seville processions means that the city's brotherhoods, of which there are more than one hundred, spend weeks and a considerable amount of money on preparing for them. Sums of up to £30,000 are spent on the decoration of the floats, on flowers, candles, costumes, musicians and precious stones with which to adorn the images of the Virgin. Naturally enough, the spectacle attracts vast crowds, tens of thousands congregating in the streets and in the windows of the houses. As the processions make their way towards the cathedral, they pass through the winding Calle de las Sierpes, then on to the Plaza de San Francisco, a stone's throw to the west of their destination and where the mayor and the city council are seated in specially constructed stands in front of the city hall. The largest crowds of all form at the entrance to the cathedral itself, where the images in each procession are blessed by the cardinal archbishop before it begins the return journey to the church from which, hours earlier, it had set out.

The foreign visitor to Andalusia may be surprised to discover that, just as flamenco is connected with the bullfight, so it is also associated with the processions. The chapel attached to the tobacco factory in Seville's Triana district, the great centre of flamenco in times past, is, for example, the starting point for the procession organized by the brotherhood known as *Las Cigarerras*, whose band plays marches distinguished by strong flamenco rhythms. But, more than this, the processions in Seville have always involved the singing of the flamenco song known as the *saeta*.

The *saeta* was originally a highly emotional song sung by prisoners lamenting their fate as well as their crimes.[12] The practice was already quite common in Seville in 1830, and is known to have taken hold in Jaén by 1865. The link with the Holy Week processions came about when the brotherhoods began to have their floats stop in front of the prisons, and the prisoners in turn directed their *saetas* to the images of Christ and the Virgin. In this context, the aristocracy had an important part to play, for from the seventeenth century onwards powerful and wealthy individuals in Spain regarded themselves as the protectors of the poor, including prisoners, and this in turn encouraged those in jail to revere them as potential saviours, as well as to express in their songs to the images of Christ and the Virgin their feelings of remorse and even identification with a mother and son who painfully brought to mind the anguish felt by their own mothers.

With the passage of time, the role of the prisoner was taken over by professional singers called *saeteros*, and the *saetas* were sung by some of the most celebrated flamenco singers. When the procession came to a halt, no longer in front of a prison but at a prearranged spot, a singer would appear on a balcony and deliver a highly emotional *saeta*. Such was the case of the legendary Enrique el Mellizo, born in Cádiz in 1848. As the procession approached, he and his three children would position themselves on the balcony of his house overlooking a street corner, and launch themselves into a series of *saetas* which invariably moved the watching spectators to a display of great emotion. It is a custom which still prevails in Andalusian towns both large and small.

The following are typical examples of the traditional *saeta*. The first evokes the suffering Christ and his grieving mother, but by implication also suggests the grief of an ordinary mother for a son who is probably in prison:

> See how he comes,
> Bent double with pain,
> His forehead dripping
> With blood and sweat.
> And his mother grieving,
> Her heart broken.

The second, sung to the Virgin Mary, focuses on her anguish, but its underlying relevance to the singer and his own mother is still clear:

> All mothers have sorrows,
> But yours is the greatest
> Because you have before you your beloved Son,
> His feet and hands tied,
> As if he were a traitor.

In the preceding pages, reference has often been made to Triana, once the home of many flamenco families, and to the participation of flamenco song and flamenco singers in the Holy Week processions. At first sight, the association between flamenco and religion may seem rather strange, for flamenco performers were originally linked with inns and taverns, with alcohol and even with drugs. Even so, flamenco singers in the past, many of gypsy origin, sang of misfortune, persecution and an adverse fate which was often shared by their audience, and in so doing they became their audience's anguished spokesmen in an environment in which high emotion was easily whipped up. In short, the singer, or *cantaor*, while expressing his own emotional misery, also took upon himself the suffering of his listeners, much as Christ took upon himself the sins of his people. As well as this, the way in which he sang was not unlike the manner in which preachers deliver their message to the congregation in nonconformist chapels and gospel halls, their voice very close to singing, their sermons full of repetitions and changes of rhythm and emphasis, all designed to have an emotional impact on their listeners. When, for example, the flamenco singer, Pericón de Cádiz, performed to a particular group and sang the line 'Why did God take her?', a member of the audience approached him in tears, embraced him and wept even louder. It was the kind of emotional response we would expect to encounter in the religious fervour of a gospel meeting.[13]

The emotion and theatricality of the Holy Week processions, so evident in Seville and other Andalusian towns, take a somewhat different but equally impressive form in the northern province of Aragón. In his autobiography, *My Last Breath*, the great film director, Luis Buñuel, observes that in certain Aragonese villages the processions are distinguished by the constant beating of drums, and he goes on to provide a detailed account of such an event in his native village of Calanda. Just before noon on Good Friday, more than a thousand drummers – in the early years of the twentieth century there were only two hundred – gather in the square opposite the church and wait in silence until the church bell tolls. The drums then thunder in unison and continue to do so for two hours until the procession begins to make its way through the streets. During this journey, the participants in the procession, which contains Roman soldiers, centurions and the image of Christ in a glass case, chant the story of Christ's agony until they return to the square around five o'clock. The drums then begin once more and continue through the night and until noon on the Saturday, after which they become silent.[14]

Although Buñuel left Spain for Paris in 1925, he often returned to Calanda and took part in the processions. He has described the profound effect the occasion, and in particular the drums, had on him: 'I don't really know what evokes this emotion, which resembles the kind of feeling often aroused when one listens to music. It seems to echo some secret rhythm in the outside world, and provokes a real physical shiver that defies the rational mind.'[15] For all his rationality and his rejection of religion from his teenage years, Buñuel reacted to the Calanda experience in an instinctive and emotional way that went beyond reason, that seems deeply ingrained in the Spanish temperament, and that, as far as religion is concerned, can be seen throughout Spanish history. He noted too that the drumming at Calanda was so intense and prolonged that, by the early hours of Saturday morning, 'the skin on the drums is stained with blood, even though the beating hands belong to hardworking peasants'.[16] When we take into account the pain and effort of those who carry the floats on their shoulders and backs, and the punishment of the flesh exercised by Spanish worshippers through the centuries, the degree of religious fervour which inspires such behaviour is more than evident.

At the same time, it is important to emphasize that the deep religious feeling which one observes in so many Spaniards often goes hand in hand with an appreciation of life's many pleasures. In *Spanish Journeys: a Portrait of Spain*, Adam Hopkins notes that, when the Holy Week processions come to an end in Isla Cristina, a small coastal town south-west of Seville, 'the young people head for the town discos'.[17] Similarly, Alfonso Lowe, in *The Companion Guide to the South of Spain*, observes that, when the procession comes to a halt, those who carry the floats can be seen enjoying a cigarette, or even a beer.[18] And it is, perhaps, no coincidence that the overall solemnity of Holy Week in Seville should be followed in the second half of April by the Feria de Abril, a week-long spree in which the Sevillians, as well as visitors to the city, enjoy life to the full. On the Prado de San Sebastián, between the old tobacco factory and the Plaza de España, more than 450 *casetas*, square tents, are erected, with wooden floors for dancing and paper roses strung across the ceilings. The surrounding streets are decorated with Chinese lanterns which are lit at night. During the day, particularly in the afternoon, people appear in carriages or on horseback, the men wearing broad-brimmed Cordoban hats, white shirts, short jackets and boots with spurs, the women in dazzling layered dresses, either riding side-saddle or passing by in elegant landaus.[19]

At night the spectacle is even greater. From around 9 p.m., and throughout the night the *casetas* are alive with the sound of dancing and singing, many of them full of guests invited by the private owners, others open to the general public. Both men and women wear traditional costume, much of it in flamenco style. The dancing is intense, passionate and extremely sexy, and alcohol is consumed by the gallon. There can be no greater contrast than that between this week of Dionysian pleasure and the religious intensity of Holy Week just before it.

In the twentieth century there have been times when a useful, if not totally accurate, comparison can be made with the religious spirit which inspired the Reconquest, the essential difference lying in the fact that the enemy was now the communist, not the Muslim. During the early 1930s the enlightened and idealistic left-wing government which followed the dictatorship of Miguel Primo de Rivera made every effort to curtail the power of both the Right and its traditional ally, the Catholic Church. In this context, liberal reforms were introduced in many walks of life and the influence of powerful religious Orders in the field of education was either restricted or removed. These were steps which, naturally enough, incurred the bitter resentment of both the Right and the Church, as a result of which they began to brand the Left as communists in the pay of Russia. When the military uprising against the left-wing government commenced in the summer of 1936, Cardinal Isidro Gomá therefore made a radio broadcast in which he spoke out against 'the bastard soul of the sons of Moscow', and, when the nationalist victory over the republicans was finally achieved in 1939, Pope Pius XII sent a telegram to General Franco: 'We lift up our hearts to the Lord and rejoice with your Excellency in this victory, so greatly desired, of Catholic Spain.'[20] This was, then, the modern equivalent of the crusade which the Christians had waged against the infidel Moor in times past.

During the Franco dictatorship which followed the war, the Catholic Church enjoyed for many years a position of enormous power and privilege. Catholicism became the established religion and all other forms of worship were outlawed in a way which, even if people were no longer burned for heresy, was somewhat reminiscent of the intolerance displayed towards Muslims, Jews and Protestants by earlier Christian rulers. Under Franco, the Church revealed a missionary zeal to rid Spain of its liberal thinkers and make it a truly orthodox Catholic country. Accordingly, the number of men and women training to become priests and nuns increased dramatically, as did enthusiasm for religious education and other associated activities. The Church and the state were entirely interdependent for at least twenty years after the end of the war. As head of state, Franco even had the power to choose bishops for Spanish dioceses. It was a period in which what has come to be known as 'National Catholicism' thrived.

During the 1960s, however, the links between state and Church began to be weakened by growing opposition, not least from within the Catholic Church itself, for many came to see the authoritarianism of the dictatorship as more of a hindrance than a help, not least in the field of human rights and social justice. By 1967 the regime had accepted the Vatican's views on religious liberty, which in turn allowed critics of the dictatorship to air their opinions much more freely. By 1973, two years before Franco's death, the marriage of Church and state which had been cemented in 1939 was finally shattered.

The advent of democracy in the years following Franco's death has meant, of course, that the influence of the Church has weakened further. There is little reference to it in the new Spanish Constitution, and, although 95 per cent of the population have been baptized as Catholics, only some 55 per cent attend church, many of them only once or twice a year. Quite clearly, as is the case in many other Christian countries, young people prefer the pleasures of the world to the strictures of religion. The religious fervour which once stirred the nation has given way to an enthusiasm for other things – football and pop music, for example. In a world in which pop stars and football celebrities are the new gods, the Church seems increasingly isolated and old fashioned.

8

Modern Andalusia

During the reigns of Charles V and Philip II, which embraced almost the whole of the sixteenth century, Spain became the most powerful country and ruled the largest empire in the world. Even so, the Golden Age, as it is generally known, was not as glittering as it appeared to be, for the sheer effort of maintaining and administering an empire which included large areas of northern Europe, parts of Italy and considerable areas of South America placed huge strains on Spain's internal economy. In addition, growing opposition to Spanish rule, especially in northern Europe, meant that in the course of the seventeenth century Spain's earlier dominance, as well as her territory, began to be eroded. It was a process of gradual decline which continued through the eighteenth and nineteenth centuries, by the end of which the country had become increasingly backward, poverty stricken and isolated from the rest of Europe. At the very end of the nineteenth century, in 1898, the last remnants of empire disappeared when both Cuba and the Philippines were lost to the United States. It was a blow which, in its way, was more devastating than Britain's loss of empire, for the latter was at least ceded by agreement, while Spain, once so great, suffered the ignominy of having her last foreign possessions taken by force. Furthermore, from the second half of the nineteenth century, Spain became a country racked by constant political unrest and military intervention: a process which has continued until relatively recent times.

From a historical and social point of view, the twentieth century has been a source of fascination for anyone interested in Spain and Andalusia. There have, for example, been two major exhibitions, the first in 1929, the second in 1992, and both centred on Seville, which clearly has a flair both for theatricality and self-publicity. This said, the most important events have been political: the extraordinary events which led to the civil war between 1936 and 1939; the thirty-six-year Franco dictatorship which followed it; and the equally astonishing return to democracy which followed Franco's death in 1975 and which by today has led to Spain's resurgence in Europe both in economic and social terms.

Present-day visitors to Seville will undoubtedly make their way to the Plaza de España, situated in the María Luisa Park and ten minutes' walk from the cathedral. Specifically built for the Ibero-American Exhibition of 1929, the great semicircular building in the *plaza* was intended to exhibit the industries and crafts of Spain. In front of it are fifty-eight tiled benches, each of which contains a map and depicts a scene associated with a particular Spanish province. Across the open area facing the building are several small bridges, their side walls decorated with brilliant tiles, and running beneath them a canal on which tiny boats may be sailed. The floor of the vast square is also laid out in patterns of attractive tiles, while the long, low building is characterized on the ground floor by beautiful arches and at either end by impressive towers, the whole in Renaissance-baroque style, even if it is of relatively recent construction. Today the building is used by various government departments.

Around the edge of the María Luisa Park are a number of impressive buildings which were also constructed for the exhibition. Such are the Museo Arqueológico, which now contains a display of provincial archaeology but which was in 1929 the Renaissance Pavillion. Similarly, what is now the Museo de Artes y Costumbres Populares, dedicated to the popular arts and traditions of Andalusia, was then the Mudéjar Pavilion. As for buildings which displayed the arts and crafts of South America, the Pavilion of Chile is now the School of Applied Arts, while many others serve as embassies for the countries with which they were originally connected. This is, indeed, an extremely pleasant part of an otherwise bustling city.

Unfortunately, the last months of 1929 witnessed the Wall Street crash and its disastrous effect on world financial markets, an event which seriously undermined the success of the Seville exhibition. As for Andalusia in general, it was, as it had been for many years, an extremely poor region in which huge areas of land were owned by wealthy landowners, many of them absentees, and where the landless peasants toiled on these estates for virtually nothing and lived in appalling domestic conditions.[1] In such circumstances, it was inevitable that, in political terms, the Bolshevik revolution of 1917, which led to the redistribution of land, should have inspired unrest in the Spanish workers, particularly the peasants in the south, and struck fear into the hearts of the rich. It was precisely the challenge presented by the rise of such democratic feeling, and the failure of the politicians to deal with it, that in 1923 led General Miguel Primo de Rivera to seize power and initiate a military dictatorship that would last for seven years. It proved, unexpectedly, to be a time of greater social harmony and, indeed, progress in terms of spending on education and public works, but, despite Primo de Rivera's criticism of the Andalusian landowners, little actually changed in the region. Indeed, the latter years of his dictatorship were characterized by growing opposition, and in 1929 the Wall Street crash delivered a final economic blow which Primo could not withstand. He finally resigned in January 1930, his departure opening the way to a new democratic regime that would last for six years.[2]

The departure of King Alfonso XIII in April 1930 meant that Spain became a republic, controlled initially by a left-wing government. Its coming to power signalled a short period of extraordinary political and social transformation, for, in its first two years in power, the government introduced measures which seriously curtailed the traditional powers of the Church, notably in relation to teaching; set about building many more schools; made divorce possible by law; and sought to improve the conditions of ordinary people, in particular those of rural labourers. Salaries were increased, the working day was shortened and the battle for agrarian reform, which was so important in Andalusia, became one of the central issues in 1932. Needless to say, the powerful landowners formed an increasing opposition to the government while the peasants flocked to join trade unions, both groups at those opposite extremes that would prove so significant in the years ahead. By 1933, however, the Left had become extremely unpopular and the government was dissolved; in the general elections of November of that year, the Right and Centre parties prevailed and, predictably, proceeded to undo the progressive measures introduced by the Left, thereby initiating a situation which, over the next three years, would descend into political and social chaos. The anticlerical legislation mentioned earlier was abandoned; the workers lost their new privileges; the landowners regained their earlier power and the land which in many cases had been confiscated from them was now returned. Inevitably, conflict between the Right and the Left became more polarized. In October 1934 a rebellion by the miners of Asturias lasted a fortnight, was ruthlessly put down by the army and led to more than a thousand deaths and the arrest of left-wing leaders, including the former prime minister. In addition, fascism, already so prevalent in Germany and Italy, began to rear its ugly head in Spain. When the right-wing government was dissolved at the end of 1935 and the Left once more won the general elections of February 1936, it marked the beginning of a year in which Spain inexorably slid into civil war. Between February and June, the general picture was one of increasing social unrest. There were a huge number of general and partial strikes. Churches and newspaper offices were attacked

147

or set on fire. People became afraid to leave their homes after dark, and many individuals of both right- and left-wing sympathies were murdered in cold blood. It was a dangerous and highly inflammatory situation which could not be allowed to continue, and so it was that on 17 July there began a coordinated military uprising against the Madrid government.

The rising began in Melilla in Spanish Morocco where a group of officers declared a state of war, arrested the local military commander who remained loyal to the government and rounded up and shot all those who resisted the rebellion. Within hours, Ceuta and Tetuán, the other two important cities in Spanish Morocco, were also in the hands of the rebels, and all republican resistance had been crushed. At this time, General Francisco Franco, who would play such a significant part in Spanish affairs for the next thirty-nine years, was in the Canaries, posted there by the government because it regarded him as a danger to the republic. On 18 July he declared martial law throughout the Canaries and issued a manifesto which was broadcast on all Canary and Spanish Moroccan radio stations and which encouraged army officers to express their loyalty to their country. It coincided with the beginning of the military uprising on mainland Spain.[3]

In Seville, it was led by General Queipo de Llano, commander of the carabineers. Having arrested those officers who were unwilling to take action against the government, he had heavy guns brought into the Plaza San Fernando. When the civil government building was hit, the civil governor at once surrendered, and the civil guard aligned itself with the rebels. As for the working classes, they were encouraged by Radio Sevilla to initiate a general strike and to take up arms against the military. They built barriers throughout the suburbs and set fire to churches, but in the course of the day both the centre of the city and the radio station itself fell into the hands of the rebels. At eight o'clock in the evening, Quiepo de Llano began a series of broadcasts in which he stated unequivocally that those who resisted the rising would be shown no mercy. By 20 July his victory in Seville was complete. Furthermore, his capture of the airport meant that legionaries could be brought in from Morocco. They became involved in a fierce assault on the district of Triana across the Guadalquivir, blasted it with cannon and ruthlessly killed all the opponents they encountered.[4]

In Córdoba the military governor employed artillery in order to force the civil governor into submission. In Granada there was an initial stalemate, for the military governor revealed his loyalty to the government, while on the streets the supporters of the Popular Front demonstrated loudly and vigorously. By 20 July, however, the stalemate had come to an end, for the military governor was arrested and imprisoned, the rebel troops went out onto the streets and by that evening most of the city was in the hands of the military. The only area which still resisted was the Albaicín, across the river from the Alhambra. Trenches were dug to prevent the approach of military vehicles and barricades were erected across the narrow and labyrinthine streets. But in the end the workers who lived there could hold out for only three days, for they had virtually no ammunition, while the military possessed hand grenades, mortars, cannons and even a small number of aeroplanes with which they were able to machine-gun the area.

Prior to this, feelings between the Left and the Right in the city were already running high, for in the general elections of the previous February the apparent victory of the Right had subsequently been annulled, and in the rerun of the elections the Left had gained a substantial victory. Tension between these opposing factions became much more heightened and, in particular, the activities of Granada's fascist party, the Falange, ensured that clashes between the Right and the Left were much more frequent. The capture of the city by the rebels meant, therefore, that in the weeks and months ahead a reign of terror commenced. They were days which saw the culmination of many years of bitterness and resentment between the lower classes and those who had exploited them. Circumstances were right for the execution of the most appalling atrocities.

By the end of July 1936, much of the northern half of Spain was in the hands of the nationalists, as were Córdoba, Seville and Granada in the south, even though vast areas of the south were still controlled by the supporters of the republic. Where the nationalists held sway, martial law was introduced, reprisals against all those associated with the Left were swift and summary executions were widespread. In this respect, the repression in Seville and Granada was particularly brutal for the simple reason that both cities contained a large working-class population which was opposed to the military rebels and which had, therefore, to be bludgeoned into submission. Arrests were made from the very first day of the uprising. They generally took place at night, as did the shootings. The executioners were not always military men but supporters of the nationalists – members of the old parties of the Right, civil guards, falangists, or bullies who merely took advantage of the situation to take their revenge on people against whom they held some grudge.

Figures suggesting the number of republicans executed during the three years of the war may be unreliable, but the cemetery records for Granada reveal that, between 26 July 1936 and 1 March 1939, 2,137 were shot, the largest number in August 1936, when 572 were killed. But not all those murdered were buried in cemeteries, and estimates have suggested that overall there may have been up to 25,000 victims in Granada, 32,000 in Córdoba and 47,000 in Seville. In Spain as a whole, there may well have been 50,000 executions in the first six months of the war and up to 200,000 during its three-year period. Needless to say, they did not end in 1939, for action against supporters of the Left continued into 1941 or 1942, several years after the war had been concluded.[5]

The most famous left-wing supporter murdered by the Right in the first months of the war was undoubtedly the poet-playwright, Federico García Lorca, already mentioned in an earlier chapter as highly critical of the Granada bourgeoisie. After the triumph of the Left in the general elections of 1931, Lorca had been appointed, as part of the new government's educational programme, co-director of the touring theatre company which came to be known popularly as La Barraca, whose remit it was to perform the great Spanish plays of the seventeenth century in the towns and villages of Spain. From the outset, the company attracted the hostility of intolerant right-wing groups who detested Lorca's homosexuality and considered the group's female members to be little more than prostitutes. Lorca himself further inflamed the Right through his declared support for the republic in the years immediately preceding the war. In 1933 he joined the Association of Friends of the Soviet Union. In 1935 he spoke of his admiration for the USSR, its art and its attempts to create a fair society. In 1936 he voiced his support for the Popular Front, and in the May Day parade of that year appeared at a window in the Ministry of Communications waving a red tie. Little wonder, then, that he became a marked man when the nationalist rebels seized his home town of Granada.

Fearing the worst, Lorca went into hiding in the house of the Rosales family, believing that, because two of the Rosales brothers were important members of the Falangist party, he would be safe there. It was to no avail, for he was arrested on the afternoon of 16 August and taken for questioning to the nearby civil government building. The military governor of Granada at the time was Colonel Valdés Guzmán, a brutal and sadistic man and a sworn enemy of the republic. It was he who must have phoned Queipo de Llano in Seville in order to determine Lorca's fate. The instruction that he should be given 'coffee, plenty of coffee' meant that he should be shot, and so it was that during the night of 18–19 August Lorca was taken away by car to the small village of Viznar, not far from Granada. There he and other prisoners were held overnight in a large house outside the village. At dawn Lorca and three other men were bundled into a lorry and driven to a spot beyond the village where they were executed. Later that day, Juan Luis Trecastro, a local landowner, boasted of having helped to kill Lorca and of having put 'two bullets into his arse for being a queer'. Three weeks later, the news of his murder began to spread. In England, H. G. Wells, president of the Pen Club, requested information of his whereabouts from the Granada authorities. They feigned ignorance, which merely confirmed that he was dead. At the end of the war, he was officially declared to have died 'in the month of August 1936 from war wounds'. His body has never been found.[6]

Needless to say, the atrocities carried out by nationalist sympathizers had their counterpart in those committed by the supporters of the republic. In this respect, the Church, because of its wealth and its traditional support of the Right, quickly became a target. Churches and convents were attacked, burned and destroyed, and individuals associated with the Church and its activities came in for brutal punishment. In Andalusia, for example, the bishops of Guadix and Almería were made to wash the deck of a prison ship before they were taken to the town of Tabernas, to the east of Almería, where they were thrown down pits while still alive. It has been estimated that in the course of the war almost 7,000 individuals connected with the Church were murdered. As for the middle classes and known fascists, they too were the object of brutal treatment. In eastern Andalusia, local mayors were forced to reveal the whereabouts of nationalists in hiding, and they were immediately rooted out and disposed of. In Ronda, 512 individuals were murdered in the first month of the war, many of them thrown into the town's precipitous ravine. And in Guadix a group of young anarchists went on an orgy of killing for five months, until they were finally apprehended on the instructions of the government. Quite often, of course, people were killed as the result of personal grudges rather than political commitment, for this was a time in which feelings ran high and such opportunities easily presented themselves. But there were many, especially the anarchists, who believed sincerely that material things, together with all the evidence of a corrupt bourgeois society, should be destroyed. If the nationalists regarded their campaign as a crusade against the 'reds', many of those on the republican side approached their task with mystic fervour.[7]

Because the military rebellion against the government was coordinated and planned in advance, the early occupation of Andalusian cities coincided with military uprisings in other parts of Spain. In the north, the rebels were led by General Mola Vidal, in the south by Franco, though, as we have seen, Queipo de Llano was also a highly influential figure in Andalusia. Subsequently, the war became much more complicated, especially on the republican side where the Left consisted of many groups – socialists, communists, anarchists, trade unions – which often failed to agree with each other, as Ken Loach's recent film, *Land and Freedom*, reveals only too vividly. Furthermore, the situation was both intensified and further complicated by the intervention of foreign powers. From the outset, the nationalists knew that they could rely on the support of Portugal, then under the control of the dictator, Antonio Salazar. The involvement of Germany also began at an early stage, for Hitler quickly realized that, if he supported the nationalist cause, he would have an ally which bordered on his continental enemy, France; this in turn would test the resolution of other European countries, and Spain would be a useful testing ground for German soldiers and equipment.

German involvement included the supply of transport planes, fighter planes, bombers, anti-aircraft guns, ammunition of different kinds and a permanent squadron of up to 6,000 crack troops known as the Condor Legion. The most notorious German action of the war occurred, of course, in the Basque region when, on 26 April 1937, German planes bombed the town of Guernica, 32 kilometres from Bilbao and with a population of 7,000 people. Forty-three aircraft in all, bombers and fighters, took part in the attack, dropped bombs weighing 450 tonnes, and machine-gunned the town. The centre of the town was destroyed, as many as a thousand people died and many more were injured. The incident caused international controversy for many years to come, and Picasso immortalized its horror in what has become one of the most famous paintings of the twentieth century.[8]

Italy also entered the war at an early stage. Although Mussolini had been cautious at the outset, there were by March 1937 some 50,000 Italian troops fighting in Spain, a number which would later increase to 80,000. In the course of the year, largely as a result of the German and Italian contribution, the nationalist position was slowly consolidated, and by the autumn their victory in the war as a whole was clearly in sight. As for the republicans, they were dependent on aid from the Soviet Union, though the war in Spain presented Stalin with a considerable dilemma. On the one hand, he could not allow Spain to become fascist, thereby creating with Germany and Italy a powerful enemy in Europe. On the other hand, a left-wing victory in which the Soviet Union had played a part might well lead countries such as England and France to sympathize with Germany against the Soviet Union. In September 1936 only a small number of

Soviet weapons were therefore arriving in Spain. By November, however, Stalin was more aware of the fascist danger. Aircraft and tanks began to arrive, as well as Soviet personnel, including technicians, military experts and pilots.

It was also in relation to Soviet intervention that the so-called International Brigades began to be formed from volunteers who wished to fight on behalf of the republic for the cause of liberty. The brigades contained exiles from Germany, Italy and other fascist countries, all strongly motivated by the desire to put an end to fascism. Many came from Britain which, like France, had adopted a non-interventionist policy in the Spanish war. The first group of volunteers, nearly all French, arrived in October 1936. Subsequently, many more entered the fray. In all, 35,000 or so foreigners fought for the republic during the course of the war, around 18,000 at any one time. Of these, there were around 2,000 British volunteers, of which some 500 were killed and 1,200 wounded in battle. They were often involved in the bitterest fighting, but by 1938 they were withdrawn by international agreement.

The strength of the international forces which combined against the republic, together with the increasing dissensions within the different groups on the republican side, meant that by the end of 1938 Franco – General Mola had died earlier in a plane crash – was able to make a final push against Cataluña. In January, Barcelona itself fell to the nationalists, and on 27 February 1939 Britain and France declared their official recognition of the Franco regime. On 1 April, Franco announced the end of a war in which all supporters of the republic were now regarded as criminals.

For the next thirty-six years Spain would become a dictatorship in which the early years were extremely harsh. At the end of the war, the economy was obviously in tatters, the infrastructure was seriously damaged and there were extremely serious food shortages. Furthermore, 1939 became a time not of national reconciliation but of revenge taken by the nationalists on those they had defeated, the godless 'reds' who had fought for the republic. In consequence, hundreds of thousands of Spaniards left the country, and those who chose to stay behind were arrested, imprisoned or executed. It has been estimated that between 1939 and 1945 there were more than 100,000 executions, while around 250,000 individuals were given long prison sentences. About 20,000 of these were made to work, between 1940 and 1959, on the construction of the huge mausoleum north-east of Madrid known as the Valle de los Caídos, the Valley of the Fallen, which, despite assertions that it was a monument to all those who had died in the war, was undoubtedly a memorial to Franco sympathizers. What else could it be when prisoners of the nationalists were forced to build it?

Those who had supported the nationalist cause did well for themselves during the dictatorship at the expense of their opponents, even though in the decade following the war the general situation was grim. In order to obtain a job or food, it became necessary to prove one's loyalty to the regime, for the Falange, the fascist party which had grown in influence before the war, became the principal means whereby employment could be secured. This in turn had a significant effect on education, for teaching was left in the hands of Franco sympathizers who taught their pupils that their country had been liberated by nationalist patriots, and in particular by their glorious leader, from the hands of godless communists loyal to the Soviet Union. As for daily life, it was a time of severe hardship. In the cities electricity was available only at certain times of the day, and, in order to conserve energy, trams and trolleybuses were not allowed to operate a day-long service. In rural areas, including Andalusia, many people barely survived on a diet of boiled grass and weeds, and there was a serious danger of widespread famine.

The outbreak of the Second World War in 1939, following immediately on the heels of the Civil War, also had the effect of isolating Spain. Franco undoubtedly wished to support Germany, but Spain's military and economic weakness made its involvement difficult. Furthermore, when Franco finally offered his support to Germany in the summer of 1940, but in return for economic and military aid, Hitler himself rejected the offer. A year later, Spain did become involved when Hitler turned his attention to Russia, one of Franco's most hated enemies. A contingent of 47,000 volunteers, known as the Blue Division, was sent to fight with the German army on the eastern front, while at home Franco made a series of inflammatory speeches in which he hailed the German enterprise. Even so, a gradual realization that Germany would finally be defeated meant that by the end of 1943 the Blue Division was withdrawn and Franco began, prudently rather than willingly, to adopt a position of much greater neutrality. But the fact that Spain had been linked with Germany during both the Civil War and the Second World War militated against it. In 1945 it was excluded from United Nations membership; in 1947 it was not allowed to form part of the Marshall Plan, the European Recovery Programme; and in 1949 it was thrown out of NATO. In effect, fascist Spain became a pariah.

The late 1940s and the early 1950s were known in Spain as the *años de hambre*, the years of hunger. The Falangist Party had entertained a dream of the countryside filled with peasant farmers enthusiastically working on their modest plots of land. The reality was that agricultural output was, at the end of the 1940s, even lower than it had been at the end of the civil war, not least in Andalusia, where agricultural workers had always worked for a pittance in the most appalling conditions. In such circumstances it was not surprising that entire families in the south of Spain should have uprooted themselves and made for Madrid and the industrial cities of northern Spain, Barcelona, Oviedo and Bilbao. Efforts were made to stop the exodus but without success. Lacking accommodation, the migrants were obliged to build primitive dwellings on the outskirts of the cities and to scrape a living as best they could. Any visitor in the early 1950s would have concluded quite easily that Spain was a third-world, bankrupt country without a future.[9]

By the mid-1950s, however, things began to change for the better. In 1953 an agreement was signed which allowed the United States to have nuclear military bases in Spain in exchange for economic assistance, and in 1955 Spain was readmitted to the United Nations. Furthermore, the Falangists in the government began to be replaced by members of Opus Dei, a Catholic secular order, whose aims, while championing nationalist principles, were economic growth and modernization. In 1959 the introduction of the Stabilization Plan meant that inflation would be controlled and external trade and foreign investment encouraged. As a direct result of this, the 1960s witnessed an economic boom which transformed the *años de hambre* of the early 1950s into its opposite, the *años de desarrollo*, the years of development. It was a period when Spain, which up to that point had been primarily an agricultural economy, became a modern industrialized society. In this context, new industries quickly developed: the motor-car industry, the chemical industry, the production of washing machines, refrigerators, television sets and the like. This, combined with the introduction of modern methods into agriculture, meant in turn that the labour force in rural areas such as Andalusia was dramatically reduced and that those who lived on and from the land experienced considerable hardship. Consequently, huge numbers moved either to the cities in search of a better way of life or left for foreign countries.

While foreign investment greatly benefited the growth of Spanish industry, the 1960s also saw the beginning of the tourist boom, notably along the eastern and southern coastline. Between 1959 and 1973 the number of visitors to Spain increased from around 4 million to over 34 million. This, of course, encouraged the construction of the hotels which, as their numbers increased steadily, would prove to be such an eyesore along such beautiful stretches of coastline as the Costa del Sol. But if the effect was far from aesthetically pleasing, it was economically beneficial, and many of those who were living in poor circumstances in villages along the coast were able to secure employment as waiters and chambermaids in the new hotels. Development along the coastal belt, together with the continuing drift away from the land to the industrial cities, served, of course, to accelerate the depopulation of the countryside, as a result of which many villages became deserted or inhabited by old people who had no desire or were unable to move away. In contrast, the cities, especially the northern cities such as Barcelona, were bursting at the seams, and, in conjunction with this, the disparity in wealth between city dwellers and those living in the much poorer provinces of Andalusia and Extremadura became much greater.

The economic boom of the 1960s also had a profound effect on Spanish politics, for the movement of such numbers of workers to the industrial cities meant that they began to organize themselves into committees and commissions concerned with the promotion of their own interests and the resolution of their grievances. As well as this, the Spanish middle class, which in the past had been relatively small and highly conservative, now contained much more broad-minded and progressive professionals – doctors, teachers, engineers, white-collar workers – who saw the restrictions of the dictatorship as an obstacle to their ambitions and their freedoms. Similarly, an expansion in the number of students entering higher education brought with it a rejection of the old values in favour of new ideas. And, finally, the resurgence of nationalism in Cataluña and the Basque Country in particular set in motion a process of opposition to centralist rule from Madrid. In every direction, then, the iron grip of the dictatorship began to be challenged.

Franco died on 20 November 1975 after a series of debilitating illnesses, his death, after more than three decades of dictatorship, marking the beginning of a new phase in Spanish history in which the social, economic and cultural character of the country would be totally transformed. It had been Franco's intention that, after his death, the existing order would continue in the hands of Juan Carlos, grandson of the former king, Alfonso XIII, who had gone into exile in 1931. The young king was duly crowned on 22 November 1975, but, contrary to all expectations, took steps to ensure that his country would now become a democracy governed by an elected parliament. Initially, things did not go well, for the first prime minister in the new regime was a long-standing Franco supporter, Carlos Arias Navarro, for whom Juan Carlos had little time.

When, under severe pressure, he was forced to resign in 1976, the king's choice was Adolfo Suárez, a forty-three-year-old who had also worked under Franco but who shared the king's belief that sweeping political reform was required. The first free elections in Spain since 1936 took place in June 1977 and in October 1978 a new Constitution was approved by Parliament. It abolished the death penalty, separated the state from the Church, and recognized the rights of seventeen autonomous regions within Spain, even if it denied them complete independence. Within a few years, Spain found herself well on the way to becoming one of the most liberal countries in Europe.[10]

Although Suárez was returned to power in the succeeding general elections of 1979, the new democracy began to experience a variety of serious problems. They were both economic – recession, factory closures, unemployment, increased oil prices, bankruptcies – and social and political – disillusioned young people, drug and alcohol addiction and growing terrorist activity, particularly by Basque terrorists. In these circumstances, and with constant disagreement within the government, Suárez had little alternative but to step down in January 1981. His successor, the rather dull Leopoldo Calvo Sotelo, lasted until October 1982, when new general elections took place. They saw the coming to power of the socialist Felipe González, a Sevillian and leader of the Partido Socialista Obrero Español, the Spanish Workers' Party. He would remain in power until 1996.

Despite, and doubtless because of, the arrival of democracy, there occurred on 23 February 1981 an incident which shook the country and served to remind the people of the threat still presented by those members of the army who wished to see a return to Francoist times. While Parliament was in full session, a lieutenant-colonel in the Civil Guard, Antonio Tejero Molina, marched into the chamber, accompanied by 200 civil guards. Carrying out the orders of more senior officers, he held the members at gunpoint for almost twenty-four hours, while in Valencia Captain General Jaime Miláns del Bosch declared martial law. The conspirators clearly thought that the king would support them, but in the event Juan Carlos instructed the officers that, as commander-in-chief, he would not, and in a television broadcast to the nation asserted his resolve that no one was to interfere with the democratic process. Indeed, the effect of the attempted coup was to strengthen that process.[11]

Between 1982 and 1996 the Partido Socialista Obrero Español (PSOE) succeeded in winning four terms of office, thereby putting an end to the influence of the Right, which had dominated Spanish politics for such a long time. This period of socialist rule was a time in which Spain made remarkable strides in terms of its modernization. In 1986, a significant step was taken when she became a member of the EEC, and shortly afterwards, of NATO. When the PSOE had first come into power, inflation had been around 15 per cent and unemployment had risen to around 16.5 per cent. In order to rectify the situation, the socialists abandoned traditional left-wing policies of nationalization and state intervention in favour of policies which emphasized sound finance, control of inflation, market competitiveness and modernization of the infrastructure. The approach had considerable success, though modernization meant cutting jobs, which affected the working classes more than most. In the 1990s government policy of this kind undoubtedly alienated the trade unions, who had earlier been enthusiastic supporters of the PSOE, and in the general elections of 1996 power passed to the right-wing Partido Popular, the Popular Party led by José María Aznar.

Paradoxically, Aznar's right-wing government has been responsible for the greatest degree of devolution to the regions in Spanish history. The pressure on the government to moderate its traditional instinct for centralism was, to a considerable degree, forced upon it by the need to defeat terrorism and to cooperate with Catalan and Basque nationalists rather than adopt a policy of confrontation towards them. Consequently, the degree of autonomy granted to Cataluña and the Basque Country has been paralleled by that given to other regions of Spain, so that today seventeen have a large degree of autonomy. In this context it seems highly ironic that the Aznar government has recently been defeated as a result of terrorist activities: the bombing of Atocha railway station in the heart of Madrid. Whether or not Islamic terrorists were responsible for this atrocity, Aznar's support of the war in Iraq and his close association with George Bush and Tony Blair have proved to be the source of his and his government's downfall, leaving the door open once again to the socialists.

As far as Andalusia is concerned, the last quarter of a century has seen progress in certain areas, though not as much as in other regions of the country. In 1992, while Barcelona celebrated the Olympic Games, Seville became the centrepiece of the 500th anniversary of Columbus's discovery of the Americas. The site for the huge World Trade Exhibition, Expo '92, was the area across the river from central Seville known as La Cartuja. In order to facilitate access to the site, five bridges of modern design were constructed over the Guadalquivir. The monastery buildings, dating back to the fifteenth century, were restored and numerous pavilions were constructed, such as the Navigation Pavilion, celebrating the voyages of Columbus. At the time, Expo '92 received enormous publicity and was generally more successful than the Ibero-American Exhibition of 1929, to which it formed a kind of parallel – 29 becoming 92 – but subsequently Seville found itself with huge debts and uncertainty over the future use of the pavilions. The Spanish, Moroccan and Hungarian pavilions are still open, and the high-tech cinema, Omnimax, with its giant screen, merits a visit, but many of the pavilions are deserted. The greatest disadvantage of the site is, perhaps, that it is across the river from old Seville, which itself seems to offer the tourist greater attractions.

Seville's appeal today lies in the beauty of its old buildings, in the liveliness of its people, in its liking for theatricality, and in its rather Romantic literary associations. It is, after all, the city of Carmen, Don Juan and Figaro. The processions of Holy Week and the exuberant April Feria which follows are unrivalled in the whole of Spain in their drama and colour. And both the Moorish buildings and monuments and the great cathedral make an indelible impression. On the other hand, the city lies at the heart of an agricultural area which remains relatively poor and continues to suffer from a high rate of unemployment, despite its trade links with Latin America.

Córdoba, which for centuries has lived in the shadow of Seville, is today a modest but in many ways attractive city. The wonderful Mezquita remains, of course, its principal attraction – where would Córdoba be without it? – attracting vast numbers of tourists, but it is remarkable too for its flower-filled patios with their fountains and overall feeling of tranquillity, another Moorish legacy. In political terms, it has the distinction of having elected a communist council in the elections of 1979, the only Spanish city to do so and an appropriate response to the many years of suffering and deprivation imposed on it by the Franco dictatorship.

In historical terms, Granada possesses a legacy which surpasses that of either Córdoba or Seville: the magnificent Alhambra, the most visited and fascinating monument in the whole of Andalusia; the neighbouring Albaicín, with its typically twisting Moorish streets; above it the gypsy quarter of the Sacromonte; and below, in the city, the cathedral containing the tombs of Ferdinand and Isabella, the Catholic Kings who defeated the last Muslim ruler of the kingdom of Granada. As well as this, Granada can boast of its association with the great twentieth-century poet and playwright, Federico García Lorca. The family house, the Huerta de San Vicente, stands on the western edge of the city and is now a museum, open to the public, while a relatively short distance away are the villages of Fuente Vaqueros and Valderrubio, where Lorca also lived. Granada, its streets, the Alhambra, the Albaicín and the Sacromonte figure prominently in his life and work, and any visit to the city seems the richer and the more fascinating for it.

Modern Granada is, though, a very different place from that of Lorca's time. From the hill above the city, the spectacle is one of increasing urbanization, of motorways and blocks of flats in the distance. But if parts of Granada are rather drab, its situation is unrivalled. To the south is the magnificent, snow-peaked Sierra Nevada which separates the city from the sea and from which Boabdil, the last Muslim king, looked back and wept over the loss of his kingdom. To the west is the Vega, the fertile agricultural plain which stretches way into the distance. From the high point of the Alhambra and from the terrace of the nearby Alhambra Palace Hotel, the view is awe inspiring, not least as the sun begins to set and the sky appears to be on fire. There are many wonderful sights in Spain, but this is one that is hard to beat.

There are, of course, other notable cities throughout Andalusia. Málaga, though suffering a high degree of unemployment, has many attractive features, including a magnificent Alcazaba overlooking the city. Jerez de la Frontera, south of Seville, is renowned for its sherry and its horses, both of which are celebrated in its two major festivals. To the south-east of Granada, on the coast, Almería is a pleasant modern city with a bustling port serving north Africa, and possesses in its massive and hugely impressive Alcazaba one of the finest Moorish fortresses in the whole of Spain. This region, though still relatively poor, is also indicative of the effort being made to improve the economy. Apart from the attractive tourist resorts along this part of the coast, such as Salobreña and Almuñecar, the emphasis has been firmly placed on the rapid cultivation of fruit and vegetables under plastic. To travel out of the city of Almería is to be presented with what at first seems to be an inland sea gleaming in the sunlight, but which is soon revealed to be a huge expanse of plastic-covered greenhouses stretching far across the plain. It is apparently the case that at present 500 lorries, each carrying 22 tonnes of fruit and vegetables, leave Almería for other European countries every day, and that two days later these are in the supermarkets of many European cities. The process is, of course, facilitated by the development of the excellent ribbon of motorways and major roads which now exists throughout Spain, and which have their parallel in a railway system which, for reliability and punctuality, is far superior to that of the United Kingdom. In the case of the high-speed train, the AVE, which links Seville and Madrid, a late arrival of more than five minutes guarantees the return of one's fare, a policy which would clearly have led to the financial ruin of the companies which operate the British rail network. This is but one example which suggests the extent to which Spain, including Andalusia, has in the last quarter of a century taken huge steps forward from a past in which the country seemed at one stage totally immured.

Conclusion

The purpose of this book has been to try to suggest the fascination of Andalusia, the magical appeal which it possesses for the inquiring traveller. Spain itself has a rich and wonderful history. To visit such places as Barcelona, Burgos, Toledo, Salamanca, Avila and Madrid is to become aware, through the existence of castles, fortresses, monuments, museums and art-galleries, of the country's varied and colourful past. But no part of Spain has quite the attraction of Andalusia, the magical pull which makes one want to return to it time and time again in order to learn and absorb more. This has nothing to do, of course, with the appeal of sun, sea, alcohol and sex which attracts so many foreign tourists to Torremolinos, Fuengirola and other similar resorts along the Costa del Sol. One could equally satisfy such appetites in various other Mediterranean countries. But nowhere else in Europe is it possible to encounter the unique historical and cultural threads which, so tightly interwoven into the past of Andalusia, also illuminate its present.

As we have seen, the presence of the Moors, longer in Andalusia than in any other part of Spain, permeates the whole of the south, and is epitomized in the glorious Arabic buildings of Córdoba, Seville and Granada. To become familiar with them, as well as with the monuments of other cities such as Almería, is to become aware not only of great beauty but also of a long history of a very different civilization which, uniquely, held sway in the south over such a long period of time. It is a magic which has caught the attention of many travellers over the centuries, including such famous individuals as Chateaubriand, Gautier, Washington Irving, George Borrow, Alexander Dumas, Rose Macaulay and Laurie Lee. Their accounts make for fascinating reading.

If the legacy of the Moors is one of the great attractions of Andalusia, the influence of the gypsies has, particularly in the form of flamenco, created a unique form of music which is now celebrated throughout the world. There is nothing more exciting than the colourful costumes, the intricate stamping of feet, the passionate and dramatic songs and the urgent and complex guitar rhythms of flamenco at its best. As well as this, the vibrant world of flamenco has influenced both Spanish composers, such as Manuel de Falla, Albéniz and Granados, and those of other nationalities, including Glinka, Rimsky-Korsakov, Debussy and Ravel. And from the gypsy world there has also emerged, of course, the fictional figure of Carmen, the dark-skinned and ever fascinating seductress who has, from the time of her birth in Mérimée's original story, been so frequently reincarnated in literary, musical and cinematic form.

The drama and theatricality of flamenco has its equivalent in Andalusia in other areas too, notably in the bullfight and in the manifestations of religious fervour which have characterized the history of the region. Although the bullfight has little appeal for the majority of foreigners who visit Spain, it cannot be denied that the confrontation between man and beast is highly dramatic, or that its unfolding is full of tension. Similarly, the religious processions of Holy Week, dedicated to the crucifixion of Christ and the anguish of the Virgin Mary, are imbued with the fervour which has coloured the history of Spain from the time of the Reconquest and which is to be seen both in individuals such as St Teresa and St John of the Cross and in the great painters of the past, such as El Greco and Murillo.

In short, Andalusia is arguably the most vital region in Spain – not in terms of its economy, which has been starved for centuries, but in terms of something more powerful which has emerged from the melting pot of history and tradition. In this particular case, the ingredients contained in that pot have often been different from those present in other parts of Spain. They have often been exotic, certainly diverse. And mixed together they have produced something which can only be described as magical.

Notes

Chapter 1

[1] For a useful survey of the historical background, see W. Montgomery Watt and Pierre Cachia, *A History of Islamic Spain* (Edinburgh: Edinburgh University Press, 1977); and A. González Palencia, *Historia de la España musulmana* (Barcelona, 1945). See also Titus Burckhardt, *Moorish Culture in Spain*, trans. Akisa Jaffa (London: Allen and Unwin, 1970); and L. P. Harvey, *Islamic Spain 1250–1500* (London and Chicago: University of Chicago Press, 1990).

[2] A detailed account of the Mezquita is provided by Alfonso Lowe in *The Companion Guide to the South of Spain* (revised by Hugh Seymour-Davies) (Woodbridge: Boydell and Brewer, 2000). See chapter 2. See also Marianne Barrucand and Achim Bednorz, *Moorish Architecture in Andalusia*, trans. Michael Scuffil (Cologne: Taschen, 1992), pp. 39–46, 70–86.

[3] See Lowe, *Companion*, pp. 51–4; Barrucand and Bednorz, *Moorish Architecture*, pp. 61–9.

[4] On Seville's Moorish monuments, see Lowe, *Companion*, pp. 91–3, pp. 112–14, 116–21 and 125–6; and Barrucand and Bednorz, *Moorish Architecture*, pp. 156–8, 162–6.

[5] All translations into English, here and subsequently, are my own.

[6] Books of various kinds on Moorish Granada are more numerous than those on Córdoba and Seville. Apart from Lowe, *Companion*, pp. 251–69, 287–306 and Barrucand and Bednorz, *Moorish Architecture*, pp. 183–211, there are important studies by Oleg Grabar, *The Alhambra* (London: Allen Lane, 1978); and Robert Irwin, *The Alhambra* (London: Profile Books, 2004). See also Michael Jacobs, *Alhambra* (London: Frances Lincoln, 2000).

[7] On the Albaicín, see in particular Lowe, *Companion*, pp. 263–9.

[8] Particularly useful are the guide books, *Seville & Andalusia* (Eyewitness Travel Guides) (London: Dorling Kindersley, 1996); and *Andalucía: the Rough Guide* (London: Rough Guides, 1997). The former contains extremely attractive and detailed diagrams and drawings of the important monuments.

Chapter 2

[1] Federico García Lorca, *Obras Completas*, ed. Miguel García Posada, 4 vols (Barcelona/Valencia: Galaxia Gutenberg/Círculo de Lectores, 1996), vol. III, pp. 634–9. The historical background may be consulted in, for example,

J. H. Elliot, *Imperial Spain 1469–1716* (London: Edward Arnold, 1963); John Lynch, *Spain under the Hapsburgs* (Oxford: Blackwell, 1964); and Henry Kamen, *Spain 1469–1714* (London and New York: Longman, 1983).

[2] On these Christian buildings, see Alfonso Lowe, *The Companion Guide to the South of Spain* (Woodbridge: Boydell and Brewer, 2000), pp. 21–2 and 26–9.

[3] The poem is entitled 'The Rider's Song' ('Canción del jinete') and is part of the series *Songs* (*Canciones*), written between 1921 and 1924. See Federico García Lorca, *Obras Completas*, vol. I, pp. 365–6.

[4] Alfonso Lowe provides a comprehensive account of the cathedral. See *Companion*, pp. 73–93. See also Richard Ford, *A Handbook for Travellers in Spain* (London, 1844 and 1846, reprinted London: Centaur Press, 1966), pp. 373–88; and W. W. Collins, *Cathedral Cities of Spain* (London: Heinemann, 1909), pp. 8–14.

[5] On the Spanish painters, see José Guidol, *The Arts of Spain* (London: Thames and Hudson, 1964), pp. 260–81.

[6] On the cathedral and the Royal Chapel, see Lowe, *Companion*, pp. 270–8; and Collins, *Cathedral Cities*, pp. 38–44.

[7] The changes to the Alhambra made by the Christian Kings are discussed by Robert Irwin, *The Alhambra* (London: Profile Books, 2004), pp. 62–7; and Lowe, *Companion*, pp. 289–90, 307–11.

[8] On the architectural features of the palace, see Guidol, *Arts of Spain*, pp. 208–10; and Lowe, *Companion*, pp. 308–9.

[9] See Ford, *Handbook*, vol. 2, pp. 546–50.

[10] On the Generalife, see Oleg Grabar, *The Alhambra* (London: Allen Lane, 1978), pp. 93–6; and Marianne Barrucand and Achim Bednorz, *Moorish Architecture in Andalusia* (Cologne: Taschen, 1992), pp. 204–9.

Chapter 3

[1] William Lithgow, *Rare Adventures and Painefull Peregrinations* (1632, reissued London: Jonathan Cape, 1928). See David Mitchell, *Travellers in Spain* (London: Cassell, 1990), p. 13.

[2] James Howell, *Instructions for Forreine Travel* (first published 1642, and *Familiar Letters*, first published 1645; reissued London: David Nutt, 1892). See Mitchell, *Travellers in Spain*, p. 17.

[3] William Dalrymple, *Travels through Spain and Portugal in 1774*, first published 1777. See Mitchell, *Travellers in Spain*, pp. 28 and 32.

[4] Richard Twiss, *Travels Through Portugal and Spain in 1772 and 1773*, first published 1775. See Mitchell, *Travellers in Spain*, pp. 33 and 36.

[5] Henry Swinburne, *Travels Through Spain and Portugal in 1775 and 1776*, first published 1787. See Jimmy Burns, *Spain: A Literary Companion* (London: John Murray, 1994), pp. 125 and 131.

[6] See François René de Chateaubriand, *Œuvres Complètes*, vol. 3 (Paris: Garnier, n.d.), p. 116.

7. Major-General Lord Blayney, *Narrative of a Forced Journey Through Spain and France as a Prisoner of War*, first published 1814. See Mitchell, *Travellers in Spain*, p. 45.

8. *Life, Letters and Journals of George Ticknor*, vol. I, Boston, 1876. See Mitchell, *Travellers in Spain*, p. 49.

9. Victor Hugo, *Œuvres Complètes, Poésie I* (Paris: Robert Laffont, 1985), p. 413.

10. Ibid., p. 504.

11. Quoted in Stanley T. Williams, *The Life of Washington Irving*, vol. I (New York: Oxford University Press, 1935), p. 329.

12. Ibid., p. 336.

13. See Washington Irving, *Complete Works, The Alhambra* (Boston: Desmond, 1899).

14. Benjamin Disraeli, *Letters 1815–1834* (Toronto: University of Toronto Press, 1982). See Mitchell, *Travellers in Spain*, pp. 59–60.

15. Richard Ford, *A Handbook for Travellers in Spain* (London, 1844 and 1846; reprinted London: Centaur Press, 1966); *Gatherings from Spain* (first published London, 1846, subsequently London: Dent, 1906).

16. In a letter to his friend, Henry Unwin Addington. See Burns, *Spain*, pp. 127–8.

17. George Borrow, *The Bible in Spain* (1842; reprinted London: John Murray, 1914).

18. Théophile Gautier, *A Romantic in Spain* (New York: Alfred A. Knopf, 1926). See Burns, *Spain*, p. 131.

19. Burns, *Spain*, p. 64.

20. Théophile Gautier, *Espagne* (first published Paris, 1845). See *L'España de Gautier*, ed. René Jasinski (Paris: Libraire Vuibert, 1929), pp. 275–8.

21. Alexander Dumas, *From Paris to Cadiz* (reprinted London: Peter Owen, 1958). See Mitchell, *Travellers in Spain*, pp. 66, 68.

22. William Clark, *Gazpacho, or Summer Months in Spain*, first published 1851. See Mitchell, *Travellers in Spain*, p. 89.

23. See Mitchell, *Travellers in Spain*, p. 100.

24. Matilda Betham-Edwards, *Through Spain to the Sahara*, first published 1868. See Burns, *Spain*, pp. 120–1, 133–4.

25. Augustus Hare, *Wanderings in Spain* (first published 1873; reissued London: George Allen, 1904). See Raleigh Trevelyan, *Shades of the Alhambra* (London: the Folio Society, 1984), p. 99.

26. Havelock Ellis, *The Soul of Spain* (London: Constable, 1908). See Mitchell, *Travellers in Spain*, p. 107.

27. W. W. Collins, *Cathedral Cities of Spain* (London: Heinemann, 1909), p. 29.

28. Edward Hutton, *The Cities of Spain* (New York: Macmillan, 1924), p. 192.

29. See Michael Holroyd, *Lytton Strachey: A Critical Biography* (London: Heinemann, 1968), p. 378.

30. Gerald Brenan, *The Face of Spain* (London: Turnstile Press, 1950), p. 43.

[31] Gerald Brenan, *South from Granada* (London: Hamish Hamilton, 1957; reprinted Cambridge: Cambridge University Press, 1980), see p. 230.

[32] H. V. Morton, *A Stranger in Spain* (London: Methuen, 1955).

[33] James Morris, *Spain* (London: Faber and Faber, 1964), p. 84.

[34] See *A Loan Exhibition: Richard Ford in Spain*, introduction by Denys Sutton, catalogue by Brinsley Ford (London: Wildenstein, 1974). The volume contains seventy-nine illustrations, mostly by Ford, a few by other artists.

[35] See Katharine Sim, *David Roberts R.A., 1796–1864: A Biography* (London: Quartet Books, 1984), p. 75.

[36] Isidore Severin Justin Baron de Taylor, *L'Alhambra* (Paris, n.d.; reprinted Granada: Editorial Turpiana, 1988), see p. 4.

[37] Philibert Joseph Girault de Prangey, *Souvenirs de Grenade et de l'Alhambra* (Paris, 1837); reprinted as *Impressions of Granada and the Alhambra* (Reading: Garnet Publishing, 1996).

Chapter 4

[1] On the social background, see Timothy Mitchell, *Flamenco Deep Song* (New Haven and London: Yale University Press, 1994).

[2] The various categories of flamenco song and dance are described in detail by D. E. Pohren, *The Art of Flamenco* (Madrid: Society for Spanish Studies, 1962).

[3] See Ángel Álvarez Caballero, *El cante flamenco* (Madrid: Alianza, 1994), p. 48.

[4] For a general account of the evolution of flamenco and its movement into different locations, see Gwynne Edwards, *Flamenco!* (London: Thames and Hudson, 2000).

[5] See Pohren, *Art of Flamenco*, pp. 59–68.

[6] Edward Hutton, *The Cities of Spain* (New York: Macmillan, 1924), p. 205.

[7] Paco Sevilla, *Queen of the Gypsies: The Life and Legend of Carmen Amaya* (San Diego: Sevilla Press, 1999), pp. 45–6.

[8] On Antonio Chacón, see Álvarez Caballero, *El cante flamenco*, pp. 179–94; Mitchell, *Flamenco Deep Song*, pp. 151–9.

[9] See Álvarez Caballero, *El cante flamenco*, pp. 229–44.

[10] There is an English translation of Lorca's lecture in *Federico García Lorca, Deep Song and Other Prose*, trans. and ed. Christopher Maurer (London: Marion Boyars, 1980), pp. 23–41. The lecture may be consulted in the Falla Archive in Madrid.

[11] John. B. Trend, 'A festival in the South of Spain', *The Nation and Athanaeum*, 14 January 1922, 594–5.

[12] On the Granada competition, see Caballero, *El cante flamenco*, pp. 211–20.

[13] See ibid., p. 305.

[14] On the Saura films and Antonio Gades, see Edwards, *Flamenco!*, pp. 123–4.

[15] See ibid., p. 127.

Chapter 5

1 For biographical information on Mérimée, see A.W. Raitt, *Prosper Mérimée* (New York: Twayne, 1970).
2 See the edition of the story by M. J. Tilsby in Prosper Mérimée, *Carmen et autres nouvelles choisies* (London: Harrap, 1981). Page numbers refer to this edition. The translations given here are my own.
3 On the topic of orientalism, see in particular Susan McClary, *George Bizet: Carmen* (Cambridge: Cambridge University Press, 1992), pp. 29–43.
4 See Jimmy Burns, *Spain: A Literary Companion* (London: John Murray, 1994), p. 66.
5 Léon Escudier in *L'Art Musical*, see Winton Dean, *Bizet* (London: J. M. Dent, 1965), pp. 108–31.
6 See McClary, *George Bizet*, pp. 51–8.
7 On this aspect of Bizet's borrowings, see Dean, *Bizet*, pp. 228–32.
8 See Carlos Saura and Antonio Gades, 'Historia de nuestra película', in *Carmen: el sueño del amor absoluto* (Barcelona: Círculo/ Folio, 1984), pp. 55–6.
9 For an analysis of Saura's film, see Gwynne Edwards, 'Carmen', in Margaret A. Rees (ed.), *Catholic Tastes and Times: Essays in Honour of Michael E. Williams* (Leeds: Trinity and All Saints' College, 1987), pp. 127–55; and *Indecent Exposures: Buñuel, Saura, Erice & Almodóvar* (London: Marion Boyars, 1995), pp. 101–15.

Chapter 6

1 For further information on the origins of the bullfight, see Andrew A. Anderson, *Lorca's Late Poetry* (Leeds: Francis Cairns, 1990), pp. 158–60.
2 See Daniel Eisenberg, 'Un texto lorquiano descubierto en Nueva York (La presentación de Sánchez Mejías)', *Bulletin Hispanique*, 80 (1978), 134–7.
3 See *Federico García Lorca: Deep Song and Other Prose*, trans. and ed. Christopher Maurer (London: Marion Bryars, 1980), p. 45.
4 See ibid., p. 50.
5 Federico García Lorca, *Conferencias*, ed. Christopher Maurer (Madrid: Alianza, 1984), vol. II, p. 96.
6 See Jimmy Burns, *Spain: A Literary Companion* (London: John Murray, 1994), p. 174.
7 On the history and character of the bullfight, see Ernest Hemingway's authoritative *Death in the Afternoon* (New York: Charles Scribner's Sons, 1932).
8 Ibid., pp. 96–8.
9 See Gwynne Edwards, *Flamenco!* (London: Thames and Hudson, 2000), pp. 161–4.
10 See Anderson, *Lorca's Late Poetry*, pp. 153–8.
11 For the poem, see Federico García Lorca, *Obras Completas*, vol. I (Barcelona/ Valencia: Galxia Gutenberg/Círculo de Lectores), pp. 617–25. It is analysed in detail by Anderson, *Lorca's Late Poetry*, pp. 153–8.

[12] Lorca, *Deep Song and Other Prose*, p. 51.

[13] Richard Ford, *A Handbook for Travellers in Spain* (London: Centaur Press, 1966), pp. 275–6.

[14] Ibid., p. 279.

[15] See Burns, *Spain*, p. 177.

[16] Edward Hutton, *The Cities of Spain* (New York: Macmillan, 1924).

[17] Kate O'Brien, *Farewell Spain* (London: Heinemann, 1937). See Burns, *Spain*, pp. 184–5.

[18] H. V. Morton, *A Stranger in Spain* (London: Methuen, 1955), p. 178.

[19] See Burns, *Spain*, pp. 185–6.

Chapter 7

[1] See Federico García Lorca, *Obras Completas*, vol. I (Barcelona/Valencia: Galxia Gutenberg/Círculo de Lectores, 1996), p. 318.

[2] On Philip II, see R. Trevor Davies, *The Golden Century of Spain 1501–1621* (London: Macmillan, 1956), pp. 117–36.

[3] Ibid., pp. 11–16, 139–48.

[4] On the history of and the legends surrounding the cathedral, see *Spain: the Rough Guide* (London: Rough Guides, 1999), pp. 490–7.

[5] On St Teresa and St John of the Cross, see Davies, *The Golden Century*, pp. 290–2.

[6] The translation is my own.

[7] See Philip Troutman, *El Greco* (London: Spring Books, 1963).

[8] On Zurbarán and the other painters discussed here, see Gotthard Jedlicka, *Spanish Painting*, trans. J. Maxwell Brownjohn (London: Thames and Hudson, 1963).

[9] See José Guidol, *The Arts of Spain* (London: Thames and Hudson, 1964).

[10] See Alfonso Lowe, *The Companion Guide to the South of Spain* (Woodbridge: Boydell and Brewer, 2000), pp. 129–32.

[11] Richard Ford, *A Handbook for Travellers in Spain* (London, 1844 and 1846; reprinted London: Centaur Press, 1966), pp. 399–402.

[12] See Gwynne Edwards, *Flamenco!* (London: Thames and Hudson, 2000), pp. 153–7.

[13] Ibid., p. 157.

[14] See Luis Buñuel, *My Last Breath*, trans. Abigail Israel (London: Jonathan Cape, 1984), pp. 19–21.

[15] Ibid., p. 20.

[16] Ibid., p. 21.

[17] Adam Hopkins, *Spanish Journeys: A Portrait of Spain* (Harmondsworth: Penguin, 1993), p. 358.

[18] Lowe, *Companion*, p. 130.

[19] Ibid., pp. 133–4.

[20] See John Hooper, *The Spaniards: A Portrait of the New Spain* (Harmondsworth: Penguin, 1987), p. 172.

Chapter 8

[1] See Gerald Brenan, *The Face of Spain* (London: Turnstile Press, 1950).

[2] For an excellent account of the period, see Raymond Carr, *Spain 1808–1975* (Oxford: Oxford University Press, 1982).

[3] The most comprehensive study of the Civil War is that by Hugh Thomas, *The Spanish Civil War* (Harmondsworth: Penguin, 1965).

[4] On the fall of Seville, Córdoba and Granada, see Thomas, *The Spanish Civil War*, pp. 221–3 and 250–2.

[5] On the killings, see Thomas, *The Spanish Civil War*, pp. 264–6.

[6] See Ian Gibson, *The Death of Lorca* (London: W. H. Allen, 1973).

[7] See Thomas, *The Spanish Civil War*, pp. 268–81.

[8] Ibid., pp. 624–31.

[9] For an excellent account of the political, social and economic problems of post-Civil War Spain, see John Hooper, *The Spaniards: A Portrait of the New Spain* (Harmondsworth: Penguin, 1987).

[10] For Spain post-1975, see Paul Preston, *The Triumph of Democracy in Spain* (London: Methuen, 1986).

[11] Hooper, *The Spaniards*, pp. 61–2.

Bibliography

Álvarez Caballero, Ángel, *El cante flamenco* (Madrid: Alianza, 1994).

Andalucía: the Rough Guide (London: Rough Guides, 1997).

Anderson, Andrew A., *Lorca's Late Poetry* (Leeds: Francis Cairns, 1990).

Barrucand, Marianne and Achim Bednorz, *Moorish Architecture in Andalusia*, trans. Michael Scuffil (Cologne: Taschen, 1992).

Betham-Edwards, Matilda, *Through Spain to the Sahara* (London, 1868).

Blaney, Major-General Lord, *Narrative of a Forced Journey Through Spain and France as a Prisoner of War* (London, 1814).

Borrow, George, *The Bible in Spain* (London, 1842; reprinted London: John Murray, 1914).

Brenan, Gerald, *The Face of Spain* (London: Turnstile Press, 1950).

—— *South from Granada* (London: Hamish Hamilton, 1957; reprinted Cambridge: Cambridge University Press, 1980).

Buñuel, Luis, *My Last Breath*, trans. Abigail Israel (London: Jonathan Cape, 1984).

Burckhardt, Titus, *Moorish Culture in Spain*, trans. Akisa Jaffa (London: Allen and Unwin, 1970).

Burns, Jimmy, *Spain: A Literary Companion* (London: John Murray, 1994).

Carr, Raymond, *Spain 1808–1975* (Oxford: Oxford University Press, 1982).

Chateaubriand, François René de, *Œuvres Complètes* (Paris: Garnier, n.d.).

Clark, William, *Gazpacho, or Summer Months in Spain* (London, 1851).

Clifford, J. and Marcus, G. E. (eds), *Writing Culture: The Poetics and Politics of Ethnography* (Berkeley and Los Angeles: University of California Press, 1986).

Collins, W. W., *Cathedral Cities of Spain* (London: Heinemann, 1909).

Dalrymple, William, *Travels through Spain and Portugal in 1774* (London, 1777).

Davies, R. Trevor, *The Golden Century of Spain 1501–1621* (London: Macmillan, 1956).

Dean, Winton, *Bizet* (London: J. M. Dent, 1965).

Disraeli, Benjamin, *Letters 1815–1834* (Toronto: University of Toronto Press, 1982).

Dumas, Alexander, *From Paris to Cadiz* (London: Peter Owen, 1958).

Edwards, Gwynne, 'Carmen', in Margaret A. Rees (ed.), *Catholic Tastes and Times: Essays in Honour of Michael E. Williams* (Leeds: Trinity and All Saints' College, 1987).

—— *Indecent Exposures: Buñuel, Saura, Erice & Almodóvar* (London: Marion Boyars, 1995).

—— *Flamenco!* (London: Thames and Hudson, 2000).

Eisenberg, Daniel, 'Un texto lorquiano descubierto en Nueva York (La presentacíon de Sánchez Mejías', *Bulletin Hispanique*, 80 (1978), 134–7.

Elliot, J.H., *Imperial Spain 1469–1716* (London: Edward Arnold, 1963).

Ellis, Havelock, *The Soul of Spain* (London: Constable, 1908).

Fonseca, I., *Bury Me Standing: The Gypsies and their Journey* (New York: Random House, 1995).

Ford, Richard, *A Handbook for Travellers in Spain* (London, 1844 and 1846; London: Centaur Press, 1966).

—— *Gatherings from Spain* (London, 1846; London: Dent, 1906).

—— *A Loan Exhibition: Richard Ford in Spain*, introduction by Denys Sutton, catalogue by Brinsley Ford (London: Wildenstein, 1974).

García Lorca, Federico, *Obras Completas*, ed. Miguel García Posada (Barcelona/Valencia: Galaxia Gutenberg/Círculo de Lectores, 4 vols, 1996).

—— *Conferencias*, trans. and ed. Christopher Maurer (Madrid: Alianza, 1984).

—— *Deep Song and Other Prose*, trans. and ed. Christopher Maurer (London: Marion Boyars, 1980).

Gautier, Théophile, *Espagne* (Paris, 1845).

—— *L'España de Gautier*, ed. René Jasinski (Paris: Libraire Vuibert, 1929).

Gibson, Ian, *The Death of Lorca* (London: W. H. Allen, 1973).

González Palencia, A., *Historia de la España musulmana* (Barcelona: Labor, 1945).

Grabar, Oleg, *The Alhambra* (London: Allen Lane, 1978).

Guidol, José, *The Arts of Spain* (London: Thames and Hudson, 1964).

Hare, Augustus, *Wanderings in Spain* (London, 1873; reprinted London: George Allen, 1904).

Harvey, L. P., *Islamic Spain 1250–1500* (London and Chicago: University of Chicago Press, 1990).

Hemingway, Ernest, *Death in the Afternoon* (New York: Charles Scribner's Sons, 1932).

Holroyd, Michael, *Lytton Strachey: A Critical Biography* (London: Heinemann, 1968).

Hooper, John, *The Spaniards: A Portrait of the New Spain* (Harmondsworth: Penguin, 1987).

Hopkins, Adam, *Spanish Journeys: A Portrait of Spain* (Harmondsworth: Penguin, 1993).

Howell, James, *Instructions for Forreine Travel* (London, 1642).

—— *Familiar Letters* (London: 1642; reprinted London: David Nutt, 1892).

Hugo, Victor, *Œuvres Complètes, Poésie I* (Paris: Robert Laffont, 1985).

Hutton, Edward, *The Cities of Spain* (New York: Macmillan, 1924).

Irving, Washington, *Complete Works, The Alhambra* (Boston: Desmond, 1899).

Irwin, Robert, *The Alhambra* (London: Profile Books, 2004).

Jacobs, Michael, *Alhambra* (London: Frances Lincoln, 2000).

Jedlicka Gotthard, *Spanish Painting*, trans. J. Maxwell Brownjohn (London: Thames and Hudson, 1963).

Jones, S., *The Archeology of Ethnicity: Constructing Identities in the Past and Present* (London: Routledge, 1997).

Jordan, Barry and Morgan-Tamosunas, Rikki (eds), *Contemporary Spanish Cultural Studies* (London: Arnold, 2000).

Kamen, Henry, *Spain 1469–1714* (London and New York: Longman, 1983).

Labanyi, Jo (ed.), *Constructing Identity in Contemporary Spain: Theoretical Debates and Practices* (Oxford: Oxford University Press, 2000).

Lithgow, William, *Rare Adventures and Painefull Peregrinations* (London, 1632; reprinted London: Jonathan Cape, 1928).

Lowe, Alfonso, *The Companion Guide to the South of Spain*, revised by Hugh Seymour-Davies (Woodbridge: Boydell and Brewer, 2000).

Lynch, John, *Spain Under the Hapsburgs* (Oxford: Blackwell, 1964).

McClary, Susan, *George Bizet: Carmen* (Cambridge: Cambridge University Press, 1992).

Mérimée, Prosper, *Carmen et autres nouvelles choisies*, ed. M. J. Tilsby (London: Harrap, 1981).

Mitchell, David, *Travellers in Spain* (London: Cassell, 1990).

Mitchell, Timothy, *Flamenco Deep Song* (New Haven and London: Yale University Press, 1994).

Morris, James, *Spain* (London: Faber and Faber, 1964).

Morton, H. V., *A Stranger in Spain* (London: Methuen, 1955).

O'Brien, Kate, *Farewell Spain* (London: Heinemann, 1937).

Pohren, D. E., *The Art of Flamenco* (Madrid: Society for Spanish Studies, 1962).

Prangey, Philibert Joseph Girault de, *Souvenirs de Grenade et de l'Alhambra* (Paris, 1837; reprinted as *Impressions of Granada and the Alhambra*, Reading: Garnet Publishing, 1996).

Preston, Paul, *The Triumph of Democracy in Spain* (London: Methuen, 1986).

Raitt, A. W., *Prosper Mérimée* (New York: Twayne, 1970).

Saura, Carlos and Antonio Gades, *Carmen: el sueño del amor absoluto* (Barcelona: Círculo/Folio, 1984).

Sevilla, Paco, *Queen of the Gypsies: The Life and Legend of Carmen Amaya* (San Diego: Sevilla Press, 1999).

Seville & Andalusia (Eyewitness Travel Guides) (London: Dorling Kindersley, 1996).

Sim, Katharine, *David Roberts R.A., 1796–1864: A Biography* (London: Quartet Books, 1984).

Swinburne, Henry, *Travels through Spain and Portugal in 1775 and 1776* (London, 1787).

Taylor, Isidore Severin Justin Baron de, *L'Alhambra* (Paris, n.d.; reprinted Granada: Editorial Turpiana, 1988).

Thomas, Hugh, *The Spanish Civil War* (Harmondsworth: Penguin, 1965).

Trend, J. B., 'A festival in the south of Spain', *Nation and Athenaeum*, 14 January 1922, 594–5.

Trevelyan, Raleigh, *Shades of the Alhambra* (London: The Folio Society, 1984).

Troutman, Philip, *El Greco* (London: Spring Books, 1963).

Twiss, Richard, *Travels through Spain and Portugal in 1772 and 1773* (London, 1777).

Watt, W. Montgomery and Pierre Cachia, *A History of Islamic Spain* (Edinburgh: Edinburgh University Press, 1977).

Williams, Stanley T., *The Life of Washington Irving* (New York: Oxford University Press, 1935).

Index

175